Also by Jennifer Toth

Mole People
Orphans of the Living

WHAT

HAPPENED

TO JOHNNIE

JORDAN?

THE STORY OF A CHILD
TURNING VIOLENT

JENNIFER TOTH

The Free Press
New York · London · Toronto · Sydney · Singapore

*f*P
THE FREE PRESS
A Division of Simon & Schuster, Inc.
1230 Avenue of the Americas
New York, NY 10020

For information regarding special discounts for bulk purchases,
please contact Simon & Schuster Special Sales at 1-800-456-6798
or business@simonandschuster.com

Designed by Lauren Simonetti

Manufactured in the United States of America

1   3   5   7   9   10   8   6   4   2

Library of Congress Cataloging-in-Publication Data

Toth, Jennifer.
What Happened to Johnnie Jordan? the story of a child turning violent / Jennifer Toth.
p. cm.
Includes bibliographical references.
1. Jordan, Johnnie, 1980– 2. Foster children—Ohio—Biography. 3. Murderers—Ohio—Biography. 4. Violence in children—Ohio. 5. Abused children—Ohio—Biography.
I. Title.

HV883.O3 T68 2002

364.15′23′0977112—dc21   200105118

ISBN 0-684-85558-5

For Craig and J. Kyle

and

In memory of Charles and Jeanette Johnson

CONTENTS

I am speaking of that crime for which there is no forgiveness. . . .

—*John Gabriel Borkman,* Henrik Ibsen

I
MURDER

1

The glory of the winter's setting sun flashed red and pink across northwestern Ohio's frozen horizon as Charles Johnson drove his tired green Chevrolet home from Sears with a space heater he hoped would save him from his wife's icy feet in bed. The two-lane rural highway was almost empty, but Mr. Johnson kept to the thirty-five-mile-per-hour speed limit. At seventy years of age, with the remains of his hair grey and the memory of thousands of wide, proud smiles recorded in deep creases in his weathered red-brown skin, life was no race to Mr. Johnson. But this evening, he was hurried. He knew his wife was anxious for him to get home.

A tall, willowy man with brown eyes regularly buffed by the wind and shining with the wonder he found in life around him, he genially bent to his wife's wishes. He smiled whenever he thought of her, even after thirty years of marriage. Jeanette Johnson, a petite, gentle woman, "held the Lord's love in her eyes," as he put it. To say that Mr. Johnson loved his wife would understate the truth. She was his world on this earth. He loved even her cold feet, though the thought of them made him shudder slightly and shake his head with a low chuckle.

A sharp cold had rolled down from Canada across Lake Erie and invaded the Johnsons' one-story aluminum-sided house earlier in the week, and hadn't budged since. The two-bedroom home had no furnace, only a woodstove and a space heater which had broken sometime during the previous night. Mrs. Johnson always wore thick white socks to bed, but Mr. Johnson could feel the cold rush to her warmth, and though she protested, he knew how she melted when he rubbed her feet in his large work-callused hands before letting the space heater take over. Her quiet, shy smile thanked him more than any words. The light in her eyes warmed his soul. She was too good for this world, he would say.

With his eyes carefully on the road, Mr. Johnson felt the sky. He said he could read the skies better than most weathermen with all their equipment, not just by looking up, but by soaking in the air it breathed. Mr. Johnson had a gift for feeling. He could feel the sky through his eyes, he told me with a humble smile, and even through his pores.

This evening the sky was hard, icy, aloof, glorious, and unyielding. Though thick clouds approached, red smoldered through their darkness. Any way it was, the sky spoke to Mr. Johnson of some truth. He let the sky guide his thoughts regularly; it was how he lived. That moment, he recalled for me, he was thinking of the subject for his next sermon as a lay minister at St. Mary's Baptist Church back in town. Redemption, he decided. Forgiveness and redemption rising like a phoenix out of the red burnings of life.

The sun was now setting at a distance not too far. A dusting of fine snow outlined the sharp, bare trees, and rested in the crevices between frozen tufts of yellowed grass in fallow fields. Almost within reach, the sky met land. He took his last full, deep breath of wonder.

Mr. Johnson's Ohio is quiet, still, flat, and vast. He visited Toledo, or "town" as he called the state's fourth-largest city, for church and a few other necessities. But he preferred the rural life and chose to live mostly within the seven-and-a-half acres of Spencer Township. When he first came to Spencer in the late 1940s, migrating north from Georgia in search of work, there were no paved roads. People relied on outhouses then. Spencer educated its children in a one-room schoolhouse down the road from where he now lived. Nature's fickle character never allowed stable prosperity to fall on the township, but even when farms suffered, people lived by neighborly goodness. There was little crime in the county. You could count the entire history of Spencer's violent crimes on one hand. In the 1950s, a man stabbed his wife to death with eighty strokes. Some years later, a fight in the corner bar left a man dead in a ditch. Spencer was then, and remains today, the kind of place where neighbors look out for one another and usually leave their doors unlocked at night.

The roads now are blacktopped, and the school closed in favor of busing children into the city, but Spencer has stayed much the same. Even as commerce and industry spread westward from Toledo, doubling the population of the counties it overtook, Spencer barely changed. The population even dropped a little, to around 1,700. City life, it seemed, stopped short just east of the township and then turned south, probably because Spencer still lacks public sewer and water lines.

On this winter evening, Mr. Johnson drove past the more prosperous and larger farms of Harding Village, where red barns stand on flat plains a few acres from their white houses with broad pillared porches. Spencer rests like a horseshoe around Harding. In recent times, politicians have been accused of drawing town boundaries here along racial lines, but in fact they were made and stiffened by religion. Around the turn of the century, invisible borders were marked between Catholics and Protestants. One group prospered; the other did not. That was well before Mr. Johnson left the South in search of opportunities. He had made his way from a very poor sharecropping family up to the Cleveland area as a teenager. Scavenging for work, he stayed in the basement of a church. He worked in the steel mills around Cleveland before the steel mills went bust, then landed a job in a glass factory in Toledo. He stayed with relatives in Spencer and commuted into Toledo until he got on his feet. Much later, he worked as the janitor of the school down the street. He had found Jeanette Collins by then, demurely nestled in a church gathering, and they were happily married. She carefully packed a baloney sandwich for his lunch every day, which he doled out to children who had "forgotten" their own lunches. There were many families in Spencer too proud to ask for subsidized lunches.

When they had saved enough, they bought a house. It was difficult in that era for a black man to do all these things with almost no education, but Mr. Johnson never spoke of those hurdles or complained. Life, to him, was a blessing and a miracle, and he did what he could to help people less fortunate.

Leaving the broad farmland, he drove into Spencer, where small houses are squeezed alongside each other in random fashion. There is no reason or plan to this township. Houses grow as randomly as weeds on land that is bought slowly and built on with almost no rules. Some houses stand near the street, others far back, their numbers skip, jump, and are interrupted by spurts of forest and fields.

This evening, his neighbors' thick chimney smoke dissipated gently into the thin air. The land lay lifelessly brown, awaiting the spring thaw. The gravel road crunched as he drove toward his yellow house, standing quietly against the gurgle of a nearly invisible creek winding under his driveway.

Mr. Johnson pulled the Chevrolet carefully into his garage. The swing set he built for the scores of children he and his wife had foster-parented over twenty years sat idle, a sad wind tinkling its chains. The sky had darkened suddenly in the early winter evening, with no flicker of light.

The house's silence made him uneasy. Jeanette did not call out his name as usual. He hurried his step to the back door, suddenly wanting to hear her voice and feel the warmth of their kitchen. The back door he would always step through was locked. It was never locked. The air felt unusually quiet and tense against his skin. He fumbled with a key. The sky went cold. He smelled something wrong. When he opened the door, black smoke rushed at him. Something was on fire.

He found his wife's lifeless body on the linoleum floor before him, her hand reaching for the door, her blood seeping toward his feet. Her eyes—he breaks, recalling the terror and confusion still staring out of her one undestroyed eye. Thankfully, he did not notice her charred legs, only the flame licking at her clothes. When he turned to get the extin-guisher, the fire was gone. He went into the bedroom and pulled a white bedspread from their mattress and wrapped it snugly around his wife. She wouldn't want people to see her like this, and he wanted to keep her warm. Briefly, and only in his heart, she was still alive. Only there could he feel the flutter of her heart, of her breath. The stillness of life and the silence of death, of what his senses knew to be true, he could not take in. Instead, he was struck by a sadness so thick and heavy that it knocked the breath out of him, a sadness so bottomless and profound that he felt irretrievably numb.

Charles Johnson does not remember walking to the telephone or dialing. But he recalls waiting on the line, hoping Johnnie Jordan would come up behind him and finish the day by killing him too. That would be a mercy. He knew it had been Johnnie. He knew it as he knew his last strong grasp of faith was draining from him. With his wife's unpro-voked, senseless death, by a child they had agreed to take into their home and foster-parent, Charles Johnson's beliefs in goodness and car-ing for others, in man's capacity for redemption, became hollow shells without the warm core that fed them. His faith remained. But for the year he lived on after his wife's death, it was a ghost of what it had always been.

III

I pray every day that I wake up soon, that the Lord gives me some reason, because I don't see no plan to this at all and I can't rest until I do. I can't sleep knowing that Jeanette is going to die again in some other person.

—Charles Johnson

At the trial of Johnnie Jordan half a year later, Charles Johnson's once tall and dignified frame appeared frail and bent, his once shining eyes, dull and vacant. His voice echoed the emptiness in his heart. He spoke to reporters with a striking lack of anger or vindictiveness. It was a tragedy, he said, not only for his wife, but also for Johnnie Jordan, a child of fifteen, with only prison in his future.

Mr. Johnson knew more than most of us could see then. Johnnie was among the first child murderers to vie for national attention after committing violent, seemingly senseless crimes, murders without motive or meaning.[1] Over the next several years, other grisly murders spilling out of schools and homes would shock America, forming an apparently new phenomenon of young, rage-filled killers taking lives with motiveless passion and little or no remorse. While juvenile crime rates were generally declining, the number of child murderers rose. Senseless murders committed by children as young as six years old assaulted communities both urban and rural, rich and poor, throughout the country.

A year and a half after Johnnie murdered Mrs. Johnson in January of 1996, a sixteen-year-old boy in Pearl, Mississippi, killed his mother and then went on a rampage in his high school, shooting nine students, killing two. In December of 1997, a fourteen-year-old killed three students and injured five others in West Paducah, Kentucky. Three months later, in Jonesboro, Arkansas, four girls and a teacher were shot to death and ten people were wounded when two boys, aged eleven and thirteen, opened fire from the woods after triggering a fire alarm. In Edinboro,

---

1. While the *Toledo Blade* and other local newspapers covered the murder, Johnnie's crime barely made briefs in national newspapers. The television magazine show *48 Hours* later did a segment on the murder.

Pennsylvania, the next month, a fourteen-year-old shot a science teacher to death in front of students at an eighth-grade graduation dance. The next month, May 1998, a teenager in Fayetteville, Tennessee, opened fire in a parking lot at his high school, killing a classmate, three days before their graduation. Two days later in Springfield, Oregon, a fifteen-year-old boy slayed his parents at home and went on to school, where he shot twenty-five people, two teenagers fatally. Then, on April 20, 1999, in Littleton, Colorado, two high school students shot twelve classmates and a teacher to death and injured twenty-three before killing themselves.

These are only the most sensational murders, those that took more than one young victim. There were, and still are, far more cases skating through the local news in which only one or a few adult lives are taken by children and which are barely noticed by the national media. In Queens, New York, for example, five teenagers, the youngest fourteen years old, beat a Chinese food deliveryman to death in September 2000, merely because they wanted free food after the Chinese food dinner they had just finished.

Mr. Johnson could not begin to fathom the crazed nature of young murderers like Johnnie, who kill in a consuming rage that not even they can understand, for reasons they cannot explain. He sought some explanation, however, hoping that in these children's stories lay some rationale, some larger truth beyond race, beyond poverty and drugs, beyond easily available weapons and gratuitous television violence. And Mr. Johnson sensed that his loss was part of a greater loss, his shock and grief the forerunner of the nation's shock and grief as his tragedy repeated itself in different forms, across socioeconomic borders, in homes and school yards and classrooms throughout the country. In response to what several news magazines referred to as an epidemic of cold and remorseless young criminals, public outrage pushed legislatures to pass harsher sentencing laws for children, "to put them away, to keep us safe," as one Ohio legislator put it.[2] Several states lowered the

2. Since 1992, forty-four states have passed legislation making it easier to prosecute juveniles as adults. Ohio and twenty-seven other states now automatically transfer juveniles accused of particular crimes to adult court. Fifteen states leave the decision to transfer up to the prosecutor. Many states have lowered the minimum age at which a child can be judged as an adult to fourteen. Kansas and Vermont have lowered the age limit to ten. But several states have not limited the age at which a child can be tried as an adult.

age of criminals eligible for capital punishment to thirteen. Some states abolished a minimum age at which children can be prosecuted as adults and incarcerated in adult prisons. The late 1990s saw the largest overhaul of the American juvenile justice system which, derived from the Elizabethan model, was initially intended to rehabilitate and save young offenders.[3]

Over the months following Mrs. Johnson's murder, the cotton and willows that framed the Johnson home in Ohio dried and withered along with Mr. Johnson. He did nothing to save them. Like the house itself, they seemed haunted by a murder too real and too empty of sense to move forward in time. A red lantern still hangs from a tree limb next to a hatchet much like the one that mutilated his wife and destroyed his world. Both rust slowly in the Ohio air.

The greater Toledo community, first angered and shattered by the murder, soon sought to move beyond the tragedy by convincing itself that the killing was a rare, fathomless, and unpredictable act of brutality. It occurred in a moment devoid of reason or understanding, in one small home, in a gentle farming community where there is little crime, where kindness was plenty and love was taught and learned. Still, the shock of a child's rage capsized the community's faith in saving children. It drew citizens away from their benevolence and made them less willing to open their homes to neglected and abused children. Lucas County Children Services (formerly Lucas County Children's Services Board), which had placed Johnnie in the Johnsons' home, as well as several neighboring Ohio foster care agencies, quickly recorded a severe drop in volunteer foster parents. Worse, Lucas County sought to avoid blame by continuing to portray the case as random and unpreventable.

But Mr. Johnson was determined that his wife's death should not be forgotten, that even though it was difficult to comprehend, it should not be dismissed as senseless. Mrs. Johnson's death deserved some greater meaning, he said. Only he believed it should be recognized as a tragedy

---

3. The system was brought into question in 1967, when the U.S. Supreme Court ruled that the juvenile criminal system had become a "kangaroo court" with arbitrary punishment. The Court ruled that juveniles should have the same due-process-of-law protections as adults. With the right to counsel, right to confront witnesses, and the privilege to guard against self-incrimination, the juvenile court system became more like the adult system. Ironically, awarding juveniles the same rights as adults made way for the tougher prosecution laws of today.

that could have been avoided. Moreover, if action was not taken to remedy the failures that contributed to her murder, such tragedies could—and would—be repeated in some other place, with some other person, at some other time.

He brought a lawsuit in an effort to reform the system which he believed killed not only his wife, but also the humanity in Johnnie Jordan. Through legal action, he hoped to draw attention to the blatant negligence and failings of county agencies in dealing with troubled children, particularly those prone to violence. He was convinced that Johnnie Jordan's rage could have been curbed and channeled if county officials legally responsible for him had been more vigilant and aware of the propensity to violent behavior that Johnnie openly displayed. And, if they had prepared his caretakers, or at least made them aware of the danger, the life of a gentle, caring woman might have been saved.

But the local government's sovereign immunity from lawsuits for negligence ultimately saved the county agencies from liability, and thus from change. And instead, the agencies rejected public examination of their actions, even internal introspection, lest reform suggest an admission of guilt.

Mr. Johnson, worn out and despondent, did not live long enough to see the case settled out of court for under $1 million. He had told me he would have neither the time nor the notion to spend the money. It was change he sought. His attorney accepted the settlement because he was not certain he could prove that the failings of Children Services and juvenile justice had gone beyond simple neglect to malice, and, equally influential in his decision, he no longer had a grieving spouse to bring home to a jury the full tragedy of the murder. But without an admission of guilt from the county, the possibility of reform fell apart with Mr. Johnson's death. No agency took responsibility or accepted blame. Worse, no one searched for a truth that might prevent another Johnnie from erupting. And the questions that haunted Mr. Johnson, the mystery of what happened to Johnnie Jordan, went unsolved in the prevailing hush and angry glares of people in the community who wanted—and still want—this story to be over, who still want to forget.

But Mr. Johnson deserves a greater effort to answer his questions than he received from the authorities. Who was Johnnie Jordan? What made this child into a killer? Why will his story likely be repeated?

Initially, I was drawn to Johnnie's story by those same questions. In my work with children, I had heard teachers and social workers increasingly complain of "superpredators," children with apparently no conscience whom they anxiously watch passing through their classrooms and caseloads. Johnnie was cited as an example. That's when I called Mr. Johnson.

Mr. Johnson taught me a great deal, and not solely about this case. Through his pain, fear, and compassion, he was able to look beyond anger and judgment as well as community pressure to let the story go, to move on and to forget. My interviews with him convinced me to continue his quest for understanding and reform, even as I watched his hope and drive fade. Though I never achieved Mr. Johnson's forgiveness of the crime, throughout this project I drew motivation from the Johnsons, their memory, their goodness, their hope, and their belief in helping children.

I began my work seeking the evil inside Johnnie Jordan, a so-called superpredator who could kill without remorse. At first, Johnnie fit my preconception. He sought gain from his crime; he wanted to be paid for being interviewed for this book. I refused. Without benefit to himself, he said, he would not cooperate. He did not care to help the public understand about children like himself, he told me, for what would it get him? Only when his former attorney intervened did he agree to our first interview.

In prison, shackled with chains too large for his arms and legs, I saw a child too small for his prison-issued jumpsuit, lost among the adult prisoners surrounding him, too shy to look me in the eye. He was a boy who still would not eat vegetables, whose worries and anxieties he did not acknowledge but came in the form of stomachaches he treated with candy. I would come to understand that he was a child who had not developed emotionally, who was capable of a monstrous act which he saw only as "a mistake," never fully comprehending its horror.

For years, I vacillated between my outrage, anger, and frustration toward the killer, and my sadness for the lost child whom no one wanted to remember or cared about any longer. It would have been easier to dismiss Johnnie as inhuman. But that is not what Mr Johnson saw in him, nor what I found in him in those first interviews—at times a child who could be soft and creative, even sensitive—at other times, cold and evil; and above all and always, confused.

When I began this book, Johnnie was a child—perhaps a morally stunted one, perhaps not. He is a monster now after years in jail, some would argue, not because of evil in his heart or in his soul, but because his rage has grown unabated until it is beyond his or anyone's control. Not even he understands his emotions, what brings them on so ferociously, let alone their origin. He is often cut off from his conscience and his heart.

When he is angry, he often laughs. He doesn't know why. It is not to turn away from his anger, he says. He does not even know at times that he is angry. "My eyes'll get watery and stuff, and then I'll flip," he told me during our second three-hour interview in prison. "That's when I know I was angry. I do the first thing that comes to my head then. It depends where I'm at. If there are chairs around, I'll throw them. If it came down to it, I could kill someone. I try not to though." Afterward, "I try not to feel too much. If I do something, I try not to have no afterthoughts. Just know it's done and over with. That's one thing that kill most people in prison—too much stress."

He had ironed his blue prison jumpsuit and combed his hair into a soft Afro, but his eyes were puffy and sleepless. He was too wary of his surroundings to rest much. He slumped forward in his chair, resting his forearms on his thighs in a tough inmate pose which instead only exaggerated his youth. He had been trying to gain weight, to look stronger, but the weight fell softly on his young frame. Later it would turn to muscle. Honesty carried in his voice, always. He had nothing more to lose, and had decided to like and trust me, he said. He didn't know why.

"I guess it's the loneliness and misery that draws me close enough to confide my secrets," he wrote me. Still, he doubted he could. "Will I have the strength, the courage, the time to explore the period of my life that was the most surprising and concentrated of all?" he asked in another letter a month later. It was the only time he expressed self-doubt.

Every week, he phoned and we spoke for the prison-allotted time. I visited him in each of his five prisons, interviewing him for four and five hours a day in weeklong stretches. As he faced rejection from the people he loved on the outside world, as they cut him off or forgot him, he became angrier, feeling as a child would that he was still entitled to their care. He came to appreciate my interest in him. By the end of this project, only his former lawyer and I had kept contact with him. I treated him like a person, he said, though often a young person.

"Why do you talk to me like a child sometimes?" he once asked with a hiss of exasperation. For as his time passed in prison, he preferred to see himself as an adult, hardened and at times mean.

"Because sometimes I prefer to see you that way," I told him.

Johnnie was silent for a moment.

"It's not who I want to be anymore, though," he told me.

Our interviews were often unsteady. Difficult questions sometimes enraged Johnnie. Several times, I wondered if he would stop cooperating with me. But he would call eventually, still angry and threatening and claiming he didn't know why he continued to speak with me.

"Expressing my feelings have always been a problem for me not only in here, but out there also," he once wrote. "This is hard telling you but, I got to tell someone or I break down or blow up insides. And I think that you're the best person for me to talk to. I feel you be the one that will get me through this sorrow." He signed the letter, as he usually did, "Respectfully Submitted, Johnnie Jordan" followed by his inmate number. He always included the time as well as the date in the upper right corner of the first page. He wrote in faint pencil, his letters so precariously slanted to the left that his words were difficult to decipher. His a's were triangles, and he bubbled the dots over his i's.[4]

At first, he bristled at questions about his past. Even in jail, he preferred the present. He did not want to go back, to remember, or to try to explain his thoughts.

"The truth is sometimes it seems at moments I can't get the words out to put in place," he wrote from Ross Correctional Institution. "Believe it or not, you have taught me a lot and gave me a lot of reasons to believe in you."

We had come to know each other better by then. It had taken some time not only to get Johnnie to open up, but to try to express himself clearly, and for me to learn how to understand what he meant when he did. We both worked hard on our communication. I began to see a sadness in him that is as deep as his anger.

---

4. Johnnie's former attorney considers him barely literate. In the ninth grade, before his incarceration, Johnnie tested at a fourth-grade reading and writing level. I have changed his spelling to make his letters more legible, but not altered his grammar.

"People tell me that I'm going to hell," he wrote one afternoon around four o'clock. "Jennifer, hell can't get worse than this cause I'm in hell now. I can only do so much to survive. At times I just want to stop, but I know I can't, I tried. I feel I'm in a deep sleep. Some kind of dream with a lot of misery, that won't let me wake up, that's how I feels, but this is real."

For much of the time, I remained a cool distance from Johnnie. I didn't want to mislead him into thinking I was primarily sympathetic toward him. He had murdered in a particularly brutal way, and I never lost sight of his crime or achieved Mr. Johnson's selfless, almost non-judgmental compassion. But one evening, during his weekly call, his voice carried the poignant loneliness of a lost boy trying hard not to cry: "I'm trying to hold on, but I don't know how long I can."

I realized then that I had become his link to the outside world. Everyone else that week had refused to accept his collect calls. Usually he told me he was "cool," he was hanging in there. This night, I heard the voice of suicide. Why? I asked. Why now, four years after the crime? Had four years of imprisonment finally broken him or had his past caught up with him? I cared more about the reason than about him until he answered quietly in the voice of a childhood he had left behind far too early, and yet was still caught in.

"It hurts, man," he said.

Still, Johnnie had not "snapped," as kids in juvenile hall put it when they recognize the horror of the crime they committed and regret their actions.

"I could get killed in here any day and no one would know about it," he said instead, and I recognized the truth in his words. No one would really care, not even for the sadness of losing another lost child. No one really knew Johnnie Jordan anymore, except me—and now, perhaps, you. His life, his story, became more important to me then, not because of who Johnnie is, but who he has become and how he became that way. His story holds clues to understanding one of the mysteries of our times: child killers without motive or remorse, without reason.

Through Johnnie Jordan, I hope to bring some light of understanding to the darkness that filled his and Mrs. Johnson's world for that evil moment, one bitter night in January of 1996.

III

Johnnie Jordan, Jr.'s Ohio is a cold place of broken glass. The sky doesn't mean much to him. His world is cement and crumbling houses, caving roofs, broken windows, smashed bottles, and slow-moving, dark-windowed cars with loud, hard music, and nineteen foster homes with parents and grandparents in between. "The hood" is what Johnnie considers his home, Toledo's ghetto. "It's cool," he says and shrugs. "That's where my boys are."

Johnnie's world had always been small, a matter of four or five blocks. Now, in prison, it's even smaller, a few cells or a floor. He doesn't like to go outside much. It's too cold or hot, too wet, or too bright. Outdoors, the air prickles his skin and makes him uneasy. It's not natural to his institutionalized life.

The Johnsons' home in Spencer Township, twenty miles from the Toledo corner that Johnnie hung on, was the farthest he had ever been from the city. He didn't like "the boondocks," as he called it. He did his best to sabotage his placement there by the social workers, until he realized that he liked the Johnsons. He even wanted them to adopt him. They had begun to expose him to something better. Johnnie enjoyed joking and playing checkers with Mr. Johnson. He warmed to Mrs. Johnson's gentle ways. His mouth watered for her fried chicken and collards. He was almost looking forward to tasting the shrimp and fried catfish Mr. Johnson talked so much about.

Two years later, with Johnnie now seventeen years old, a good meal to him is a Coke with Little Debbies. He has never seen an ocean or a mountain. But now, with chains and shackles, through blackened windows of prison transport vans, he has traveled as far as the outskirts of Columbus, Ohio, in the center of the state. He has learned more about the world while in prison.

"You know there's a place called Akron?" he asked me. "Akron, and it's in Ohio. There's a place called Canton, Ohio, too."

The Johnsons, although neither were educated beyond elementary school, could have taught Johnnie all that and much more. They might even have saved him, but slowly. First, they would have had to understand Johnnie's dangerous world. Because even though they passed through the same Toledo streets and the same country roads, Johnnie and the Johnsons experienced profoundly different worlds.

Johnnie never really knew Mr. Johnson's Ohio of picturesque skies and friendly smiles. Though he lived in Mr. Johnson's world for a while, Mr. Johnson's world never lived in him. Johnnie never understood love and kindness, or the wonder, brilliance, and mercy that filled Mr. Johnson's life. And Mr. Johnson did not know Johnnie's world of using and being used, of blood and meanness, a jarring world with no reason and no sense. When he found out, it was too late.

2

Early morning, well before dawn, the air lay too still against Johnnie. The absence of movement and the sense of time suspended made him restless. He could not silence an agitated buzzing in his head, pierced only by angry thoughts echoing into others more bitter than the last. The outside world seemed to be closing in on him. He lay for a moment trying to tame his thoughts. Then, abruptly, he wondered why he bothered to control his anger. What would happen if he allowed himself to cross into a darkness he could feel inside of him, a darkness he thought was a secret? He tumbled into a troubled sleep, and let go.

When sunlight struck him across the face in midmorning, Johnnie woke with a thin grey mist in his head. He suspected it gathered before his eyes had opened to the day. But he could not know. He had conditioned himself to forget his dreams. As long as he could remember, he hated sleep because of the violent, ugly dreams which often left him with no images at all, only a mean feeling. Nightmares were worse. These he remembered, but he never shared them with anyone—not his sisters or brothers, his boys on the street, not his counselors nor any of the adults, including his parents, who have all been paid by the government at one time or another to care for him. How could he describe the pitiful look on his mother's face behind bars or his father crying out for his help from the dead of night? Experience taught him that adults would only ask if his parents had beaten him or had sex with him. He didn't want to think about those things. When he was younger, they would tell him not to care about his parents, because his parents were bad. But he did care. If they tried to reassure him after a screaming nightmare that his parents were okay, he got mad. He knew better. He knew without seeing or hearing that his mom and dad were strung out again somewhere, cold, homeless, and pitiful, while he was warm and dry in some foster home. He thought hard for a moment, trying to remember which foster home he was in now. The old people, it finally came. Charles and Lynette—or something—the Johnsons.

To keep nighttime hauntings away wherever he was, Johnnie exhausted himself as much as possible before allowing sleep to take him. He stayed up late, sometimes until five or six in the morning, when the sounds of the wakening house, the crackling of bacon, the shouts of one foster mother or another, came to him. With the morning noises, he would allow himself to drift into a light sleep. As a result, he was habitually tired. Deep sockets ringed his bloodshot eyes. Rivers of lines crested his forehead with worry and ran down his puffy cheeks, which were still padded with baby fat. He did not recognize furrows on his face as signs of sleep deprivation. He thought it was just the face he was born with, one he would carry the rest of his life, which, he believed, would be short. He knew he was tired, but he did not know what it was to be refreshed.

Today there was a mean edge to the greyness left by his dreams. He heard voices outside. Were they talking about him? His lips and eyes locked in an angry frown that fractured any softness in his young face. He didn't care, he told himself once, and then mumbled it aloud. But the scowl would not go away. The cloud hovering behind his eyes now seemed so thick it crowded his head. He could not clear his mind, not this time.

Why do I care, anyway? he thought. They were going to move him, no matter what he did. He had tried to tell himself that maybe the Johnsons would change their minds and decide to keep him. But after last night, when Johnnie came home past eleven o'clock, an hour after curfew, and Mr. Johnson got on him about it, the chances were not good that he could stay. Johnnie liked Mr. Johnson, but not when Mr. Johnson criticized him. He did not like people telling him he was bad all the time, and lately that was all they said.

I hate the stupid boondocks, throwing an old issue of *Vibe* magazine across his bedroom floor. *Nothing to do out here. It's boring.* When bored, he became angry and he didn't know what he might do. But he did not care now. His mind was set on what was wrong with everything around him, especially the Johnsons. They would not let him keep the dog that followed him home recently. *No matter what, Mrs. Johnson*

wouldn't let that stupid dog stay in the house. I'm not any stupid dog.
Johnnie's stomach churned, sending hot blood through his limbs.

He'd better leave, he thought. He'd better walk around outside. The
voices in the living room were probably talking about how bad he was.
Nobody ever stopped by to visit, but Mrs. Johnson had a visitor this
Monday morning, probably here just to talk about him, he bet. He
would almost have liked to be at school now, to keep the boredom and
anger away, at least for the time being. But Johnnie had not been registered in school for several months.

He finally got out of bed about one o'clock. He shuffled into the
bathroom, head down to bury the scowl he could not shake or hide,
moving quickly to avoid any greetings. The bathwater ran smooth and
warm. He took care of his hygiene now, since a group home taught him
how and explained the dignity of cleanliness. He felt a little better. But
while his toothbrush cleansed his mouth, the foul taste he always got
when this feeling came over him refused to be washed away.

He had missed breakfast. He wasn't hungry anyway. He never had
much of an appetite.

"You can have some cereal," Mrs. Johnson chirped when he entered
the kitchen.

Johnnie grunted.

"You want me to fix you something?"

"No," Johnnie said, grabbing a cereal box. He did not notice which
one. It all tasted the same to him, everything did. He kept his eyes
down.

"You iron my shirt for me?" he asked Mrs. Johnson in a mumble.

"Sure, Johnnie," she said with that bird in her voice she always had.
Only the bird sounded a little too high-pitched in his ears today.

That reminded him of the visitor's voice he thought he heard. Who
was over? Who had she been talking to? He saw no one. He didn't want
to ask.

"Someone here?" he blurted out suddenly, surprising himself.

"No, nobody's been here today," Mrs. Johnson told him evenly.

She did not sound like she was lying, but he did not believe her. He
put his drained cereal bowl in the sink and went to his room with the
freshly ironed shirt. But his scowl deepened, and a flicker of apprehen-
sion lit Mrs. Johnson's face as he passed.

He flipped around the television channels restlessly in his room, hoping something would catch his attention and zap his mind free and empty. But the television droned on hopelessly as he flew from one colorful image to another. His ugly, aggravated feeling was coming on stronger now. Time was moving too slowly. He wanted the afternoon over. Maybe he'd call J.R., a group home counselor to whom he had grown attached. He'd make J.R. come get him and take him somewhere for a while. He started toward his bedroom door, to get to the phone. But J.R. would be out of town until tomorrow, Johnnie remembered in a sudden burst of anxiety.

J.R. should have come yesterday when I told him to, he mumbled to the TV. He felt the blood in his stomach rising and churning. *I told him I'm gonna do something bad.*

Johnnie did not know what he would do, not then, and not now. He knew this feeling was dangerous, but he could not think of anything to control it. He felt nauseated, and for a moment wondered if he had eaten too much chocolate. He loves chocolate—and hates it. It tastes so good, he eats too much and always becomes sick. Still, the sickness does not stop him. That's why he sticks mainly to Little Debbies, the marshmallow kind. But he had eaten no candy today, and recognizing that made him even more agitated. There was no reason for this sickness. *J.R. should have come.* He turned on his boom box, blaring the volume above the TV. J.R. would not like him turning to his gangsta rap, so he did. Even during the day, everything Johnnie did purposefully was to dull himself. Except listen to music. Johnnie found himself in his music. Gangsta rap had his soul wrapped up in its beat, its anger. It made him bold, proud. It understood him. Now he hoped the sound would pound the bad feeling out of him.

But the gangsta rhythms were making him feel bigger instead. Bigger and meaner. He'd better leave for a while. Walk around, get some air, like they taught him at the group home. He put on his coat. As he walked toward the front door, he saw the Johnsons' neighbor, Eva Holston, in her sweatpants and yellow jacket talking to Mrs. Johnson. He turned instead into the bathroom and washed his face, not wanting to walk past them to the front room.

"Did you say hi to Johnnie?" Mrs. Johnson asked her guest when he emerged. The two were sitting together on the couch waiting for the *Oprah Winfrey Show* to begin.

"Hi, Johnnie," Miss Holston said with a pleasant wave. She didn't know the boy well, but she sensed he was trouble, being in foster care and all. A boy that age in foster care had been through a lot, she reasoned, and was more than likely troubled by his life. But he was quiet, and respectful of the Johnsons. He was even polite when they all sat down to supper a couple of times at her house across the street after Mr. Johnson helped clear her land of fallen timber. Of course, Johnnie slumped down awkwardly at the table and mumbled only short responses to questions. He also watched people closely, as if following their lead. Maybe he was just shy and this was his way of minding his manners. Still, there was something swirling beneath all that quietness, something loud inside the child. She could not put her finger on it. What was his problem? Where was it? It had to be there somewhere. The Johnsons didn't see it. They only saw the good in people. They trusted too completely. Holston wondered why the foster care people would put an older boy like this with an elderly couple in their twilight years who just wanted the peace they had earned.

"Hi," Johnnie mumbled back to Holston. In her memory, he seemed to be crouching in the dark hallway, watching them before he hurried back to his room. And, she remembers, Mrs. Johnson's eyes grew big.

Mr. Johnson was puttering around the house, fixing a curtain rod in the kitchen that had lost a nail. He could not find the hammer, so he used a small hatchet to do the repair. As he finished, he placed his tool behind the stove and looked in on the women, who were now talking over *Oprah*. This would be a good time to run to Sears for the new space heater. His wife had asked him to hold off on the trip a few days. He was not certain why. He was more concerned about the hazards of their smoking heater on what promised to be a cold, cold night. Now that his wife had company to pass the afternoon, it would be a good time to make the run.

"I'm going to Sears," Mr. Johnson said, walking into the front room. Mrs. Johnson stood up suddenly, her nervousness barely cloaked by her quickness. She looked around the room briefly before meeting Mr. Johnson's eyes. Then, smiling quietly to her husband, she let him go.

Eva Holston was surprised Mrs. Johnson had such an obviously difficult time allowing her husband to run his errand. The Johnsons had been arguing with Johnnie, she knew, but that was normal in any fam ily with a teenager. She also knew better than to ask what was upsetting her friend. Family business stayed within the family. The Johnsons treated all their foster kids as family. It was private. Holston respected that.

Mr. Johnson walked in his slow, deliberate step, through the back door to his Chevrolet waiting in the garage. As he reached for the car door, he stopped cold. He was not sure why. His feet took him back toward the house. When he heard his wife's voice, a tremor of relief washed over him. He shook his head, freeing himself of a strange, anxious feeling. Then he turned back to his car and drove away.

III

Eva Holston had been ready to leave for quite some time, but Mrs. Johnson kept encouraging her to stay. Finally, Holston said she had to go, that a friend was working on her house.

"That boy." Mrs. Johnson suddenly leaned forward, her voice straining in an earnest whisper. "That boy, did he leave?"

"Who?" Holston asked. She was surprised that Mrs. Johnson would refer to the boy living with them in that way, and was even more surprised at the edge in her voice. "Johnnie?"

Mrs. Johnson nodded.

"I don't know, Mrs. Johnson," Holston said. How strange Mrs. Johnson was acting, she thought. She considered her neighbor a sweet, simpleminded woman who depended on her husband to connect her to this world on occasion, and to complete her sentences most of the time. But Mrs. Johnson's words haunt Eva Holston today.

"I'm going to go on across the road then," she said, pulling herself to her feet. Mrs. Johnson rose too, smiled, and nodded gracefully. Together they walked to the front door.

Outside, the silver-grey light seemed blinding. When Holston looked back, Mrs. Johnson was a shadow against the deeper blackness inside.

A figure moved behind Mrs. Johnson toward the bathroom again.

"Johnnie, how you doing?" Holston called out a final time.

"Alright," he said. His answer was short, his face hidden in darkness. Mrs. Johnson stepped forward into the daylight for a moment, long enough for Eva Holston to see a brief smile, then returned to the darkness. She hesitated a moment before she closed the door.

As Holston walked away, she thought about what her common-law husband had said just the night before: "Something ain't right with that boy." She didn't know why she thought it, so she shook the thought free.

III

Johnnie returned to his room. He did not think about going out any-more, or wanting to feel better, or about the Johnsons wanting him moved out. He didn't care if Mrs. Johnson and Eva Holston were talking about him. He heard the women clutter and cluck good-bye, and the door finally shut. He turned Tupac Shakur up louder and louder on his boom box until the aluminum sides of the small straw-yellow house shook. Mrs. Johnson didn't tell him to turn it down, as he expected she would.

Instead, she had gone to her bedroom for her Bibles and returned to read them at the dining room table. She lay one open on her pink table-cloth to Psalm 121, verses 1 through 8.

> I lift my eyes to the hills—
> where does my help come
> from?
> My help comes from the Lord,
> the Maker of heaven and
> earth . . .
> The Lord watches over you—
> the Lord is your shade at
> your right hand;
> the sun will not harm you by
> day
> nor the moon by night.
> The Lord will keep you from
> all harm—
> he will watch over your life;
> the Lord will watch over your
> coming and going
> both now and forevermore.

As the music grew louder, she turned to her second Bible. Later, a detective would come to believe she intended for Johnnie to read this passage from Galatians (6:7–10) in hopes of deterring him. He still catches his breath thinking that Mrs. Johnson had sensed what was about to happen.

> Do not be deceived: God cannot be mocked. A man
> reaps what he sows. The one who sows to please his
> sinful nature, from that nature will reap destruction;
> the one who sows to please the Spirit, from the Spirit
> will reap eternal life . . . Therefore, as we have
> opportunity, let us do good to all people . . .

As Mrs. Johnson sought refuge in her Bibles, Johnnie sat listening to his gangsta rap while a darkening cloud gathered strength, preparing to sweep through his mind.

III

"That's when I started getting these thoughts in my head about killing," he told me later.

The evil thoughts grew harder and deeper and sharper. He tried to shake them, but they were lodged in his mind. He walked to the doorway between the kitchen and the front room, where Mrs. Johnson had returned to watch television.

Bang her over the head. That's all. Bang her over the head.

I could, he thought, as if replying to the voice in his head.[1]

Naw, man. Don't do it, another thought spoke to him in a voice higher than the last.

Do it! said the first voice. This was a man's voice, and spoke as clearly as his father.

Johnnie sat on the couch with Mrs. Johnson. He no longer heard the music still rapping in his room, or the television. He saw her laugh at the TV but didn't hear the laugh. He could only hear the strange voices arguing: one telling him to kill her, the other cautioning him not to. He

---

1. Johnnie believed these voices to be real. A psychiatrist later concluded these voices were the manifestation of a struggle going on inside his conscience.

even saw where the voices came from, he says now. On his right shoulder sat a little devil in a red coat, holding a black pitchfork. On his left stood a little angel in white. Just like in the cartoons. Though he sat facing the television, he felt he was watching himself from the corner of the ceiling above as the angel and the devil argued.

He went to the kitchen where his eye caught the hatchet, behind the stove, which Mr. Johnson used to fix the curtain rod. It seemed to be waiting for him. His arms felt heavy and strong.

What would it feel like to bang her over the head once? he wondered. Just once. It seemed irresistible.

Do it.

He took hold of the hatchet in his right hand as Mrs. Johnson entered the kitchen, a strange, small smile on her face and in her eyes. He hid the hatchet behind his back.

She tripped slightly as she walked past him but did not fall, then began washing dishes from his breakfast. She was planning to make his favorite dinner that night, fried chicken, believing it would be his last night with them. She was counting on the foster care people to take him to a group home in the morning.

Mrs. Johnson's back was turned to Johnnie when he began to move toward her.

Should I do it? Johnnie asked himself.

Do it, a voice said again.

But at the last moment, Johnnie changed his mind. He returned to the living room, passing the Bibles Mrs. Johnson had left in plain view. He glanced briefly in their direction before standing in front of the television, which droned on, voiceless and meaningless to him. He saw only the greyness in his mind. Nothing was better. He felt he had to free himself of this mean agitation inside of him.

He went back to the kitchen. Once again, just inside the doorway, he faltered, and returned to the front room.

The television flew to a blur of voices and flying colors now, as his music throbbed the house.

I don't care, he thought.

For the third time, he entered the kitchen. He raised the hatchet over Mrs. Johnson. Relief washed through him as he smashed the blunt end of the hatchet on the back of her small skull. The room seemed to echo with the thud, and then turned eerily silent. For a moment, no one moved. Nothing moved. Johnnie's arm rang with excitement, but his mind fell still and confusion washed over his burning fury. Mrs. Johnson shook with the force of the blow, then stumbled backward, one step, two steps, before turning to look him full in the face. Her brown eyes were lit with surprise, her eyebrows high, her mouth slightly open.

Why? A whisper passed in the thin air, though Johnnie does not know if the word was actually spoken. Her gasp was quickly swallowed up by the air which seemed to be fleeing the room.

Why did I do that? he thought. A stillness enveloped them both.

The voices in Johnnie's head stopped. Everything was quiet. Neither moved for what felt like a long time.

"I didn't want to hit her again," Johnnie said later. "But I, I didn't know what to do. I—I was scared. The way she looked at me—" He broke off for a moment, the first and only time he did so in his taped confession to the detectives.

Mrs. Johnson did not scream as he struck her a second time. She did not utter a word as she fell and struggled to get up. Johnnie met her eyes. The confusion and surprise staring back at him only fed his anger and stoked his rage into a fury. His arm flew as if the hatchet were weightless, crushing her right eye, then shattering her skull and then, turning to the hatchet's cutting edge, slashing at her skin and muscle. Each blow was directed at her face—her eyes and her mouth—ten blows was the coroner's estimate, maybe fifteen.

Johnnie doesn't remember how many times he struck her, but he thinks it was more like twenty or thirty. Blow after blow, he found, she would not die. He had wanted to hit her just once. But life was more difficult to extinguish, even in Mrs. Johnson's fragile body. Every time she moved, he struck again. When her blood gurgled, he struck more. He did not understand how much it took to destroy a body or a life. And he did not know that rage could take him so fully, or that the fury washing over him would feel so good.

"I wanted it to work out like I hit her one time and she pass out or something and I put her in her closet somewhere and it won't—you know what I'm saying? You don't see no blood or anything," he said later.

But she was still there. Her body was there, spilling red blood across the kitchen floor. She finally lay still, next to the deep freezer, her arms reaching for the back door.

Johnnie's thoughts came back to him, out of the blurring fury. He had been there, watching himself, every blow, like an observer in the corner of the kitchen. Now his thoughts and sight returned to his body completely.

Johnnie does not understand what the word "panic" means. His knowledge is as uneven as his education. He learned the term "paranoid" from a psychologist, but he claims not to understand the word "panic." But he says he paced back and forth through the small house, from the kitchen to the front room and back, frantically thinking about what to do next.

"Not running," he says, "but going through the house paranoid and stuff. I was frightened. You know what I'm saying? No wetness came to my eyes. You know what I'm saying? I didn't feel nothing for Mrs. Johnson or what I had done."

For a moment, he was amazed and even scared of himself, wondering what had allowed him to kill like that, without feeling sad. But his fear quickly took a more practical turn. Where could he go? He had to run before Mr. Johnson came home. He knew he couldn't hide Mrs. Johnson's body. He had to leave. But he had no money even to catch the bus into town.

He searched the Johnsons' bedroom bureau until he found Mrs. Johnson's shiny black purse in the bottom drawer. He tore at the snap and dumped the contents onto the bed. A half roll of cherry Life Savers tumbled out with a few yellow and green hard candies, then the Sweet'n Low packets she carried for her husband, who was diabetic, and finally some money. Johnnie grabbed the bills and most of the change, $12.49 in all, though he thought it was at least double that amount.[2] He had never stolen like this before, from a lady's purse, and it felt strange to him, stranger almost than the murder.

He grabbed his jacket and gloves and returned to Mrs. Johnson's body with her money in his pocket. He stood before her for several

2. Police reports say Johnnie took $7.49, because that was the amount of money on him at the time of his arrest. But Johnnie spent some money before he was apprehended.

minutes, but remembers thinking nothing, feeling nothing. Still no tears came to his wide eyes. He was too preoccupied, seeing what he had done. He turned away briefly. Then, with a fluttered glance, he thought he saw her catch a shallow breath. He looked hard, straining to see signs of life. She seemed to move very slowly.[3] He believes he heard the gurgling of her blood too, over the bleating boom box and the growling television.

He remembered the kerosene Mr. Johnson had brought into the house the night before, when the wind howled outside and Johnnie had said he was cold. He removed the yellow cap, placed it on the kitchen counter, and poured the oily, transparent liquid over Mrs. Johnson's body, from her feet up to her face. She did not move nor make a sound. He flicked on a Bic lighter and placed it to her leg. It flamed for a moment but quickly went out—not once, not twice, but three times, until he found a piece of cardboard, lit it, and touched its orange flame to her leg.

Mrs. Johnson was on fire when he ran out into the cold night, leaving the bloody hatchet in a wooden cupboard in the front room, next to the photo album now splattered with blood. He had not meant to hide it so much as to put it away.

Mr. Johnson would be home soon, Johnnie figured, and he was right. The green Chevrolet had already turned off the highway and onto Spencer's quiet back streets. Mr. Johnson had finished marveling at the sky, finished outlining his sermon in his head. He was still living in a gentler world that no longer existed. It did not occur to him that the figure walking in the middle of the road far ahead might be Johnnie. He turned right, heading home, as Johnnie continued up the road.

III

Johnnie displayed almost no emotion when he confessed. He was mechanical, matter-of-fact. Not regretful, not mean, not angry, not scared. Nothing. It was the most bizarre confession Detective Denny Richardson of the Lucas County Sheriff's Department had ever heard.

3. The coroner reported that Mrs. Johnson was probably dead from the beating. But Johnnie believes he saw her breathe. An autopsy reports no soot in her lungs, which if present, would indicate she was still breathing when Johnnie set her on fire.

After a half hour of relating the bloody details to detectives, Johnnie was asked what had spurred his lethal outburst.

"Have you had it in you a long time?" Richardson asked. "Or did something happen that day?"

"It just—she—she ain't do nothing to me," Johnnie says in his taped confession. "It just that something went through my head. She—she was a nice lady. I'm—I'm sorry that I did it—did that to her. It's just something that went through my head that made me do it. She didn't do nothing to me."

"And why are you telling us this today?" the detective continued.

"Because I guess I need help," Johnnie said. He did not want to do anything like this again. He thought he might. And he thought the police would get him help. His probation officer had said they would.

Now Johnnie wishes he had not told the truth. He wishes he had just run away. If he had been caught, he would not have confessed. Nothing he did, he says today, made him deserve what happened next. Nothing. Rather than blossoming with time, Johnnie's regret diminishes.

3

The frigid January air, sharp and cold, slapped Johnnie as he left the Johnsons' home. He zipped up his black Jacksonville Jaguars jacket and buried his gloved hands in his jeans pockets.

Blue-white stars pierced the early evening sky. Johnnie kept his eyes on his white sneakers, almost glowing in the darkness, as he shuffled down the road. He thought of nothing, not where to go nor what to do. He walked straight down the middle of the country road, lined with a prickly warren of barren trees.

He did not dwell on what he had done. But he knew. He did it. So what? He guessed she died there. He didn't know. It just happened. Like everything else in his life. Things just happened. There wasn't a reason or cause; there never was, only excuses later.

Thin, icy air swallowed the white vapors of his breath. He had walked almost a mile down Irwin Road before his feet began to get numb. He wished he had that dog with him now. The stupid stray dog had followed him home, but because it was so raggedy, Mrs. Johnson didn't want it in the house to mess up her floors. He had tried to get rid of that stupid brown mutt, he recalled with a small smile playing on his lips, but the dog kept following him. At night, Johnnie would see the dog curl up outside, sometimes under his window in the snow, sometimes under the porch, waiting for him until morning. Before he named it, Mrs. Johnson complained to his social worker, who told Johnnie that she would take the dog to live with her sister. Tamara Cusack, his case-worker, did take the dog, but he knew she didn't take it to her sister's. He knew she lied, but he liked her. She was pretty. She was getting married. He frowned. He didn't like her getting married. Probably that dog got hit by a car by now, it was so stupid. He didn't even like dogs.

Yellow headlights spotted Johnnie just in time for the car to swerve and avoid hitting him. He hadn't noticed the car until the lights blinded him, filling his eyes and making his heart jump. Where would he go? For a moment he thought of calling Mr. Johnson. He was the only one who would have come and gotten him before. But no, not now. Mr. Johnson would not come for him now. The thought was brief and jarring. He grew nervous, agitated. No one here for me now, he thought. Mr. Johnson would soon be coming along the very road Johnnie walked and not even know, Johnnie thought. He wanted to leave before Mr. Johnson saw him, before he found out. Were there any buses to take him into Toledo? He didn't know their schedule. He was walking toward Oak Terrace, the public housing project.[1] That was where he usually went at night. It was the only action he had found in Spencer. His "boy" Stacy would know the bus schedule.

Johnnie's feet moved faster as the darkness closed in, passing Pargo's pool hall and bar, a squat whitewashed cinder-block dive with red neon beer signs in its small iron-barred windows. A cluster of apartment lights burned yellow holes in the dark night just beyond at Oak Terrace. Johnnie weaved through the back yards of the low-rise buildings strung together on tight curving streets that more often than not wound up going nowhere but a circle, until he reached 9845 Oak Place. He ignored some teenage boys pushing each other around in the halls and knocked on the front door of apartment 2A.

Ora Jackson, Stacy's sister, let him in. She noticed nothing different about Johnnie as she kept chatting on the phone—he was polite, quiet, and sometimes, with that smile, charming, she remembers. Did she know when the buses ran into the city? She shook her head. Could he use the phone? She ended her conversation for him. But the phone rang before Johnnie could use it, and she was drawn into a new conversation. While she was talking, Stacy, who was almost twice Johnnie's age,

---

1. In an effort to disperse the inner-city poor of Toledo, Catholic Charities established the Oak Terrace Housing Development on the corner of Irwin and Angola Roads in the 1960s. The Lucas County Housing Authority took over the development in 1973. Using a federal grant, they renovated the eight multifamily apartment buildings hoping the new rural environment would revitalize Toledo's destitute families. With the projects, Spencer's poverty rate has grown to 13.2 percent, almost matching the rate of 15.3 percent in Lucas County, which includes Toledo.

came home and Johnnie asked for a ride into the city in his car. At first, Stacy refused. It was cold out and he was tired. But when Johnnie offered him $5, Stacy agreed.

Johnnie rode in the back seat of Stacy's Ford, on the driver's side, and asked about bus schedules.

"You okay?" Stacy asked

"Why?" Johnnie asked.

"You're acting kind of weird," he told Johnnie.

Johnnie shrugged. He didn't think he was acting any different, and Stacy didn't pursue it. Instead, he turned the radio on and they listened to music as the winter evening dropped quickly into night. He let Johnnie off at the 7-Eleven store on the corner of Hawley and Western, across the street from Libbey High School, a regular hangout where kids gather at the corner after school and in the evening, the older ones smoking and looking for trouble, the younger ones drinking Slurpees or sodas and pedaling their bikes past tumbling houses and litter-strewn lots. The East Indian family that owned the store was wary of the youths. When the older boys, daring to be challenged, boldly slipped gum and candy in their pockets, the owners would look the other way. The East Coast Crips and the Bloods had made deep inroads in Toledo.

Johnnie gave Stacy his $5, maybe a little more. Instead of going into the store, he walked down Western, hands stuffed in his jacket pockets. He had left his gloves behind.

He still didn't know where to go. He stopped thinking about buses. He stopped thinking about getting away. Maybe tomorrow he'd try to head out of the city. Now he just wanted a place to sit and get warm. He decided to call on one of his girlfriends.

Katrina was pretty and bright.[2] He saw her more regularly than the others, although she was older, almost in her twenties. Most of Johnnie's friends were older. All of them, it was reported in his probation records when he was fourteen, had found themselves in conflict with the law at one time or another. But Johnnie never felt he had good friends or anyone he could trust, not even Pebbles, as he called Katrina, who had no criminal record and was generally known in the neighbor-

2. Katrina's name has been changed to protect the identity of her child fathered by Johnnie.

hood to be a good girl, a girl with a future. He didn't like talking much to people, especially about himself. He figured that when he told people something, they acted like they understood when they didn't. So he gave up. The nearest to a best friend he had would have been Jerry, but he doubts he ever knew Jerry's last name. They met in detention at St. Anthony's Villa and later hung out on the streets together. "That's why I liked him," Johnnie recalls. "He got in trouble like me." Eventually, Jerry's mother had sent him to live with family in Mississippi, to get him off the city streets.

Katrina saw a softer side of Johnnie, one that he only allowed girls to see. "Stay sweet," she would write to him later, "and pray." Johnnie would just laugh. Johnnie liked her well enough, but she meant little to him. Nobody he had sex with meant anything to him. But Katrina liked Johnnie a lot. She's not sure why. He had a handsome smile. Maybe the way he acted so cool appealed to her. He walked around like anything could happen and he would not care. He was tough, but he was also sensitive. He'd stand up for her, even fight for her. He was loyal.

Katrina was alone in her mother's small house when Johnnie knocked. His visit wasn't unusual. He just showed up sometimes, especially when her mother was at work. They watched television for a while. She asked if he was hungry, and prepared something for him. He had seconds, though even then he could not remember what he ate. After more TV, they "kicked it."

"And that don't mean we talked," he said later, with a half smile.

He fell asleep after sex. It did not occur to him to tell Katrina what he had done, or to ask her help. She elbowed him awake abruptly when she heard her mother coming home. Johnnie dressed quickly and climbed out the window. Katrina's mother didn't like Johnnie. No one knew why exactly, nor did they expect otherwise.

Johnnie was feeling better now, smoother, less jittery and sensitive. The cold no longer bothered him. His feet took him through the four-block area where he had grown up with more than a dozen different foster parents. He retraced his path to Libbey, the large brick high school, and continued along the high wire fence, over a frozen creek and deep into a tunnel under rickety train tracks. The dark woods on either side of the road frightened him. People never scared Johnnie; only monsters in the wilderness did. Once past, he relaxed in the familiar streets, with garbage in the road and plastic bags tumbling dry and dead in the empty wind. Many of the houses were boarded up, their brick steps crumbling. Plastic sheets covered some windows. Chairs rusted on front porches and signs warned of fierce, nonexistent dogs. Grey electrical tape held together the fractured glass of a beauty shop. A low storefront church proclaimed its Bible message of the day: "believe on [sic] the Lord Jesus Christ, and thou shalt be saved . . ."

Johnnie tried to read the words, but they made no more sense to him than the preacher at the Johnsons' church. To believe in a person named Jesus was all it took to go to heaven, his stepgrandmother once told him. But Johnnie was too honest to pretend to care about someone he never met, someone who had never done anything for him. He never really thought about death, even though he had often thought about killing himself. He didn't understand death any more than he understood life. For Johnnie, life was what stood before him at any given moment. And now, all that faced him was the night.

He wondered where he could go to keep warm. Frankie Cooper on Buckingham, he thought. He liked Ms. Cooper. She was tough on him, but straight. He knew she cared. Of all the foster parents who had taken him in, Ms. Cooper and Mrs. Johnson were his favorites. It did not occur to him then that Frankie Cooper was the only other person he had ever truly thought of killing, that Ms. Cooper almost had been his first murder victim. He only had good thoughts about her now, much as he did about Mrs. Johnson. But he decided against visiting Ms. Cooper. She might want to know why he was out so late. Instead, he headed toward the home of another boy. In the morning, he'd work his way over to another girlfriend's. He had no plans beyond that.

Johnnie still did not realize that he was on the run. He wasn't thinking about getting caught. He never thought of turning himself in. His mind was clouded and dull, back to normal. Johnnie generally strove to be lost from himself, and he succeeded most of the time. And now, he would not allow the fresh memory of the murder to surface. He would not open the night to examination or emotion. Life would just happen to him, as it always had before. It didn't matter. Nothing did.

4

Mrs. Johnson, she had the stars of heaven shining in her eyes. That pure light came right out of her eyes. I don't expect you to understand. Sure, she seemed simple in the mind, but so she was in spirit, simple and pure as a child of heaven. Now don't you put my name in that book. I don't want no devil-child coming after me. That's what he is you know, a child of the devil. There ain't no other truth or reason, and if you're looking for any, they called excuses.

—A church friend of Mrs. Johnson's

Teresa Edwards met Jeanette Johnson through business, as she calls it, the business of foster care, and they quickly became good friends. For a year and a half now, they talked on the phone every other day around five-thirty in the afternoon, when their kids started to settle down. Teresa was drawn to Mrs. Johnson's gentle nature, her good laugh, her sincerity, and her life wisdom. Like Teresa and Teresa's mother, who also foster-parented children, Mrs. Johnson took in children because she couldn't bear the thought of an unwanted and homeless child. For too many people, foster care had become a business, a means to make extra money on the side. But for Mrs. Johnson, it was a calling, a response to need.

After Teresa adopted her young son, she drew back from foster parenting. She had the responsibility of her son to consider now, not just her own safety to think about. She had to be more selective about who she let into her home with her own child. But she and Mrs. Johnson remained close. Teresa would not leave her son with many people, sometimes not even with her mother if she was dubious about the foster children staying there. Mrs. Johnson was one she trusted most to care for her boy overnight on weekends when Teresa needed to get out for a breath of adult fun.

Teresa heard from Mrs. Johnson one evening about a child the Lucas County Children Services had placed in the Johnsons' home. Johnnie Jordan was a quiet and sad young man, Mrs. Johnson said, but seemed to be a fairly good boy. She didn't know his official case plan, his personal background, or why he was in foster care. She knew only that the caseworker from Lucas County Children Services who asked her to take him sounded desperate.

Mrs. Johnson admitted that she and Mr. Johnson wanted to settle into a more peaceful retirement. A teenage boy was a little too much for them at the moment. But the caseworker's pleas touched Mrs. Johnson's heart. She could not help worrying about how the boy must feel if he was so unwanted. In the four decades she and Mr. Johnson foster-parented, she had never turned a child away, nor asked that one be taken from her home, no matter how difficult the child might have been. So now, when the caseworker promised that the child would be in their home only a few days, Mrs. Johnson agreed to speak to her husband. Together they decided to accept Johnnie Jordan.

Teresa had known Johnnie before. Five or six years earlier, he had been placed in her mother's foster care. He always seemed very confused, even lost. Since then, she had come across Johnnie occasionally, in the traffic of people coming in and out of friends' houses or on the street. Each time, he was living in a different foster home. His smiles became rarer, and he seemed more confused and distracted as the years passed. The sweetness in him appeared to be drying up. He was no longer the young boy who had been quick to give her a fresh smile. Teresa had heard that Johnnie flirted with gangs, even joined the Crips and fell into dealing drugs and selling guns, but they were only rumors and she would not lower herself to pass them along.[1] At the Johnsons',

---

1. Johnnie had been a member of the Crips since he was twelve years old. While his foster care and juvenile justice records often made note of his affiliation, Johnnie did not feel a real connection to the gang. He joined almost by default after his older sister, who ran with the Crips, got into a fight with a girl who was associated with a rival gang. The Crips mounted a drive-by shooting at their rivals and Johnnie, then twelve, participated in the raid. But the gang never became a substitute family for Johnnie. He does not think he was influenced so much by his peers when he was younger, but he was more influenced by his siblings and doing what he needed to take care of them.

maybe Johnnie had changed. Mrs. Johnson sounded like she was okay with him. Three days passed without incident. The few days promised by the social worker extended to more than four weeks, and in that time Mr. Johnson gradually brought back Johnnie's smile, his playfulness. Maybe, Teresa thought, it would be alright after all.

Johnnie, for his part, had liked Teresa Edwards ever since he had been a foster child in her mother's home. She was kind to him, sometimes taking him out to eat, sometimes letting him visit her home. She looked young, and she wasn't overly strict. More than anyone he met, he would have liked her to be his mom. For her, he would have tried.

Johnnie was not surprised to run into Teresa again at the Johnsons'. Many foster parents knew each other and visited each other's homes. But he was surprised the day she brought over her ten-year-old adopted son. Johnnie did not know she had adopted anyone. He didn't think about it enough to realize he was jealous. He would play with her boy when they spent the night at the Johnsons'. He might as well; there was nothing else to do out there in the boondocks. But he found the boy annoying, constantly talking and happy. It didn't seem fair to Johnnie.

Late Friday afternoon, three days before the murder, Edwards dropped her son off at the Johnsons'. They had agreed to baby-sit him for the night. The house smelled of the warmth and goodness of dinner. Johnnie asked Teresa if he could speak with her, and walked her out to her car. He told her that he knew his caseworker's plan was to transfer him to a group home. He did not want to leave the Johnsons', and he was agitated. The institutions his caseworker had mentioned as possibilities were outside Toledo, away from Johnnie's family. The caseworker thought Johnnie's family was a bad influence and worried that he was hurt by the street gossip about the trouble his parents and siblings were constantly involved in. But Johnnie didn't want to go.

"I didn't do anything wrong," he complained to Teresa. "Why can't I stay?"

Teresa had no answer.

III

When Teresa came the next morning for her son, she sensed tension in the home. There was an edginess to Mrs. Johnson that Teresa had not seen before. They chatted about the weather, about church, regular things, but Mrs. Johnson did not relax. She wanted Teresa to stay longer. Usually, Teresa would snatch up her son and be off, but this Saturday, Mrs. Johnson took Teresa's coat and practically forced her to sit down. Mr. Johnson was there, but he was different too; quiet, not kidding in his usual way.

Teresa stayed for several hours. Johnnie and Teresa's sons were hand-paddling, slapping at each other's hands. The slaps grew harder and the mumbling fiercer before Teresa raised her hand to the boys and told them to settle down. They did for a moment. Then an argument erupted loudly.

"I asked her to be my mom first," Johnnie burst out. "Before you."

"What?" Teresa asked.

"Remember, I asked you," Johnnie said defiantly. "You picked me up one day. We were driving down a long street. Remember? I asked you to be my mom!"

Teresa felt the anger in his voice. He wasn't asking her to recall a memory. He was speaking with a bitterness he had harvested for years.

"Yes, you did," Teresa said, remembering the ride down McCord Road when she had picked him up from her mother's house. But she wasn't sure what to say, and she did not like the tone of Johnnie's voice, so she sternly brushed him off.

Teresa and Mrs. Johnson continued to talk about church. The Johnsons were going that day, as well as the next day.

"She is my mom! I asked her first," Johnnie burst forth again. This time he was even louder and angrier.

Teresa looked at Johnnie then, straight into his eyes. She had to force herself not to flinch from the pool of anger smoldering there.

"Johnnie, you did ask me first, but when you asked me, I was in foster care myself. I wasn't thinking about adoption then."

Teresa refused to pay any more attention to Johnnie and turned back to Mrs. Johnson. After a few more moments, she stood up to leave.

"Sit down. You always in a hurry, girl," Mrs. Johnson insisted. "Sit down."

This is not Mrs. Johnson, Teresa thought. "Really, I have to go," she said.

Mrs. Johnson looked strained, but with a sad smile, she replied, "Of course."

"Could I go home with you?" Johnnie suddenly asked.

"Yes," she agreed, thinking that a trip away from the Johnsons might ease the tension in the house. Then she thought better of it.

"Wait until I get in contact with Children Services," she said, "and I'll get back with you Monday." Johnnie knew she wouldn't.

After church on Sunday, Mrs. Johnson complained to Teresa that Johnnie's attitude had abruptly changed for the worse. He had turned nasty and angry when he spoke. His tone, even more than his words, chilled Mrs. Johnson. A devil was inside him, she whispered to Teresa on the phone the day before the murder.

Johnnie did not want to leave the Johnsons, and he certainly didn't want to go to a home away from Toledo. He stayed out beyond curfew that night. When Mr. Johnson chastised him, he became sassy, cursing Mrs. Johnson. Mr. Johnson told him that he did not allow such words in his house. Far from repentant, Johnnie swore at his foster father. He was full of pent-up anger; he knew Mr. Johnson had phoned Children Services on Friday and asked that the foster care agency immediately take Johnnie from his home after Johnnie had let loose a similar temper tantrum. Told that Johnnie's caseworker was not available, a panicked Mr. Johnson called again later that morning, and a third time in the afternoon, each time leaving urgent messages.

Mrs. Johnson told Teresa how she and her husband had called the social workers repeatedly for help but had gotten nowhere. Teresa offered to call the agency herself on Monday.

She then asked to speak to Mr. Johnson. "Call 327-3200," she advised him in a whisper. "The twenty-four-hour crisis number."

III

On Monday morning, January 29, 1996, Teresa kept her promise. She phoned Children Services and spoke to a young man. She said the Johnsons wanted Johnnie out of their home right away. But there was nowhere for him to go, she was told. Besides, Johnnie would be going to a group home within a few days. That is what they had told the Johnsons two months ago. Desperate, Teresa told the social worker she would take Johnnie into her home for a couple of days if necessary.

But the young man warned Teresa about Johnnie's history. Johnnie had been violent in the past. There were "sexual issues" involved. He needed intense therapy to curb his anger. In short, putting Johnnie in a home with a younger child was not a good idea.

Teresa was astonished. She was flabbergasted to hear that Johnnie's troubles ran so deep and that he was so dangerous. She was certain the Johnsons had also been kept in the dark.

"I'm going to call Mrs. Johnson. I know she is not aware of all this," Teresa told the agency official. The social worker said nothing.

But the Johnsons' line rang in an empty house and Teresa became swept up in her busy day. Usually she phoned Mrs. Johnson in the early evening anyway. She would try then.

At six o'clock, Teresa was on the phone with another friend when the line beeped with a second call. It was her mother. Had she heard?

She couldn't believe her mother's stark words. Immediately she rang the Johnsons, her heart pounding and fluttering, hoping the news was not true. Twice, three times, the phone rang. Mr. Johnson answered.

"Girl, I'm trying to, I—" He broke off. Teresa felt her heart freeze. "I–was trying to find your number."

"Is it true?" She asked. "Is it true that Johnnie killed my friend?"

For a moment there was no sound. Then a deep, hollow breath.

"Lord have mercy," Mr. Johnson cried, not with bitterness or anger, just a breath he couldn't seem to catch or grasp, a breath that had escaped him. "Lord have mercy. My wife is on fire."

5

62-year-old 5'2" female weighing an estimated 120 lbs. Right eye has been destroyed. The skin is charred on the right side of the face, chin, neck, torso, right arm.

—Coroner's report

As Detective Ernest Lamb walked through the narrow grey halls of the Lucas County Sheriff's Department in downtown Toledo Friday night, he felt a shiver up his spine. A neat, good-looking man with broad shoulders and an easy, relaxed smile, Lamb is not likely to let his senses shake him. But they did this time. The phones lay too quiet. The office was too still. Toledo is always less active than Detroit or Cleveland, but this quiet felt unnatural, like the air before a storm.

"Something's gonna jump," he told the other detectives, adjusting his overcoat to meet the cold beyond the glass doors through which they passed into the weekend. "We've been going along smooth sailing. Something's gonna jump sooner or later, and I just hope it doesn't get me."

They all laughed.

It did not occur to him that he was the on-call detective.

|||

At 6:35 P.M., Monday, just after dinner, the call came. At first, Lamb thought the dispatcher was joking; nothing this violent happens in Toledo, let alone in Spencer Township. Sure, there were murders, suicides, rapes. But those were more direct hits of simple violence. The dispatcher described a crime scene way more grisly and ugly involving an older woman. Maybe if the victim had been younger and the body had been found in Toledo, he wouldn't have been so shocked. But even then,

such a murder would be extremely rare, and never involve an elderly woman. Not in his town. Given his prediction from three days ago, he thought someone might be pulling his leg. Sometimes Dispatch will pull a gag, and now, three days before his first anniversary as a detective, he suspected a prank. Besides, in his eighteen years on the force—seven years as a jail officer, almost ten patrolling the streets, and finally as one of the first black detectives in Toledo—he never heard anything like this: a structure fire, a body hacked and set ablaze. He had been called to burglaries, one suicide, but nothing like this.

From his house on the border of the township, Lamb reached the Johnsons' home in five minutes. He knew as he approached 125 Irwin Road that this was no joke. The fire chief's car and the paramedic truck waited, their drivers standing together in the cold. From their strained faces and shifting efforts to keep warm, Lamb knew they did not want to go into the house.

"You've got a murder on your hands," a paramedic told him as he walked toward the house. The seriousness of his expression made the scene all too real. This was not what Lamb wanted. This, his first homicide case, promised to be too big, with too many eyes watching. If you don't solve your first case, he knew, it hangs over your head for the rest of your career.

Deputy Sheriff Phil Williams, the patrol officer who was first on the scene, met Lamb at the door and briefed him quickly outside. His eyes were big, full of the crime scene. Some of the strong, nauseating odor that had overtaken Williams when he arrived ten minutes earlier had been aired out of the house, but it remained powerful.

The body was in the kitchen, Williams told Lamb. It had been set on fire. It looked like the victim had been hit with something. And, Williams told him, they had a suspect—one Johnnie Jordan, a fifteen-year-old foster youth who had been placed in the Johnsons' home.

The rancid smell of burning flesh struck Lamb as he walked into the kitchen. His foot skidded on the linoleum floor, slick with kerosene and blood. He did not see a human body at first. Only by way of his imagination could he make out Mrs. Johnson's charred leg sticking out of a bedspread, and then he recognized her outstretched arm. Lamb bent to uncover her head, exposing her mutilated face and mouth, the bludgeoned back of her head. Some wounds were deep, others shallow. What kind of person would do this to an elderly woman? he thought as he gently re-covered the body with the white bedspread. Lamb would no longer think of Johnnie as a juvenile, not after seeing the body. He would conduct the search for the killer as he would for any murderer who left such a gruesome scene.

Mr. Johnson had been pacing back and forth the length of the house, shaking his head, his eyes fluttering frantically as if looking for something. Not even Eva Holston, who had rushed over from her niece's home across town when her husband phoned, could convince him to sit down, and she could not bring herself to follow him into the kitchen. Why, Lamb asked, did he suspect Johnnie Jordan? Mr. Johnson took a breath. He and his wife were having problems with Johnnie Jordan and had asked Children Services Board, which placed him in their home, to remove him. The social workers had procrastinated for weeks, promising they would take Johnnie soon. They told the Johnsons to hang on. Lamb shook his head. He knew the most brutal crimes were often committed by the young kids now. It's the times. CSB knew that too.

Lieutenant Kirk Surprise arrived to take charge of the scene, leaving Lamb to search for the murder weapon. Something blunt, but also sharp. In Johnnie's room he found a small black book, a title pasted to the front: "Johnnie Jordan's Life Book." Inside were newspaper clippings of his parents' various crimes and his own, as well as some school awards interspersed with a few diarylike entries in which he had written what he had eaten and done various days rather than fragments of personal introspection. Nothing in the last several entries indicated anger. A piece of cardboard with phone numbers and addresses fell to the floor from inside the book cover. The latest newspaper article recounted Johnnie's arrest for assaulting a city bus driver.[1]

Lamb showed Mr. Johnson the newspaper clipping. Mr. Johnson shook his head in disbelief.

"This is the first time you heard of this?" Lamb asked incredulously. "You never knew this kid had a violent temper?"

"No," Mr. Johnson said.

---

1. Johnnie's caseworker had given him the black book and insisted he use it as a diary to relieve his feelings. Johnnie did not understand what she meant. Instead, he used it as a scrapbook, almost proudly recording his family's various run-ins with the law, reported in newspaper clippings from the *Toledo Blade*.

Lamb was appalled that the Johnsons had not known the dangerous history of the boy they had taken into their home. The social workers knew, he bet, but they did not tell the Johnsons because if they had, the couple would have refused. It was an old game. They do not reveal all of the facts about kids when they desperately need a foster placement. With this kid, they must have been desperate.

Though the foster care agency was Johnnie's guardian, Detective Lamb did not call the agency to inform it of the case. He did not think Children Services would be much help. Experience had taught him that CS was rarely as informed about a child in their care as a parent would be, or as Lamb thought they should be. Furthermore, it could complicate matters. While parents might later complain of this omission, he knew Children Services would not.[2] Instead, he asked Mr. Johnson where Johnnie might have gone. Johnnie sometimes talked about a young man known in the projects as Red. But Mr. Johnson did not have an address or a phone number.

As Lamb began his search, he noticed the two Bibles open on the dining room table. It seemed like the Scripture was talking to Johnnie Jordan, Lamb thought. This lady had a premonition that she would be murdered and the Bibles were open to verses meant just for him. She knew this kid was bad, that he was dangerous. Later, Lamb would wish he had instructed the crime-scene photographer to take pictures of those Bibles before Lieutenant Surprise sent him to search for the suspect.

Lamb and his partner, Detective Bruce Birr, stopped first at Pargo's, the local bar, a few miles from the Johnsons' home. The patrons, like himself, were African-American, but Lamb, a well-muscled man, sharply dressed and with a commanding presence, knew he stood out as an unwelcome outsider. A hush fell over the bar when he entered. Three or four customers looked at him, then puckered distastefully before turning away. Lamb identified himself loudly and asked if anyone knew Johnnie Jordan. He got only "the sneers," as he calls the reception. No one replied. He asked again, less politely now. Still nothing.

"Any of you know Mrs. Johnson?" he asked. Heads turned back to him. People began to stir, looking at each other and then to Lamb.

---

2. Some states require police to inform parents when their child is arrested. None require police to inform parents when their child is only a suspect in a crime.

"You mean the nice old lady down the road?" one man asked.

"Yeah, that nice old lady was just beaten with an ax and set on fire by this Johnnie Jordan," Lamb replied.

This got their full attention. They gave Lamb the next lead. Across the street, in a low-rise building in the projects, he would most likely find Johnnie.

Oak Terrace would take hours to scour. Outside, Lamb saw a group of young gangbangers ducking into doorways at the sight of his car. Their tough act couldn't hide their innocence. "Wanna-bes," the local sheriff called them, laughing at the attitudes they adopted but had not grown into yet. They claimed not to know Johnnie.

Lamb and Birr began knocking on doors. They got the same cold response that had greeted them at the bar at first. Nobody offered to talk to him and his white partner. But when Lamb mentioned Mrs. Johnson's name, and how she had been killed, Ora Jackson stepped forward quietly and motioned the detectives into her apartment. There they spoke to Stacy Kaynard, who said he had driven Johnnie into town earlier. Stacy also said that after he dropped Johnnie off, he had called his sister from the 7-Eleven to see if she needed anything. Based on the time of that phone call, the detectives knew Johnnie was less than an hour ahead of them.

Lamb immediately radioed his lieutenant and received authorization to call in the Fugitive Task Force—a five-man law enforcement unit led by the FBI and designed to apprehend dangerous criminals. Anyone who had seen the battered and burned body of Mrs. Johnson would have no doubt that the murderer, no matter how old, was indeed very dangerous, and probably desperate.

6

Mrs. Johnson was lying there in a pool of blood. Worst thing in my life I ever seen. The house was full of people—police, fire, rescue. Everyone was quiet. Only sound was someone from the coroner's office snapping pictures and Mr. Johnson pacing back and forth, back and forth.

—Eva Holston, neighbor

As one of the five law enforcement agents of the Northwest Ohio Fugitive Task Force, Detective Denny Richardson's mandate is to apprehend violent criminals from other jurisdictions outside of Toledo and assist in investigations of their crimes. Richardson, a Toledo police officer with twenty-four years of service, had logged four homicide cases during his four years on the Task Force. He is always on call.

About eight o'clock Monday evening, Task Force chief Wendell Hissrich of the FBI called Richardson, briefly described the crime scene at the Johnson residence, and sent him to the 7-Eleven at the intersection of Western and Hawley, the corner where Johnnie was last seen. There, Hissrich and Richardson met the other members of the Task Force—Danny LaCourse, a Lucas County sheriff's deputy; Roger Rettig, a Toledo police officer; and Mike Belcik, a police officer from a neighboring town.

Johnnie Jordan was dangerous, running from a particularly brutal murder, they were told. Few crimes leave perpetrators more desperate than murder, particularly a slaying as crazed as this one.

Driving his Ford Bronco toward the ghetto, as Detective Richardson calls the neighborhood where Johnnie was presumed to be hiding, he thought how the statistics fit this crime. Most juvenile offenders, especially violent ones, commit their crimes between 3 P.M. and 9 P.M. In contrast, adult criminal activity is most frequent between 9 P.M. and midnight.[1] Most homicides are committed on Monday or Tuesday nights, particularly when it's raining, although this particular Monday night was clear.

Richardson was neither surprised nor did he feel inconvenienced by this sudden call to report to work. Duty was a way of life for him. He had reenlisted in the Marine Corps in 1967 to serve in Vietnam. With the air of a greying sea captain, his muscular forearms tattooed, he was a man whose rough exterior put people more at ease when they found themselves in dark corners of the night. Less apparent was his knowledge in legal matters, gained from years of experience.

Lamb told the Task Force they were searching for Johnnie Jordan, whom he described as a fifteen-year-old African-American, about five feet six inches tall and weighing 150 pounds. He was thought to be wearing a hooded blue, white, and black football jacket. In a Polaroid snapshot provided by Mr. Johnson, Johnnie appeared as a child with a soft, smiling face, a thick torso and skinny legs—not exactly the portrait of a gruesome killer. He apparently had no family to seek help from. There was only one lead. The suspect might return to the Campbell-Buckingham-Hamilton area near the 7-Eleven store, the neighborhood that Johnnie knew as the hood.

Looking through Johnnie's "Life Book" earlier, Lamb had seen that Johnnie had once been in the custody of Frankie Cooper, a foster mother on Hamilton Street. The five members of the Task Force made that their first call.

Johnnie was not there, but Ms. Cooper reluctantly told Detective Lamb that the "child" might be at a friend's place on Buckingham Street. She said little else. She told the police she didn't know the address and could not give a firm description of the house.

In three vehicles, none marked, the officers circled the Buckingham area for about fifteen to twenty minutes. They stopped the first young man they saw, and asked if he knew Johnnie Jordan. He pointed them to the 1500 block of Campbell Street, where another friend of Johnnie's lived. Again, they were not given a house address. That lead did not pan out either.

---

1. Confirmed by the *Juvenile Offenders and Victims: 1999 National Report,* issued by the Office of Juvenile Justice and Delinquency Prevention. p. 34.

Lamb and Birr returned to the Johnsons' home to search for more clues and evidence, while Richardson and the others continued to cruise the four-block area in their white Ford Bronco. Around midnight, as Richardson and Hissrich turned onto the 1200 block of Buckingham, their patience paid off.

A figure cutting through an empty lot attracted their attention. He did not seem to be in a hurry, and his jacket did not fit the description they had been given. In fact, he looked nothing like their suspect. But they halted their vehicle at the curb when the figure reached the street. Richardson rolled down the window, calling him over to the car. Crossing in front of the stark high-beam lights, the suspect looked like a man, older and duller, not at all like the picture of a young Johnnie with a quiet smile. Still, his height and weight matched. The style of the jacket was about right, though the colors were off. Without identifying themselves, they asked his name.

"John Black."

The two detectives got out of the car.

"Could I see your ID?" Richardson asked.

"I don't got none."

"Where do you live?"

"Hamilton Street," he told them. "I'm a foster kid there."

The officers recognized Frankie Cooper's address, and they knew they had Johnnie Jordan. Ms. Cooper had a foster child living with her named John Black, but none of the children in her home were over the age of eight. They invited Johnnie to ride with them to Ms. Cooper's. He nodded agreeably.

Not once did Johnnie try to run. He doesn't know why. "I didn't think, man," he would say later. "I seen them, but I didn't know they were the police. I was right outside one of my boys' houses, and a week ago before that he got shot on his front porch [by gang rivals]. I was right out front of his house and I saw that jeep pull up and it was just sitting on the corner, wasn't doing nothing. There was no stop sign or nothing. I be wondering and keep looking back, wondering why they're sitting there. But I got in that frame of mind, I don't care, and kept walking. I wasn't even worried about the police. I was worried about a drive-by [shooting]. I don't know why I didn't run. I wasn't thinking fast. I was in my own little mood. I know any other time I'll run, cuz I'm good at running from police, but that time, I don't know why I didn't run." Nor did Johnnie change his story or back off from the simple answers he gave the detectives. His body was fluid, not rigid. He did not appear scared. He was letting life happen to him. The detectives found this behavior strange, but to Johnnie, it was normal. There was nothing he could do even if he thought he wanted to.

Ms. Cooper did not want to answer the door when the knocker sounded again around midnight, though it felt like the banging shook her whole house. She did not want to alarm the younger children, so she opened her door. She did not like the story the detectives told her. She did not want to believe Johnnie Jordan was capable of murdering Mrs. Johnson. And she certainly did not want to help the police. But she knew she could not stay out of this one.

With her coat draped over her nightgown, she went outside into the cold, looked briefly into the police car and identified Johnnie. He secretly hoped she would protect him, that she would take him in and lie for him. But the anger in her eyes told him otherwise. He felt sad, but only for a second. He did not really expect her to react any other way. He did not think about what he would do next. Thinking ahead had something to do with hope, and he was too wary for that.

When Lamb saw Johnnie sitting in the back seat of Richardson's car, he was struck by how young the boy looked. He had difficulty attributing the brutal murder of an old woman, but a child this young, so dull, so relaxed, was even harder to grasp. The detective looked for certain mannerisms in Johnnie, signs that he was lying. Even the coolest criminals will let something slip out if you watch closely enough, he believed. Johnnie was one of the coolest he had seen. Not cool, he later recognized, but unable to feel. Johnnie's lack of emotion made him seem eerily dead.

III

The police read Johnnie his rights and handcuffed him. He did not ask why. With no witnesses to the murder or proof of his guilt, the officers arrested him on a technicality: for violating his parole.

Several months before, his parole officer had issued a warrant for Johnnie's arrest after Ms. Cooper, then his foster mother, called to say she had heard that Johnnie was carrying a gun. The police went to his school, where they searched Johnnie and his locker, and then combed through his room at Ms. Cooper's house. They found nothing. They did not arrest Johnnie, but his parole officer kept the warrant so police could haul him in without a problem if they suspected Johnnie of a crime, and as a way to warn Johnnie that he was being closely watched. It was a game Johnnie knew well but didn't care much about.[2]

Inside the Lucas County Sheriff's Department, Johnnie was taken to a conference room on the first floor. The windowless room did not intimidate him. From earlier stays in juvenile detention, he was familiar with a stark room like this, with its long table, plastic chairs, and chipped blackboard. He looked to the barred windows, to the dark night outside, and waited for the questions.

During the first hour, the Task Force officers acted almost friendly, as they breezed in and out of the room, chatting with Johnnie casually, even joking with him. They were observing him closely, and like Lamb before them, were amazed at his behavior. He showed no emotion. They could tell the kid probably had a rough life. But his outward serenity was unbelievable, inhuman even, after such a brutal murder.

Johnnie sat at a metal table, his handcuffs off. Lamb asked if he was hungry. Johnnie said no. But he accepted a ginger ale after a bathroom break.

Lamb was nervous. He knew he had to get a confession from Johnnie, and the best chance for that was tonight, before Johnnie had rest and time to concoct stories. No evidence at the Johnsons' house linked Johnnie to the slaying. The detectives did not have the murder weapon. Not only did they need a confession; they had to get the confession right, so that it would stand up in court.

The rules for interrogating adults and juveniles are the same in Ohio. But Lamb felt out of his league. Though he is as well trained as any detective on the force, there is no preparation, guidelines, or special training about how to interview juveniles. Johnnie Jordans were still a relatively new phenomenon. Lamb asked several detectives to join him in interviewing Johnnie. All declined, but suggested he ask Detective Richardson, who had earned their respect long ago on many other cases. Richardson agreed.

---

2. Johnnie says that he had two guns, but had rented one to a friend and buried the other by a fence in back of Ms. Cooper's house. Out of respect for Ms. Cooper, he says, he would not take the guns into her house.

Lamb began by "Mirandizing" Johnnie, reading from the Juvenile Waiver of Rights form:

"Johnnie, you have the right to refuse to make a statement or to answer questions. If you remain silent, your silence cannot be used against you in a court of law. Do you understand?"

"Yes," Johnnie said.

"Anything you say can be used against you in a court of law. Do you understand?" Lamb continued.

"Yes," Johnnie repeated.

"You have the right to the presence of a lawyer or parents or both during the questioning.[3] If you cannot afford a lawyer, a lawyer will be appointed for you before questioning, if you so desire. Do you understand that?"

"Yes."

"Unless you are willing to give up the above rights, no statement of yours can be accepted and no questions will be asked of you. Do you understand?"

"Yes."

"The above rights stay with you and may be claimed now or at any time during the questioning. Do you understand that?"

"Yes."

Lamb asked Johnnie to read a paragraph aloud, to show that he understood and was sufficiently competent and intelligent.

"I have read the statement of my rights shown above. I understand what my rights are. I am willing to answer questions and make a statement. I do not want a lawyer or a parent at this time. I understand and I know what I am doing. No promises or threats have been made to me and no pressure of any kind have been used against me," Johnnie read haltingly.

Later, Johnnie would say that he did not understand what it meant.[4]

---

3. This line, alerting juveniles to the right of having their parent or parents with them, is the only difference between the adult waiver form and the one for juveniles in Ohio. Child advocates contend that the adult wording is not easily understood by children.

4. A study of adolescents' understanding of Miranda rights by Thomas Grisso, a forensic psychologist at the University of Massachusetts Medical School, found that generally juveniles fifteen years and older in calm circumstances can comprehend their rights as well as adults. But fourteen-, fifteen-, and sixteen-year-olds with emotional disabilities like Johnnie's often misconstrue the meaning of these rights as younger, less mature children do. In Grisso's study, one subject interpreted the right to remain silent as meaning he should remain silent until he was told to talk.

He says he does not recall a word of the statement now. He only remembers that at that point he knew he could have called someone if he wanted. But he didn't have a parent to call. And he didn't think a lawyer would help him any more than he could help himself if he could convince the detectives he had nothing to do with the murder.

So Johnnie began answering the questions alone with the detectives. He told them he was in the ninth grade at Libbey High School, that he lived with the Johnsons, that he left their house about two-thirty in the afternoon, and that Mrs. Johnson was still alive and well at the time. Short lies floated easily out of him. But as the hours wore on, he felt a little more strained. He wondered whether he should tell the detectives what actually happened.

Richardson thought Johnnie was on the verge of confessing that night, or at least thought about it. He wondered if Johnnie figured he could control the truth with what he said. Just as young children have difficulty distinguishing between fictional stories and reality, some older children believe they can revise or change the truth with their stories. Abused children often linger in this stage of development. Was Johnnie stuck in that strange stage, or was he a mean criminal behind those dull eyes? He did not appear developmentally delayed, but he did not seem crafty either.

III

Richardson tried to push some buttons. He told Johnnie that Mrs. Johnson had been killed. Johnnie did not flinch. He did not seem upset. He simply said he did not know that she had died. He was not in the house at the time.

Where had he been?

At a girlfriend's house.

Lamb was taken aback. He hadn't thought of a girlfriend. Johnnie seemed too young. They asked for her address. Johnnie could not give it exactly, so they invited him to show them the house.

About 1 A.M. they reached Katrina's house and woke up her family. She was nervous when her mother brought her down to meet the detectives. Johnnie sat coolly in the back seat of the patrol car, knowing what was going to happen but seeming not to care.

Yes, Johnnie had been at the house, Katrina said. But the time she gave was clearly after the murder, so his visit was not a valid alibi. Johnnie was returned to jail and booked for breaking probation.

Lamb was growing frustrated. He knew that Johnnie was lying. Watching him closely, he noticed that Johnnie, despite his surface cool, was swallowing a lot: a strong indicator that he was making up his story. Lamb had also checked into Johnnie's past and learned that Johnnie had the background of a kid who was likely to wind up in a police interrogation room. There was the abuse, the trouble in school, the learning disabilities, parents who were criminals themselves. Johnnie was ripe to strike out at society. But none of this, nor his lies, were enough to convict him. It would not be hard to place Johnnie at the Johnsons' house at the time of the murder, but there was nothing to prove that he actually killed Mrs. Johnson. There were no witnesses, no weapon.

Lamb feared that Johnnie could not be held in jail long enough to get a confession. If Johnnie had a parent to ask for, or a lawyer, his release would already be in the works. Fortunately for the police, Johnnie had no legal parents. His guardian in foster care was the State of Ohio. And even if he had parents, Ohio law would not require police to notify them of his arrest.[5] Lucas County Children Services was Johnnie's legal guardian, but the police did not consider calling the agency. Not because they thought social workers might have tried to protect Johnnie as a parent would—they never did when it came to the police—but because it simply did not seem pertinent.

Approximately six hours after Johnnie was taken into custody, Richardson and Lamb played their last card. They told Johnnie that they were going to take all his clothes to the crime lab and have them tested for DNA to match Mrs. Johnson's. Richardson pointed to a maroon stain on Johnnie's white sneakers and told him that he thought they would probably find their evidence there. If not that stain, he added, then in some fiber on his pants.

Richardson thought they had Johnnie then, but Johnnie kept silent. He put on the jail jumpsuit and slippers, turned his back, and let them close the cell door behind him.

---

5. Some states require police to notify one or both biological parents of a charge against their child. A three-judge panel of the Virginia Court of Appeals ruled in March 1999 in favor of a juvenile who appealed his conviction because the authorities contacted only his mother and failed to contact his father, whom he had not known since birth.

III

Johnnie sat on his cot in the dark cell for a second before he fell to the pillow and exhaustion swept him into sleep. His last thought was of Mrs. Johnson, but a Mrs. Johnson alive and well and smiling at him. He almost smiled back. Then everything went blank in a dull, steel grey.

7

Everyone who works in this business has to be stupid. You have
to be a dreamer or you get chewed up and thrown away.
—Gary Edwards, director of Homes with a Heart, a foster
care agency which briefly cared for Johnnie

Ed Pendleton went to work Tuesday morning with little on his
mind. He had served as a parole officer for four years and was good at it.
At age forty-one, and after fifteen years in the juvenile corrections field,
he still had the energy and optimism to handle the thirty troubled kids
in his caseload. Raised in a small town in Alabama, Pendleton had struck
out for a bigger city, a more needy town. In Toledo, he had found one. It
was difficult work, but he liked his job. It was important.

If he had been aware that this morning would be the last time he felt
secure and happy in his vocation, he would have savored it. Though he
played a pivotal role in this case, the satisfaction of his career would
diminish over the next few hours. He would lose faith in a system he
once trusted, respected, and to which he gave his heart and his time. The
comfort of doing right was stolen, and in its stead a vapid feeling of
loneliness and betrayal came to haunt him.

It's too late to change his profession. He has a family to support and
promotions keep rolling in. Today, working as a supervisor in the same
office in which he once found such personal reward with far fewer
kudos is sometimes difficult for him. He sees himself not as the hero
that the Toledo community considered him, but as another cog in a failing and destructive system. He wishes this one day, which helped earn
him promotions, had never happened. More deeply, however, he knows
that the day was inevitable. Johnnie Jordan just happened to be the
name attached to the youth who brought it.

III

Inside the Parole Department offices, the smoothness of Pendleton's day soon fractured. His supervisor, Marilyn Young, rushed toward him in what seemed a flurried second, pulled him through the winding crevices of the parole office's green cubicled halls, and then into her office. She had heard about the murder of Jeanette Johnson informally from a friend at police headquarters. The suspect's name, Johnnie Jordan, sounded familiar. She put the pieces together, linking him to her office. Johnnie Jordan, Pendleton's parolee. She tried to ease the sting of the words as she broke the news to Pendleton.

Pendleton sank down into a chair, stunned. He had just seen Johnnie at the Johnsons' in the latter part of last week in what appeared to be a very relaxed atmosphere. They had played checkers. As he was preparing to leave, Mr. Johnson had taken up the game with Johnnie. The two joked and laughed. Mr. Johnson and Johnnie seemed to have a fine relationship, like a father and son, or more like a grandfather and grandson. Either way, a good relationship of the kind Johnnie probably never had. Together, in overlapping and disjointed sentences, they had told Pendleton a story about how Johnnie had tried to catch a wild turkey because he wanted to feed it. They laughed so hard, Pendleton could hardly make out their words. When Pendleton was at the door, Johnnie told him he wanted to stay with the Johnsons. He said he felt accepted by them. Still, Pendleton knew that any kid with Johnnie's background would not be easy for the Johnsons to handle. His problems would remain, and without proper treatment would almost certainly get him into further trouble. He wanted the Johnsons to be careful.

Pendleton does not recall warning Mr. Johnson that afternoon of the anger boiling inside Johnnie, although Mr. Johnson remembers that he did. In any case, it was Children Services' responsibility to inform foster parents about the children they were taking into their homes. Pendleton had not suspected that the agency had failed to do so, though later it did not surprise him that it had not. He knew the difficulties caseworkers had finding troubled children temporary placements, let alone more permanent homes. There was no place for such children in the foster care system. Later, Pendleton found that Johnnie's caseworker had told the Johnsons only that because of Johnnie's "runaway behavior and adjustment problems in foster care, his case plan was designed to address Johnnie's unstable placement history." They were not told that Johnnie had been in juvenile detention for striking a bus driver, or that in detention he had to be restrained by staff twelve times, or that he had been physically aggressive with adults as well as other children, or that a psychologist had found Johnnie "lacking coping skills. Was aggressive, hostile, angry, withdrawn and dangerous."

The Johnsons never asked Pendleton about Johnnie's criminal history. It did not occur to them. They simply assumed Johnnie was on probation for truancy and running away.

If Pendleton did warn the Johnsons of Johnnie's anger, he says, it wasn't because of Johnnie's behavior during that visit or any other. It was the pattern of anger emerging in Johnnie's files that troubled Pendleton most. For Johnnie had always presented himself as a mannerly young man to Pendleton, even polite and soft-spoken, gentle. He was never disrespectful toward him. Some kids direct their anger at probation officers. Not Johnnie. Some kids do not respond to intervention. Johnnie seemed to. He still wanted to please people. He wanted help. Some kids are so clearly angry they can't think straight. Not Johnnie, Pendleton thought. Johnnie's main problems were his anger and his inability to address its cause.

The pattern Pendleton saw in Johnnie's files, one that he had seen many times with other children and would see many times again, flashed like a warning sing to Pendleton. He had seen many kids come and go through his office and knew the unpredictability of their lives. Some of the worst would make it. Some of the best would not. One truth remained, he says: if the problems do not change, the behavior does not change.

While Pendleton saw reasons for real concern in Johnnie, he thought Johnnie was beginning to change for the better. His next placement, in a therapeutic home, could save him. In such a place, he would be forced to face the causes of his anger, unlike at the Johnsons', where Johnnie had been successfully dodging the Lucas County Children Services' psychiatrist. On his last visit, Pendleton had insisted that Johnnie visit the psychiatrist. Johnnie agreed. He even called to make the next available appointment with her. Progress, Pendleton had believed. He was wrong, he thinks now. It was already too late.

Sitting before his supervisor, Pendleton remembered the first time he met Johnnie, at the Cuyahoga Hills Boys School, several years before. He was with J. R. Robinson, a counselor, who had brought Johnnie a mess of barbecued chicken wings with special red sauce. The grease mingled with the sauce, the meat slid off the bone and almost dissolved in your mouth. It was enough to make Pendleton's mouth water. But Johnnie was acting shy. He refused the food at first. But after J.R. coaxed him into a taste, and then another, Johnnie dug in like any kid. Johnnie did really well at Cuyahoga Hills, well enough to be granted early release by the board. Still reflecting, Pendleton then remembered when Johnnie first exhibited serious behavior problems several months ago, after Johnnie had read a newspaper story reporting that his father had been picked up on charges of sexually molesting children. Johnnie had badly wanted to return home so he could take care of the family. Pendleton did not want to think anymore. He knew he had a job to do.

III

Pendleton walked the few blocks around the white marble Lucas County Courthouse to the Child Study Institute (CSI), Toledo's juvenile jail. He waited for Johnnie in the Ping-Pong room.

Shackled in metal arm and leg cuffs, Johnnie shuffled forward to meet him, sliding to keep his feet inside the jail slippers. His face looked puffy and worn, swollen and unhappy. He fell limply into a chair, as though coolly surrendering to the environment. He spread his legs in the tough, defiant inmate fashion. But when he looked at Pendleton, his head slumped forward.

Pendleton began talking about Mr. Johnson, and the pain he was feeling. He told Johnnie how difficult it was for Mr. Johnson, not knowing what happened to his wife, how she was murdered. It would be best for Johnnie to speak up if he knew something, Pendleton said, so that Johnnie could get help.

Those words triggered Johnnie's confession. He knew Mr. Johnson was hurting, but most of all, he wanted help. He did not want to kill again. He needed help. Within eight minutes of Pendleton's arrival, Johnnie told his story.

Pendleton listened to the end, then said he would call in the detectives. Johnnie should repeat the account to them. Johnnie nodded. He asked Johnnie for the detectives' names.

"Detective Lamb and some white dude," Johnnie said.

III

Only after Pendleton returned to his office and phoned the detectives' bureau did he allow himself to dwell on his role in Johnnie's life. For months and years to come, he would feel guilty that he had abused the trust Johnnie had placed in him, by acting as a law enforcement agent rather than the African-American big brother that Johnnie considered him to be. Johnnie trusted few adults. One was J.R., the counselor Pendleton had assigned to Johnnie after they had bonded at River Road Group Home; the other was Pendleton himself. Johnnie did not lie to anyone he cared about personally. Unfortunately for Johnnie, the people he cared about worked for the government. Even though he was guilty, Johnnie had no one in his corner, no one to talk to or prepare him for what was coming. A more privileged child, a boy with a family, or even just with a parent who had pushed for his release the night of his arrest, would probably not have confessed. And he would almost certainly have gone free if a clever, expensive lawyer had taken the case before Pendleton stepped in. That unfairness of the justice system often saddened Pendleton. But he was used to that truth. What shook Pendleton today was the contradictory role he had played in being a law enforcer and a parent to the same kid at the same time.

It almost did not seem fair to Pendleton that Johnnie, a child with diminished intelligence, who confessed, out of trust, to the rage and murder inside of him, would now be viewed as just another criminal. Pendleton felt Johnnie was mentally ill. That didn't mean he should have been allowed to go free. But if he had been given the right mental health care, if the issues of abuse and anger had been addressed before, as they should have been, this would not have happened. On top of those problems, Pendleton knew no one had helped Johnnie cope with the trauma of being taken from his family and put in foster care. Studies have been done on the effect of losing a parent or sometimes both parents to death. But there is no research demonstrating the harm to a child who has lost a parent and been thrown into a patchwork system of government care that is ill-equipped to raise children. Pendleton knows what emerges from it, he sees the result in his office every day: needy children suffering from depression, self-hatred, distrust of adults, an inability to make new intimate connections, and a tremendous loss of a sense of structure. Mentally these children are in jeopardy. And the systems they are thrown into only make them more fragile.

Pendleton sees Johnnie's patterns in many other kids in the reports that are wedged in his files. Pick up any of the folders, he says, and the story reads almost identically to the next one. There is physical abuse. There is emotional abuse. There is sexual abuse. The faces and the names change; the problems don't. Many of these kids are, or have been, suicidal. It doesn't take much to see the link between suicide and homicide. In both, the kids are desperate, on the edge, and need serious help—help that society and the government don't give them.

It wasn't like this when Pendleton began working in juvenile corrections, in 1976. There were angry kids then too. But not like this. Probably around 1986, he began to see the youths become more violent, probably because their parents used more drugs, and harder drugs. Who knows what chemical effects these drugs have on fetuses. Certainly the lack of parenting was destructive, perhaps more destructive than even the abuse. That's when he noticed the juvenile system was beginning to explode with hard-core kids like Johnnie.

The number and severity of cases overwhelmed and numbed the child welfare agency that was designed for a smaller, less violent population. Today, Pendleton believes, society does not want to spend enough money and time to help kids like Johnnie. There are too few people to watch over the cases, too little cooperation among the various agents within the system. Lucas County Children Services failed Johnnie. The Lucas County Mental Health Board failed Johnnie. And the juvenile corrections agency failed him.

Johnnie was mentally feeble for a long time in foster care, a period during which the agencies could have saved him with psychiatric care and greater attention, Pendleton believed. Instead, all the pressure and all that stress boiled up and hit Johnnie at once, and he just couldn't cope. Johnnie just lost it. He could have fit into society. Maybe he still could, with intense help if it began immediately. But time would slip away quickly. The only psychiatrists to meet with Johnnie would draw up evaluations for judges and prosecutors and defense attorneys. Pendleton knew Johnnie would never truly get help now. This murder would define Johnnie, and prison would inevitably forge him into an even more hardened criminal.

We are creating other kids who will follow in Johnnie Jordan's path, Pendleton thought, and we are failing them, too. Their victims fall to shadows and lines on the tortured faces of these children. Pendleton sees the scars clearly, and he is afraid.

8

I don't know if it was his upbringing or if he was messed up in the head. It didn't matter. I knew I didn't want this kid walking around free.

—Detective Ernest Lamb

Pendleton's call found Detective Lamb at the crime lab, where he was assembling the last and least likely pieces of possible evidence for testing. He had gotten little sleep, driving home around 4 A.M. Tuesday and returning by 8:30. Throughout the restless night and into the early morning hours, he painstakingly reviewed the case in his mind. Without DNA, only circumstances linked Johnnie to the crime. The evidence was barely enough for prosecutors to bring a case, and certainly not enough for a conviction. The police probably could not hold him much longer. Lamb believed the opportunity to obtain Johnnie's confession had been lost the night before. When Richardson pointed out the few bloodstains on Johnnie's clothes, and told him they would tie him to the slaying, the detectives thought Johnnie was close to admitting the murder. But Johnnie Jordan remained silent.

Richardson was also in the crime lab and equally dejected. He had slept only a few hours on a cot in the detectives' office after bagging evidence taken from Johnnie's person, clothes, and possessions the night before—a black T-shirt, blue jeans, black and white Reebok tennis shoes, an Apex black and white Jacksonville Jaguars jacket with "John" tagged inside it, white socks, a mobile pager, a marijuana pipe, and several rocks of crack cocaine. Johnnie was using the weed; he was dealing the crack. They also took from him seven dollar bills and change.

But the lab had found no proof of blood or human tissue on the clothing. And the spot of blood on Johnnie's leather sneakers, which caused a momentary flicker in Johnnie's eyes when Richardson pointed it out, could not be conclusively matched to Mrs. Johnson's because human blood on animal tissue like leather cannot be accurately typed and assessed. Even the cap of the kerosene can had no fingerprints because of the greasy fuel that spilled over it.

When the detectives' secretary relayed Pendleton's message that Johnnie was ready to talk, Lamb and Richardson hurried across the street to the Child Study Institute. They waited in the same room where they had questioned Johnnie the night before. Johnnie was brought in without handcuffs, looking very much the same as he had a few hours earlier.

Lamb brought a tape recorder and an adult confession form from the police bureau. He had forgotten the Juvenile Waiver of Rights, so he hurried next door, to an office in the juvenile prison, and returned with that form.

At 11:17 A.M., fifteen minutes after Pendleton had called, Lamb asked Johnnie if he could turn on the tape recorder. Johnnie agreed. There was no preinterview and little talk before the recorder was activated. Richardson began by introducing himself, Lamb, and Johnnie. Lamb read the Miranda warning, asking Johnnie if he understood each paragraph, much as the night before.[1]

At Richardson's request, Johnnie read the last paragraph of the Juvenile Waiver form aloud: "I am willing to answer questions and make a statement," he said, his low voice picking through the words haltingly. "I do not want a lawyer or a parent at this time. I understand and know what I am doing. No promises or threats have been made to me and no pressure of any kind has been used against me."

---

1. Studies have shown that children, especially those twelve years old and under, are more likely to waive their rights than adults. In one study, 90 percent of juveniles waived their right to counsel compared to 60 percent of adults. In the 1962 Supreme Court ruling in *Gallegos v. Colorado*, the Court found that a "14 year old boy, no matter how sophisticated . . . is not equal to police in knowledge and understanding . . . and is unable to know how to protect his own interests or how to get the benefits of his constitutional rights." Yet today courts generally see children as competent to make their own legal decisions. This has led to some controversy, particularly because children are far more eager to tell adults what they want to hear and offer false confessions. For example, in the 1999 Ryan Harris case, two children, ages seven and eight, falsely confessed to killing an 11 year old in Chicago after being encouraged by detectives and enticed by a McDonald's Happy Meal.

Then Johnnie answered Richardson's questions while eating a box lunch. His voice remained slow, a monotone, slightly softer in some places, slightly harder in others. Never was it angry or tearful. It was flat, Richardson thought, and bizarre.

Johnnie told the detectives that the last time he had attended school was ninth grade at Libbey High School. He was not sure of Mrs. Johnson's first name, maybe Jean. But the rest of his facts were clear and correct. He had been living with the Johnsons about a month and a half. He was at the Johnsons', he said, "because my old foster mother kicked me out."

He needed no warming up or encouragement. He answered most of the questions in half sentences or fragments until Richardson asked him to tell his story about the crime.

"Yesterday, the twenty-ninth," Richardson said. "Going back to sometime in the afternoon hours, would you go over what happened, where you were at, who was at the house, and what happened from there?"

Johnnie was stumped.

"It was about . . ." He stumbled as he tried to recall. "I don't know what time . . ."

"That's okay," Richardson said. "As close as you can get to the time will be fine."

"I'd say about four," Johnnie replied. But then he decided to begin earlier, because what happened that afternoon, in his mind, had started when he woke up that day.

After that, Johnnie had no difficulty. He was almost eager to tell his story. It bothered him somewhat when the detectives interrupted to ask for specifics. Most of the time, he had to ask them what they meant. But then he would quickly return to his account.

He had tumbled out of bed about half past noon, taken a bath, thrown on his clothes, watched TV, and listened to the radio.

"Her friend came over and they were sitting up there talking and stuff. And I had walked by because I was just about to walk out the door. I had my coat on. I went in the bathroom and washed my face. And after that, Mr. Johnson already had left and it was just her and her friend. And after I got through washing my face, I went back in the room. And then I started getting these thoughts in my mind. And I went back up in the room."

"You started getting thoughts about what?" Richardson asked.

"Killing her," Johnnie said plainly. "And then I went back. . . I went to the TV room where she was at. We were sitting down watching TV. Then, I was sitting up there. . . I was sitting up there on the couch just thinking. And then I got up, and then I went in the kitchen and had the ax from upside the stove."

"You grabbed an ax alongside the stove?"

"Whatever that thing was. And I was standing in the kitchen at first with the ax right here. And she had . . ."

A juvenile jail guard interrupted by knocking on the heavy door and poking his head into the room. He needed to have Johnnie take some drug tests.

It was worse than poor timing. The interruption almost cost the confession. Richardson calmly pointed out they were in the middle of taping. Could it wait? he asked firmly. Johnnie was silent, but less patient. Richardson feared he might stop the confession, but in fact, that never occurred to Johnnie.

"Where was I at?" Johnnie asked as the door shut.

Richardson reminded him.

"And I was standing in the kitchen after I grabbed it, because I was sitting up there thinking, Should I do it, or shouldn't I do it. And then she walked towards me. But she walked towards me, then I acted like, that way she wouldn't see the ax, I had moved back into the TV room 'cause she went in the kitchen where I was standing at and started washing dishes and stuff. So I went in there, when she was washing the dishes. She had her back turned and I was thinking, should I do it or not. I started to run up to her the first time and do it but I had turned back around. Something made me turn back and say don't do it. I went back and sat down. And then something made me do it again."

Johnnie took an audible breath before continuing.

"I went back and sat down again. And then the third time I did it, I hit her with the hammer part. And then she just backed up and looked at me. And I didn't want to hit her again but—I didn't know what to do. I was scared. The way she looked at me, I was."

Johnnie did not know what to say then. He didn't understand what he felt when Mrs. Johnson looked at him, only that at that moment something passed between them in their eyes. It struck him during the confession, a feeling he did not understand.

"I was then sorry I did it," he said after a moment, "because of the expression on her face. She couldn't even say nothing."[2]

Johnnie's mind would later replay that moment when he put his words to what happened. This thought, as much as her expression, haunted him. The look in her eyes, the emptiness of her mouth.

"So I swung and hit her a couple more times," he resumed. His blows struck her mouth and then her eyes, the places he couldn't bear to face. "And as she was laying down on the ground and she started bleeding and stuff. And I was just sitting there watching her 'cause she was still alive, but I didn't want to, I didn't mean it, I didn't want to kill her but it, something went in my mind that if I don't, I'd end up in jail like I am right now. 'Cause she'd probably tell or something. But she—" His voice was higher. He didn't finish his thought, he just went on.

"So I, after that, I went to go get my gloves and my coat out of the room. I was gonna go get my gloves and my coat and getting ready to walk out the front door and she was laying in the kitchen. I looked back and I seen her and she was still moving and breathing and stuff, so I grabbed the kerosene heater, I meant the kerosene from on the side of the garbage can by the back door, and I poured it on her. And I had lit a match or I had lit something. I didn't know if it—you saying she, it burned her but it didn't seem like it was gonna burn 'cause the kerosene kept putting it out. So I poured it on there and lit a match. And I left, went down to my boy Stacy's house to use the phone. And tried to see if any buses run out there . . ."

He continued with the story. When he paused at the end, Richardson asked Johnnie what gave him the idea to kill her.

---

2. Johnnie's defense attorneys would not emphasize this statement of remorse because they feared the court would view it as unsubstantial and shallow since Johnnie said he regretted hitting Mrs. Johnson at that moment, but then he set her on fire. "There wasn't much remorse in that one statement," attorney Ron Wingate later explained. "In court it could open a whole new can of worms. With the lack of skills Johnnie had showing any remorse, it wouldn't come off. Johnnie had a certain coldness about him. In the first fifteen minutes, he'd always come across aloof and cold. After two or three hours alone with us, he'd warm up and you could see the little kid."

"Had that been going through your head for a long time or did something just happen that day?"

"It just, she ain't do nothing to me," Johnnie said, seemingly bewildered. "It's just that something had went through my head. She was a nice lady. I'm sorry that I did that to her. It's just something that went through my head and made me do it."

"Had you ever had those kinds of thoughts before?"

"I had it one time, but I actually didn't do nothing about it. I was actually talking to somebody about it."

Johnnie later said he thought Richardson was getting somewhere, that they were going to figure something out, for Mrs. Johnson, and for himself. What, he didn't know. But Richardson did not pursue that course. Instead, he asked how much time had passed between Johnnie's first blow and the next several.

"About three seconds," Johnnie said. "After we stopped, I had stopped looking at her. Because I was shocked. I was thinking, Why did I do that?"

"Next time you hit her with the hatchet, where did you hit her at?" Lamb asked.

"The first . . . the second time? In her face," Johnnie answered. "I think I hit her in her mouth." He wasn't sure, it was all a blur as he saw it. His only perspective remained from the corner of the ceiling where he had watched himself kill Mrs. Johnson.

Mrs. Johnson had fallen next to the deep freezer. "The plan wasn't to—it didn't work out the way I wanted it to work out. See, I wanted it to work out like, I hit her, like one time, and she'd pass out or something. And I'd put her in the closet somewhere . . . and it won't . . . you know what I'm saying. You don't see no blood or anything. But it didn't work out like that. Because when I seen the blood, I didn't know what to do because there was so much of it."

"Did you panic?"

"Huh?"

"Did you panic?"

"I was frightened," Johnnie answered. "You know what I'm saying. I just didn't know what to do right like, not running but, going back and forth from the house. Paranoid and stuff."

The detectives tried to go through each blow. But Johnnie couldn't remember each one. He remembered only hitting her again and again, every time she moved.

"So the next blow, where did you strike her at?" Lamb persisted.

"I think in her face. I kept hitting her in her head and stuff," Johnnie told him.

"How many times did you think you hit her in the head while she was moving?"

"About ten," Johnnie said. "I don't know. I just kept hitting her till she, till I didn't see her move no more when she was still breathing."

"She was still moving when you doused her with the kerosene?"

"She had stopped, but she was still breathing," Johnnie answered. Though the coroner later found it was unlikely Mrs. Johnson was still alive or breathing at that point, Johnnie is sure she was. "She was just making that little breathing noise 'cause the blood that was coming out of her mouth and stuff . . . she was like gurgling and stuff."

"Then what did you try and ignite her with first?"

"Huh?" Johnnie asked, stumped by the word "ignite."

"What did you try and light it with first?"

"I tried to just light a match and put it down there, but it kept on putting it out," Johnnie said. Finally he used a piece of cardboard. When he ran from the house, he thought that the fire was out.

"When did you take the money from her purse?"

"After I hit her like three times," Johnnie said. After he thought she was dead, and had to escape. He didn't know exactly how much he took from Mrs. Johnson. He guessed about $15 or $20. Leaving the house, he placed the hatchet in a cupboard by the front door and closed it.

"Now when you were thinking about doing this, were you thinking about just killing her at first or were you thinking about taking her money first, or how did that go?" Richardson asked.

"I was like, I told you," Johnnie was getting frustrated. "I wanted—my intention wasn't to kill her. I was just intending to knock her out or something. But it ended—it just didn't work that way."

"But once you saw that look on her, you knew that you couldn't stop then," Richardson said.

"And I seen the blood and stuff, I knew I couldn't like stuff her in the closet and leave the blood right there. And there was so much blood I couldn't get it up. I wasn't going to intend to get it up," Johnnie said.

"And why are you telling us about it today?" Richardson asked.

"Because I think I need help," Johnnie said, his voice low, almost sounding ashamed.

For Johnnie to admit needing help frightened him. He did not know how help would come, or what it would look like. He never imagined he needed therapy or a psychiatrist. Today, in prison, Johnnie still says he needs help and that he was tricked into confessing with the promise that help would be given to him. But still, not in the form of therapy. "I don't need no psychiatrist," he says. "I need help." Then too, no matter what, he wanted no one to think he was crazy. He'd rather go to jail the rest of his life or be executed than for anyone, including himself, to think that he was crazy.

After his plea for help, the confession tape is silent for long moments. There seemed nothing to say.

Then the detectives returned to some details to make sure the story was coherent. They asked Johnnie if he had been high on drugs. He told them he had not gone out before the murder so he didn't have an opportunity to get high. They also asked where he put the ax. He drew them a map of the Johnsons' front room and the cabinet he placed it in. They radioed a patrol officer who quickly went by and retrieved the hatchet, so slimy with Mrs. Johnson's blood and flesh that Johnnie's fingerprints were untraceable.

"When you first hit her and she turned around and faced you, why didn't you just walk away then?" Lamb asked for the final time.

"Because it wasn't that easy," Johnnie answered.

"Now don't you think that first blow would have been a little less trouble than what you've gotten into now?" Lamb demanded, his outrage steaming under by his words.

"Yeah," Johnnie mumbled sheepishly.

III

Richardson rewound the tape. Johnnie listened to it to see if there were any additions or corrections he wanted to make. There weren't, Johnnie said, his voice low. It was the last official record of Johnnie's young voice, pure if only in truth.

The confession lasted twenty-nine minutes. Within the hour, Lamb and Richardson closed the case. Around noon, Lamb left the building, relieved to have solved his first homicide.

He wanted nothing more to do with Johnnie or any kid like him. He was chilled by how cold and callous Johnnie was at his age. He would not have believed a young kid could be like that. Now he knew better. In the subsequent months, he came to believe that in these times the coldest crimes are committed by the young kids out there. There may not be a greater number of juvenile crimes, but those that are committed are much worse, more cruel, much more violent and ugly. Lamb wasn't sure he wanted to know what triggered Johnnie and kids like him. He didn't know if it was in Johnnie's upbringing, or if Johnnie was just messed up in the head. It did not really matter to Lamb.

After the confession, he had nothing more to say to Johnnie Jordan. He last saw Johnnie at the trial. Only one thought lingers with Lamb still.

The two Bibles. He should have taken pictures of those Bibles, he thinks now, because everything was there. It seemed like the words were talking directly to Johnnie Jordan. About the things you do to people, you'll pay for in the end. This lady had a premonition that this was going to happen. She had two Bibles and they both were open to saying the same thing, and it seemed like it was meant just for him. It was spooky. This lady knew it was coming, and was reading about Johnnie Jordan in the Bible, Lamb says. She knew this kid was bad, that he was dangerous.

9

Ellen Jones, director of Lucas County Children Services, began the clear, brisk morning like many others, except this Tuesday she got into the office at 9 A.M., late by her standards. A meeting had held her up, but Jones prefers black-coffee meetings at dawn to those at more reasonable hours which fracture her day. Often she rises at four in the morning. She was brought up to wake early and work hard. She barely flinches at the cold and darkness of Ohio winters. She lights up mornings with her red suits, her firm and determined air, and her easy smile. Jones was the first African-American director of Children Services. She was, in fact, the best-liked and most respected director of the department that most people could remember, until that Tuesday.

There was a strange atmosphere in the office that morning. People moved awkwardly, she thought, different from the usual flow of business punctuated by sparks of laughter, frustrated thuds of fists on desks, and defeated sighs. A case manager moved swiftly to her side.

"There's a rumor," she whispered to Jones. "One of our foster parents got hurt or killed and one of our kids did it."

Jones's round eyes grew wide. Her bright lipstick-red smile fell and the dimples fled from her round cheeks. Holding her breath, she called her agency's Placement Office, the office charged with assigning and keeping records of kids in foster homes. It couldn't be true, she told herself. Her heart sped wildly with the dial. The police would have called, she tried to tell herself. Someone would have called. But as she waited, she knew how the bureaucracies work within themselves, spinning in their separate spheres. She also knew the kids they all dealt with. And she knew the worst was only too possible, even probable.

The Placement Office also heard that something had happened at the Johnson home. Ellen Jones did not know the Johnsons. If they had come to one of the foster parent training sessions, they had not introduced themselves to her. There were over two hundred foster parents in Lucas County, yet still not enough to handle all the kids needing a home. Exacerbating the problem was a high turnover rate. Most foster parents didn't last long. Even the ones who had been taking in kids for decades were fleeing the system now. They were getting less support from the foster care agency. They did not feel that the caseworkers listened to them. And they saw how the kids were getting meaner and scarier, more troubled, less controllable. The agency was having a very difficult time recruiting new foster parents. They were in such straits that they turned a blind eye to foster parents taking kids just for the money, even if it was, at most, $13 a day. Most of these people used whatever money they were given for themselves.

Jones did not know Johnnie either, but she knew foster kids. She had been a foster parent herself. After she lost her four-year-old daughter to a rare and fatal illness, she and her husband adopted a child. Then, while she was working in juvenile court, she was asked to take in a troubled teenage girl. She did. Then twenty-two years old, Jones was scarcely older than her foster child. She parented the girl as well as her own child while earning a law degree at night. For many years, she worked as a referee in juvenile court before taking over a group home for troubled kids. Now she was director of Children Services, the agency that over-saw all foster children in Lucas County, including Toledo.

That morning, Jones directed two of her staff members to go to the Johnson home and report back with a firsthand account. She did not think to call the police. While the buzz in the office became more animated, Jones waited anxiously for her social workers to call. The Jordan kid? She heard people in the office asking one another. Well, he had a nasty past. But the Jordan kid? There were other kids who had shown more rage, ones who had been more violent. The Jordan boys were pretty quiet most of the time. The girls caused a little more trouble. One was probably in a gang. Another kept running away and threatening to attack adults. And the youngest recently squeezed a bird to death. Who was his caseworker?

Within an hour, the worst was confirmed. Johnnie Jordan had killed Mrs. Johnson. Jones made a brief announcement to the staff. No one can remember what she said, but everyone remembers the silence that followed.

"It was like a death in the agency," one staffer said later. "Or more like something died within the agency. The shock, and this realization that the victim could have been me. Everyone had started to notice that we are in a dangerous profession, talking to these kids, transporting them from one home to another, dealing with their anger, love, and grief." Even a four-year-old could be frighteningly violent, she had found in her own casework.

Many of the caseworkers cried at their desks. The range of emotions was fierce. For many, it was like a colleague had died, Jones says. "Mrs. Johnson was their comrade who they lost in battle." Others cried for Mr. Johnson, who was left behind. Only a few cried for Johnnie.

Tamara Cusack, Johnnie's primary caseworker, seemed to hate Johnnie from that day forward, some of her colleagues indicated. She seemed to see his crime as raw murder and was furious. They thought she felt personally deceived and that it reflected badly on her. "She couldn't see through to the kid anymore," one fellow worker said.[1]

The Jordan family caseworker, Donna Lewis, had an almost opposite reaction. She immediately collapsed in tears. "My heart literally bled for him," she said later, "for the Johnnie Jordan I knew." She visited him in jail, but was required to write up reports of her visits for her superiors—reports that would later be used against him in his trial—until she was forbidden by the agency to have any more contact with the youth.

"I understood," she said, almost relieved. "I needed to keep my distance for professional reasons."

Johnnie never understood why Tamara Cusack and Donna Lewis stopped talking to him or visiting after his juvenile court hearing. He didn't comprehend the blunt legal letter their agency sent him when he was awaiting trial in adult court, saying they were no longer responsible for him, that he was now an emancipated minor, an adult in the criminal court's eyes. Children Services was no longer his guardian and therefore would have no further contact with him. He didn't understand the words at first. Then he felt scared. When he figured it out, he got angry. No one cared, ever, he thought.

In the wake of the crime, Ellen Jones did one thing that morning

---

1. Cusack did not return my calls and, through the CSB director, said she did not wish to be interviewed.

that she felt in her heart was right but sensed would rebound against her. She took up an office collection, $500 in all, for Mrs. Johnson's funeral. She knew Mr. Johnson had no money for his wife's burial. In fact, he had no savings at all. As an attorney, she recognized that her act conceivably could be seen as an admission of guilt. "But sometimes you have to do the right thing. You just do," she says today.

But the agency's board of directors did not agree. They saw it as the wrong thing to do, as precisely a confession of fault. And for that, Ellen Jones was targeted as the agency's scapegoat for the Johnnie Jordan fiasco. Soon after, she was forced to resign.

III

While Jones took the fall for her workers and bosses, the entire agency was targeted by the media. The *Toledo Blade* scoured Jones and her staff, largely neglecting the other services that also had failed Johnnie, including the mental health agency and the parole office. In the firestorm of blame and criticism, the various services each sought to shift the blame to others.

The lesson, as Jones saw it, is that the government makes a lousy parent. The real tragedy is not that she was fired and her agency blamed, she said, but that this kid whom she did not know wanted to be loved very badly. He wanted a permanent home. He wanted the Johnsons' home to be that place. The softer the kids are, the harder they fall, she says. If he had been a less sensitive child, if he had not felt the sting of rejection so profoundly, if the government agencies, all of them together, had intervened earlier and more energetically in his case, he might have survived. And so might Mrs. Johnson.

10

"Mrs. Johnson? You mean to tell me someone killed Mrs. Johnson? Mrs. Johnson?" The local fire chief could not shake his dismay. He went into the kitchen, the air still heavy with dark smoke, and knelt down to the body, searching for a pulse.
—Spencer fire chief Tim Lewis, the Johnsons' neighbor

Denny Richardson has seen the worst in men, and he has seen some pretty rotten men. Usually he leaves his work at the door when he goes home to his wife and son. But some crimes and some criminals stick with him. Those who sadistically torture their victims, especially children, top his list of evil persons. Those who lose control on the spur of the moment and commit crimes as a result are in another category. A third group are criminals who, provoked by anger or fear, or motivated by greed, plan and execute a crime. Richardson recognizes that his personal distinctions make little difference. Those found guilty of serious crimes all go to the same place. They are all put behind bars together.

He has no illusions about the rehabilitative powers of prison. Rehabilitation does not occur in the system today. That's okay with him. He believes an individual can learn to change his or her signals and maybe behavior, but not their insides, not their fundamental nature. The inner person is still there.

That is why Johnnie's case stuck with him. Richardson did not understand the kid who had confessed to him. He had no doubts about Johnnie's guilt, or the integrity of his confession. But he needed to comprehend the crime, for his own peace of mind. Johnnie fit into none of his categories neatly, and yet all of them partially. Three days after Johnnie's confession, Richardson drove out to the Johnsons' house to

see if he could make some sense of it. The case was closed, his responsibilities ended, but in his mind, it was not complete.

To Richardson, the flat, emotionless confession of the boy as he ate a
box lunch was entirely detached from the gruesome killing. Striking
someone in the face with a hatchet to murder them takes a special kind
of person. It's easier to murder from a distance, from a car, or with a
gun. That's almost a game. But to kill while the victim looks into your
eyes, and without being angry with her, or having any motive to kill
her, and then to set her on fire—that must take a special kind of person,
he thought as he drove out to Spencer Township.

Perhaps a half-dozen people Richardson encountered in his lifetime
as a police officer have frightened him. He has been threatened by many
more, but takes none of those seriously. The quiet ones are most dangerous, not those who threaten. The men who look at you with a certain
coldness, those you know will kill if they get a chance, those are the
dangerous ones. Johnnie was a quiet one. But he didn't have that evil in
his eyes.

Richardson considered for a minute whether he was afraid of Johnnie Jordan or should be. No. Not now. But after the boy served time,
maybe. If Johnnie received a life sentence, he could go free by the time
he was fifty-two. Society shouldn't have to take that risk.

During the confession, Richardson had sized Johnnie up fairly
neatly. Relatively bright. Street-smart. He might not do well in school,
but he wasn't as dumb as his IQ test scores indicated. He was well spoken, given his origins and upbringing. But Johnnie surprised him with
his confession. Richardson predicted that if Johnnie did confess, it would
be a sanitized version of the murder. His confession wasn't that. It was
raw. Johnnie didn't try to soften or excuse his actions at all. Nor did he
hype it with street bravado. He was factual. But it was not guilt that
produced Johnnie's honesty. It was clear that Johnnie Jordan did not
hate the lady he had beaten to death. She was a nice person, he said, and
she had treated him well. But he never imagined or cared how she must
have felt, even afterward. He seemed incapable of relating to her, of
identifying with her and showing mercy. Johnnie had made eye contact
with his victim, and only when recounting those moments did he show
a trace of emotion. He approached her several times but then changed
his mind, another action that surprised Richardson in view of the utter

brutality with which he struck her again and again. He drove her to the ground and took her money. And then he returned to set her on fire. It fit no pattern; it was typical of nothing he had ever encountered or read.

Times were changing though, he knew. Like Lamb, Richardson was noticing the increase in serious crimes committed by juveniles. Ten years earlier, kids were arrested for relatively petty crimes, maybe arson, maybe burglary. Now it was murder and rape. Crimes that were meaner, more cruel. The juveniles were often even colder and even more emotionless than older, hardened criminals. It had nothing to do with acting cool. It was in their personality, the detective believed; the way they live. Empathy and sympathy were just not part of their souls.

The highway to Spencer Township was empty that Friday as Richardson drove, except for a few trucks. Ohio was brown and dry and cold all over. Even during the day, white dustings from the frozen sky clung to the withered clumps of brittle grass, which stubbornly resisted even booted feet. The few clouds looked within reach. The sky was white, not grey. It began shedding large white flakes as Richardson pulled up to 125 Irwin Road, once the Johnsons' home. As he got out of his Ford Bronco, there was no wind, but the air cut like ice, strangely sharp, as if haunted with a memory of the murder. That's when the tragedy hit him, before he entered the small yellow house. He saw no tragedy in Johnnie's eyes, or in the autopsy report, or in the confession or photos. All held their own horror. But before this closed-off home, the tragedy became real and yet void of any sense or reason.

The scene inside disturbed him. Black charred marks on the kitchen wall indicated to him that Mrs. Johnson had tried to pull herself up after she was struck and set on fire, but had fallen back to the floor.[1] Johnnie thought she was still alive, her blood gurgling, he had said, when he lit her clothes with the Bic lighter. He had asked Johnnie how she reacted when he poured the kerosene on her. And he remembered that for some reason, Johnnie did not give an answer.

Later he would learn that Johnnie showed moments of remorse in the privacy of his cell. It softened his opinion, perhaps, but only slightly. Yet with all the facts of the case obvious and clear, its larger truth still

---

1. Here Richardson's analysis differs from the coroner's report, which found that Mrs. Johnson was probably dead by the time Johnnie poured kerosene on her.

eluded him. What was going on inside Johnnie? The kid had been ready to explode. If he hadn't killed Mrs. Johnson, he would have killed someone else. Richardson was certain of that. And if no one can figure out why, he thought, Johnnie will not change and most probably will murder again.

Richardson found no more answers to the crime—not that day, not later. His conclusion was simple. Johnnie Jordan operates differently from normal people and even normal criminals. He never fit in, his emotions never fit life. Even as a criminal, he fit nowhere. One part of him is a monster. As for the rest? Richardson didn't know.

II
THE BEGINNING

11

I just had a feeling that something wasn't right after a while. I talked to my wife. I says please be careful. She said, what happened? I said I don't know what we got. We just got to be careful.
—Charles Johnson

Johnnie Jordan, Jr. struggled for his first breaths under a cloud of skepticism. No one looked forward to his birth, it seems. And after a difficult labor by his drug-addicted and malnourished mother, doctors and nurses doubted he would survive. Some even doubted that his death would be a loss.

Even before he was conceived, social workers had been tracking his parents and their two older children. The Jordan family was known in Toledo not only among child protective service workers and justice officials who had jurisdiction in their neighborhood, but also among doctors and nurses who too frequently treated Johnnie's older sisters for burns, broken collarbones and shoulders, ringworm, loop-shaped wounds suggesting whippings, and other suspicious accidents. Police and social workers filed reports after responding to calls from concerned teachers and neighbors. Help was offered periodically. Food stamps and welfare checks, the Jordans accepted. But parenting and drug rehabilitation classes, budgeting help, counseling, and homebuilders programs, they rejected. Still, the Jordan case lingered in a thickening file as various welfare agencies alternately watched and ignored the family as it self-destructed.

By the time Johnnie was born, at 3:04 A.M. on April 28, 1980, the Jordans were already at war with the Lucas County Children Services Board (CSB), the government agency charged with taking abused, neglected, or unclaimed children into protective custody and foster-parenting them until, hopefully, they are adopted or reunited with their biological family. The Jordans fought the agency's advice as well as its directives. They resented its interference and they refused to comply, sometimes willfully and other times through laziness—both of which resulted in their children's frequent removal from their home and placement in foster care. The parents could not always "command" where their children lived, Johnnie's father says with what he takes to be a knowing wink, but they always retained psychological and emotional "power" over their children.

On the cloudy April day of Johnnie's birth, a brisk wind whisking the sky with brief spells of sunshine, Johnnie's exhausted six-pound body was viewed with at least one sad shake of the head.

"A violent beginning," a nurse was overheard saying. "Violent beginning to a violent world. He hasn't a chance."

Her young assistant timidly objected to the comment.

"Look at where he came from," the older nurse pointed out firmly. "You can see right now where he's going."

Whether predicting the future or reflecting the past, she knew Johnnie's world before he did. Many others did as well. They also knew that the lives of Johnnie's parents were over, for all fruitful and hopeful purposes, by that time. But no one decisively intervened.

Johnnie's Parents

Marilyn Monroe Jordan was fourteen years old when she first saw her future husband, Johnnie Jordan, Sr., onstage. He walked with a swagger and flashed a great white smile that reminded everyone of James Brown. His looks made her heart stop, but it was his sly, self-assured charisma that carried the show. He was a talented singer and a good impersonator.

Johnnie Sr. always has been a natural performer. His grandmother boasted that he jumped on stage as soon as he could walk. His early acts were a great hit in his hometown of Toledo. In the 1960s and well into the '70s, he entered every one of the many James Brown look-alike contests and talent shows in the city, and won most of them. His impersonation of the singer earned him the nickname Little James Brown. Social service workers of the same generation still remember his quick, smooth moves and his singing. He had some talent, they say. And he was known to be full of dreams. He was going to make it big, he told people. While still a teenager, he took his act as far as Detroit, on his way to New York. That's as far as he made it before he met Marilyn.

III

Johnnie Sr. claims he did not know Marilyn's real age back then. She was just a beautiful lost child named Marilyn Monroe. She spoke little of her home life, only that she wanted to get away. Later she refused to tell social services anything of her childhood, except that her mother was dead and that she did not get along with her father. No matter how pressured, she kept her past to herself. Not even her husband knows for sure whether Marilyn Monroe is her real name.

Johnnie Sr. brought Marilyn back to Toledo when his mother called and asked him to come home. She said she was dying of cancer. Johnnie Sr.'s relationship with his mother has never been good, though he would like you to believe otherwise. To support his conviction that he is a good and productive father, he would prefer the world to think that his life always has been relatively normal, even that he came from a good background. But that is far from the truth.

Johnnie Sr.'s mother was a prostitute. She had four sons and five daughters, each by a different, absent, father. When Johnnie Sr. was ten years old, his mother brought him to the wide and cracked stone doorstep of Johnnie and Lorraine Saunders's two-story home on the crumbling tumbledown West Side of Toledo, where large old houses settle unevenly on narrow streets.

"This is your son," she announced to Johnnie Saunders. "He's named Johnnie, after you. I can't handle him anymore."

Mr. Saunders wanted nothing to do with the boy. He admitted to Lorraine that he had had a one-night affair with the child's mother, but he did not believe he had fathered the boy. His wife urged him to take the child in nonetheless. He refused. He thought he had good reason. Beside a lack of proof that he had fathered the child, the boy was already trouble.

Johnnie Jordan, Sr. had tangled with the law and his caretakers early and often as a kid—petty theft, burglary, joyriding in stolen cars. He passed through reform schools, detention facilities, and several foster care placements. He was convicted of two felonies and five misdemeanors as a juvenile, a record he now laughs about and casually dis-misses with a wave of his hand.

When his mother refused to pick him up from court after one scrape, the clerk called Johnnie Saunders. As usual, he was out, but Lorraine answered the phone. She went directly downtown, planning to grab Johnnie by the ear and impart some of her stern discipline before returning him to his mother. But her resolve failed her when she found the skinny eleven-year-old alone, head down, his feet dangling from a hardwood bench in the echoing hallway of the vast courthouse.

When he saw her coming, Johnnie Sr.'s eyes lit up like a blue sky and his smile widened to a full half moon, Mrs. Saunders remembers. He jumped off the bench and ran to her, and from that moment, she was hooked. He made her his stepmother. He made her laugh and told large stories. He was just a boy in need of guidance. He had the heart and spirit of a wonderful child who had found his way into trouble. With some love he could make his way back, she thought.

When Mr. Saunders came home that night and found a boy he did not recognize as his son in his living room, his wife's home-sewn orange curtains fluttering at an open window, he thought he was being robbed. Even when he was told it was Johnnie, the child who claimed to be his son, Saunders wanted the boy gone. But Mrs. Saunders persuaded him otherwise. Though neither his two previous marriages nor their own eighteen-year marriage had produced any children, she told her husband that his indiscretion required him to accept the boy as his own.

"His mother says he's your child, so you have to take responsibil-ity," Ms. Saunders argued.

But more important to her was the look in the young boy's eyes. "He thinks you're his father," she whispered to her husband. "He's got no place to go."

"The Lord must have had his hand on my shoulder from that day on," Lorraine Saunders says today. "Because I couldn't have gone through all that came next without Him."

Lorraine Saunders

If she had the choice to go down to the courthouse for young Johnnie Sr. again, Lorraine Saunders can't say she would. She only shakes her head. That bittersweet day she claimed not only a stepson, but was later held responsible, by social services and her own heart, for Johnnie Sr.'s seven troubled children, who were yet to come.

When she took young Johnnie Sr. in, she had only her experience from a caring small Southern community to guide her. Her adult years in a larger town with a disintegrating social fabric taught her something else altogether. Toledo today is a far different place from the cohesive world where she grew up.

Lorraine was raised in a North Carolina town that took care of its own, in a family that sacrificed for one another. When she was two, her mother died and Lorraine's fifteen brothers and sisters raised her with love and kindness. They gave her all that they had, she says, and more. When she took in young Johnnie Sr., she only knew her family's example. And later, "when religion found me," she says, she had no choice but to live by her beliefs.

"I was living with my husband for seven years before we were married," she says, a spark of humor brightening her age-misted eyes. "Come to find out when I was saved that we were living in sin, so we had to get married.

"But by me being saved by Jesus Christ, I also knew I had to keep going downtown for Johnnie's kids. I had all the hope in heaven and earth in those days. Now, I'm just tired," she finishes limply. The light in her eyes dims.

For most of her married life, Lorraine was alone in her parenting and foster-parenting. Her husband eventually accepted but never really claimed Johnnie Sr. or, later, his grandchildren, as his own. He was gone from the house most days and nights.

"That's why my grandmother say they stayed together so long," Johnnie Jr. laughs. "Because he never be there."

Johnnie Jr. knew from early on that his grandfather, who had a record of petty crimes dating back to the 1940s, owned a second house where neighbors say he pimped.

"Yeah, I don't know how long he be doing that," Johnnie says, "but ever since I can remember." He laughs fondly at the hazards of the old man's vocation. "He constantly be getting bones in his body, fingers, legs broke, like every week. He mean, he cuss you out in a minute, cuss anyone out for no reason. But he cool though."

At seventy-eight, Lorraine Saunders is retired from a local hospital, where she worked in the kitchens. She suffers from a variety of ailments that includes diabetes and arthritis. Most days, she has difficulty walking. Yet she still tries to raise two of her youngest step-grandchildren, Johnnie Jordan, Jr.'s younger siblings.

For years before she retired, she had foster-parented several children, including a teenage mother whose baby boy Mrs. Saunders adopted. Later, Children Services convinced her to take in five of Johnnie Sr.'s seven children, including Johnnie Jr. The older children were soon carted off to detention facilities for their behavior. They returned to her home more dangerous. One intentionally set her house on fire, and another ran away with Mrs. Saunders's adopted infant. Three of the five children, including Johnnie Jr., were finally removed from her home for good. Recognizing that raising even the remaining two kids was beyond her ability, she tried to give them back to Lucas County Children Services.

"I was getting too sick to get out of bed. They were getting into so much trouble and violence and I knew I couldn't handle them," she says. "I tried to give them up. The social workers said, 'We can't take them back, they're yours. We gave you legal custody.' I didn't understand when I took them in that I was adopting them."

Financially drained, Mrs. Saunders begged for relief. Finally, Children Services offered some help. "They gave me day care and things like that to give me a break every once in a while," she says, sighing heavily. She knew it was not enough; the children were in critical need of psychological help. "I try to get the children to their therapy. They got both individual and group, but I just can't do it. It's no CSB anymore, just me." And no financial assistance. "They asked if I would fight it out just a little longer."

Three years later, she has little fight left and, it seems, even less time.

III

Through branches of dim light breaking into her creaking house, Lorraine Saunders reaches from the couch for the phone. Though it is beside her, she cannot catch it before its eighth shrill ring. She's exhausted. On the other end of the stretched cord, a teacher tells her that one of Johnnie Jr.'s younger brothers declared his intention to shoot a classmate today.

She speaks softly into the receiver but says very little. "He's forever threatening somebody," she says after she hangs up, her eyes downcast. "We've been having problems with him since the incident," she says. "Wanting to act like *him*." She turns her head discreetly. She can hardly speak Johnnie's name.

Johnnie Jr.'s little brother has threatened to kill many classmates and teachers. He recently stabbed another child with scissors. He is seven years old. His face mirrors Johnnie's—when Johnnie's was young and soft—from the high arched eyebrows to the tired lines running down into his puffy cheeks. He is small for his age, as Johnnie was. Both were born prematurely, and in their preteens neither caught up to their peers physically. Like Johnnie, his torso is disproportionately large compared to his legs. He stands less than four feet tall and seems to weigh only as much as a bag of cheese puffs. Jeans hang from his skinny frame. He does everything his grandmother tells him to, running to answer the door or the phone, checking the oven. He appears to be a sweet and dutiful child. His large brown eyes have a scared, doe-eyed look that pulls the world toward him. Thoughts reflect immediately on his open face. He seems incapable of lifting the revolver he claims to have buried out back, the one he plans to use to shoot a child who teased him that day.

Almost visibly, his heart lifts and races at the mention of Johnnie Jr. He wants to hear about his older brother. In his world, Johnnie was never mean, just "bad," and that word now holds a coveted meaning in his child's mind, tied up with love, confusion, and respect. Johnnie always played with him and hugged him. He was better to him than anyone else. To prove that he is proud of Johnnie, and that he still loves him, he acts like Johnnie as best he can. He wishes he knew Johnnie better, and what Johnnie thinks.

But the moment Johnnie Jr.'s name is brought into his stepgrandmother's home, the seven-year-old boy is sent upstairs to do homework. He goes obediently, without protest. At the top of the stairs, he strains to catch words of the conversation below. His grandmother does not notice him listening, his small head poking through the faltering wood banister.

Lorraine Saunders does not know if Johnnie's younger brother wants to be like Johnnie, or whether he simply thinks that because he is a Jordan, he should be bad too. She's inclined to the latter. She is sure

about one thing though, that something went terribly, terribly wrong
with all of the Jordan children. She doesn't know where or when, but
she is positive that in each of the children the wires in their brains were
crossed in exactly the same evil way.

"All the children are sweet on their outward appearance," she says,
"but on the inside, they're all very, very mean. They're fighters. And you
can be certain when you do something good, something nice for them
like go buy them clothes, they're going to react in a mean way. I don't
know whether they're not used to good treatment or they think bad
treatment is love. Something went wrong. If you don't treat them badly,
the way they were treated at home, you don't love them. The worse
they're treated, the more you're loved. When you do something really
nice, they're going to retaliate with something bad. No mean words, no
sign of anger. They'll just set fire to the house or try to hurt somebody."

But Johnnie Jr., Lorraine Saunders felt, was better than the rest. He
was the one with heart. Even after the murder, she thinks Johnnie is less
dangerous than his siblings. One of Johnnie's sisters has a fascination
with dead babies and keeps a scrapbook of news clippings on infanti-
cides. Another sister shot a member of a rival gang. A juvenile court
judge agrees with Mrs. Saunders's assessment, adding that "Johnnie's
siblings almost make Johnnie look like a saint." All but the youngest of
the seven Jordan children have juvenile records of violent behavior; but
Children Services told Saunders nothing of those problems when the
foster care agency convinced her to take the siblings into her home.
Now she cannot believe she left her own son alone in the house with
the children at times. She worries about the damage that is yet to
expose itself.

"I did not know they had any problems of this kind or any other,"
she says. "They [Children Services] held it back from me. To tell you
the truth, if I had known things was as bad as they were, I never would
have taken any of them. That's the truth."

Still, she works hard to keep the two remaining children fed and
clothed, and takes them to church regularly. But she does not believe
anything she can do will stop Johnnie's little brother from following
Johnnie's murderous path. It is just a matter of time. She dresses the
children as nicely as she can so that they are never ashamed. She feels
that it was shame, wrought by teasing, which hardened Johnnie's heart.

Many social service workers worry for Mrs. Saunders. They know she lacks the strength, health, and money to raise Johnnie's two siblings, let alone the capability to wean them from their violent ways. But the foster care system that reared Johnnie Jr. and his brothers and sisters for a time no longer wants to have anything to do with the family. After convincing his stepgrandmother to take the children in, they washed their hands of the Jordans, despite the risks to Mrs. Saunders and unknown others. Meantime, Mrs. Saunders worries for the next victim, just as she hurts for the last.

She cries when she thinks of the murdered lady. She tries to convince herself that Mrs. Johnson must have been sick anyway, because she was so thin and such a tiny bird of a woman. She knows better, but she still tries to ease her pain. She cries for all of the Jordan children, but Johnnie tears at her heart most, she admits. He's so young and his life is ruined, she says in a whisper.

She imagines the Johnnie she knew before the killing. She is not sure he still exists. Of all the children, he was the best. He was the sweetest, the most sensitive. His smile is identical to his father's. He always tries to make her laugh, even today, and he usually succeeds.

"What's up, old lady?" Johnnie says by way of greeting in a collect call from Ross Correctional Institution.

"Speak for yourself," she shoots back. But the light comes back into her eyes, and even some laughter slips free, until she sees one of his younger siblings scurrying to hear. Mrs. Saunders stops laughing, not wanting them to think Johnnie is having fun in prison, or enjoying himself in any way. Sometimes she lets the young ones talk to their brother, but only for a few minutes, and only while she's in the room. He always makes them laugh too.

The collect calls are expensive, so Mrs. Saunders rarely takes Johnnie's calls. She has never visited him in prison, because the prisons are too far away. She did not attend a single day of Johnnie's trial. She could not bring herself to testify on his behalf despite his lawyers' requests. She's relieved that Johnnie himself never asked her to appear. She could not stand before the court and the public after the hideous murder and tell how Johnnie cared for her and for his siblings, how he would sit on the crumbling front steps of her house waiting for his brothers and sisters to come home, and how they would run to him and he would toss them about as if he were their father. Only in private, with no one to overhear, will she say that he was a sweet-natured and gentle, playful child. She cannot even tell her friends how he was quiet, how he is simply not the type that you would picture doing anything like *that*— maybe his sisters, but never him.

Her friends do not want to hear it. Even her religious friends, she says, do not want to think that this could be true. It would be easier if he were just evil. That would make more sense. But Mrs. Saunders does not see evil in Johnnie. The monster in him, she says, she never knew. She simply cannot reconcile her image of Johnnie with the murderer. And, she cannot face him, except briefly on the phone when she does not have to justify to anyone else that she still talks to him. She knows that she is all Johnnie has left, the only person permitted by prison regulations to send him care packages twice a year and money for necessities. She does neither. She is the only one who will take his collect calls, and then only sometimes.

She wonders how all this happened. How the family fell apart. Sometimes she thinks she can see the Jordans' violent future clearer than their past. Then she closes her eyes.

The Jordans

Johnnie Sr. and Marilyn lived together for seven years in Toledo. They had two of their seven children before they married. For some time, Johnnie Sr. worked as a security guard and occasionally a mechanic until his life on the streets and in drugs made it impossible to keep a regular job. Two years before Johnnie Jr. was born, a caseworker found the Jordans and their two daughters sharing one bedroom with a space heater and an overflowing portable toilet. The bedsheets were stained "pitch black" with dirt, according to a Children Services Board report. There was no baby formula in the apartment for the infants. Marilyn fed them table scraps she chewed first to soften. One of the children had boils on her body so severe she was taken to the hospital. At first, it appeared the baby was afflicted with syphilis chancres, but doctors at Mercy Hospital in Toledo found it was an extremely serious diaper rash worsened by a staph infection.

Seventeen months later, a concerned neighbor called social workers again. They found the children "failing to thrive." Hospital records show that at nine months old, the Jordans' second child weighed only ten pounds. Marilyn continued to feed the children only table scraps.

With almost no other income, the Jordans used their welfare checks for drugs, according to social service records. They traded and sold their food stamps for heroin, crack cocaine, and methamphetamine. They refused the counseling, money management, nutrition-aid, and parenting classes offered to them by social workers. Nonetheless, the Children Services Board closed the family's case, blindly hoping—without any reason—that the Jordans might right themselves. Quietly the agency anticipated more trouble. They sat back and waited. It was during this time that Johnnie was born.

Early Years

Johnnie was born into a turbulent life. His parents moved the family often from apartments to abandoned houses, running from trouble and finding more. Soon after Johnnie, his four younger siblings were born.

Before Johnnie developed memory, it is difficult to know what went on inside the houses where he lived. The Jordans claimed to have had a normal, happy home. Neighbors attest to the opposite, calling the Jordan home a drug den. Violent and abusive men lived with the family periodically, entering and leaving at all times of the day and night. Johnnie's sisters say they were molested and raped by some visitors. More than one neighbor claims the Jordans sold their children for drugs. Johnnie says he does not remember being abused in this way, but he thinks one of his sisters was. School records show the children rarely attended classes, and when they did, they were almost never on time.

Johnnie is not sure what to think of his home life during his early years. He figured it was normal, because his parents told him so, and because he had nothing to compare it to. His parents beat him and his siblings sometimes. The children usually went hungry. He never learned how to wash himself or brush his teeth. Sometimes his parents played mean games with him, he says, but refuses to elaborate. All this seemed normal to Johnnie, and he has hidden these memories in his mind this way. In foster care, he never said his parents had abused him.

But now at eighteen, talking to inmates with more normal pasts, and reflecting on his role as a new father, Johnnie finds weird memories return to him in the night. They confuse him.

"But lots of kids don't have the parents they should have," he tells me in a phone conversation from prison.

"Did you?" I ask.

"No. I have to wonder if they ever really loved me at all. Some of the things they did. I will always be there for my daughter. I would do anything for her. I know they wouldn't for me. My mom, I haven't seen her since everything happened [two years earlier]. She knows where I'm at too."

"Did they abuse you?"

Johnnie does not answer.

"Emotionally, did they abuse you?"

"Yes," he says quietly. "And other ways too."

Those ways, Johnnie still refuses to talk about, even to think about. He knows they are there in his mind, but he has sealed that part off, he says, and refuses to go there for himself or anyone else. When the subject is pursued, he gets angry. He doesn't know why his sisters "told on" his parents, he says. "If you ask a child over and over about something, they might begin to believe it's true" when it's not, he complains. Johnnie prefers to be dubious about his sisters' recall of abuse, though hospital records found one of Johnnie's sisters had an enlarged hymen when she was eight, indicating sexual abuse. He is confused about which of his own memories are real and which memories he thinks might have been planted by suggestion.

"I mean I love them to death, they're my parents," he insists. "Even my mom, I want to see her. Even if it's not right what she did."[1]

III

Johnnie Jordan, Sr. raises his head with a disturbing smile when his son's words are repeated to him during an interview in prison.

1. Johnnie's mother was on the streets. I left messages to reach her through friends, family, and in places she was thought to be living, but she did not return my calls and told some family members she did not wish to be reached. She had not spoken or written to Johnnie since his arrest.

"He was closer to me than to his mother," he says, seeking approval.
"Didn't he get along with his mother?"

"He was alright with his mother. I didn't see no hostility in my family really. We raised our kids to be loyal." A smile creeps across his face.

Spoken by Johnnie Jordan, Sr., "loyalty" is an ugly word. It echoes crimes he has committed but conditioned his children to accept and to hide from outsiders who, he taught his children, would not understand. He has woven abuse and pedophilia so deeply into the family culture that in his children's minds these conditions have formed part of the foundation of their understanding of love. Some pedophiles are sorry for the damage they cause. Even while committing the abuse, some feel guilt and shame. Not Johnnie Jordan, Sr. A psychiatric evaluation reports he shows no remorse at all, and no real concern for his children. The way Johnnie Sr. figures it, he was betrayed by his children, and betrayal is worse than any abuse he may have committed.

Johnnie Sr. once may have been handsome, as people who knew him in his youth say, but it is difficult to find anything attractive about him today. His smile is transparently false, particularly when he means to be charming. At times, he has Johnnie's face—but it is worn, deflated, and cunning, without the warmth or uncertainty that sometimes flashes in his son's eyes. Where Johnnie Jr.'s eyes are often confused and angry, his father's are cool and mean even when he tries to be soft.

He stands less than five feet five and wears a small, unpressed prison jumpsuit, double-cuffed above torn yellow suede shoes. His hair is long, in the form of a ragged afro. He shuffles into the interview with his hands in his pockets, wearing a slight smile, half defeated and half pretense. He hides his thin, tapered fingers under a table or in clasped fists. Only when angry do his hands flare, revealing long, sharp nails carefully manicured into clawing hooks. For self-defense, he says.

"I love my kids," he says fiercely. His words are sharp and threatening rather than reassuring. The more emphatic he becomes, the colder and deader his eyes. Nothing bad happened to his children while they were in his care, he insists.

Medical reports and court testimony say in fact that many bad things did happen to them, many horrible things, I remind him.

He grows angry, his eyes flat and matted. He looks away, then puts on a James Brown laugh and the gloss returns to his eyes. His wide grin breaks long dimples across his face as he shrugs. If something bad did happen, he says, he wasn't responsible. Left there, Johnnie Sr. would be simply an ugly man. But his malaise runs to a deeper meanness. Cruelty lies in his knowledge of what his abuse has done to his children, and still he smiles. He knows that he has destroyed them, and he doesn't care. He knows what he has done to his children, why they have all wound up behind institutional bars and, the lucky few of them, with psychiatric care. He is fully aware of his manipulation and its cruelty.

He relishes his power over his children. He raised them to protect him. Certainly they are more concerned for him than he is for them. He confuses their names, their ages, and even stories about them. He and his wife gave two of their children the same name, as if they forgot the one who is just four years older. Johnnie Sr. remembers only one of his children's birthdays, and that because it is close to his. He doesn't care much about protecting Johnnie Jr. He hasn't had a visitor in two years. He talks to me only in the hope that it might somehow lead to his release from prison.

Disloyalty brought him to where he is now, he claims, not his crimes. This is what he wants to talk about first.

"The only problem I got right now, that hurt me to my heart," he says, "is why my children lie on me like that. I'm here for something I didn't do, and it hurts me each and every day. If I live to be ninety-nine and I get out of here, I'm going right to their homes and ask them why they lied on me like that," he says. He intends his words to be pleading, but they sound threatening.

He is serving thirty-six to eighty years in prison. The prosecutor, John Weglian, still bristles discussing the case. Usually a jovial man, his dark eyes scowl at the mention of Johnnie Jordan, Sr. Weglian was a defense attorney at one time, but even appreciating that side of the law, he says he could never have represented Johnnie Sr. It was one of the worst cases of child abuse he has ever encountered, but very difficult to prosecute because of the incomplete records kept by Children Services. If the abuses had been documented properly, Johnnie Jordan, Sr. would have received a life sentence, Weglian believes. Instead, Children Services had provided evidence that was based almost solely on word of mouth. Only a few weeks before the trial, Weglian and an investigator he hired tracked down the Jordan children's medical records on their own, running to various hospitals in Toledo to collect files on the children and reports from doctors and nurses concerned about possible abuse. Children Services should have collected the same records long ago but did not.

Weglian was forced to make the two youngest Jordan children, each under age eight, face their father in court and testify against him. Before the judge, they showed their looped scars from whippings, spoke of the knife their father used to cut them, and told how he waited for them on their way back to their grandmother's after school, to routinely lure them into an abandoned house with promises of money in exchange for touching and sex.

The older children were too afraid to face their father in court. One of them agreed to testify at first, but suddenly appeared at Weglian's office a day before trial to tell him she couldn't. She worried not only for her safety, but also for that of her own children.

Johnnie Jr., who was awaiting his own trial for murder, refused when his lawyer approached him with Weglian's request. He remained loyal to his father, even if his testimony could have lessened his own sentence as part of a deal offered by prosecutors.

Still, Johnnie Sr. maintains he is innocent. "There are so many beautiful women out there, why would I mess with kids?" he asks.

The way he tells it, he was set up.

"I got locked up because I had gone to donate plasma," as he describes selling his blood. "When I went there, they say they got a warrant for my arrest. 'For what?' I asked. 'Rape,' they said. I say, 'You got to be jiving me, man.' The things I had going for me, ain't no way I would have blown all of it for that. I made good money, as an entertainer in Toledo."

He cannot recall the name of the lounge or club where he supposedly worked. None in Toledo have any record of him working around that time. People who knew him say he was unemployed.

He was forty-two, already convicted of felony for burglary and theft, as well as twenty-one misdemeanors, when he was arrested on three counts of rape and three counts of felonious assault involving three of his children. He was convicted on one count of rape, two counts of felonious sexual penetration, and three counts of felonious assault for cutting his children as a form of punishment.

The sentence was not harsh enough, Weglian says, considering the torture and abuse suffered by his children. But it is amazing that Weglian won that much punishment. Faced with many of the same charges but claiming a religious awakening, Johnnie's mother, Marilyn, plea-bargained her way to only two years in prison. Weglian hadn't enough time to gather the necessary records before her trial, which took place more than a month before her husband's, so they had to let her get away with a relatively light sentence. It still bothers Weglian.

III

Johnnie Jordan, Sr. had turned forty-five the week before I met him, and he was proud to have made it this far in life. He does not think his son will.

He had heard about Johnnie's arrest for murder while he was awaiting trial in the county jail in Toledo, across the street from where Johnnie was behind bars. His son flashed before him on TV. He couldn't believe it. Johnnie was his one child least likely to hurt anyone, he says. He was softer than the rest of his kids; he cared more about others.

Something just went wrong in his son, that's all, he says. Did Johnnie murder in a moment of crazed rage?

"No, no," he answers himself. "My son ain't hardly crazy. No. Not by a long shot. No Jordan is crazy. I can say he's angry about something, but about what I really can't say."

When asked why he thinks Johnnie exploded in violence the moment he did, his father tries to offer another self-serving explanation.

"I asked him why he did it and he said so he could be with me [in prison]," he says. "I told him that was the wrong way to do it." He laughs.

The way Johnnie Sr. sees it, his son was a happy child, a normal child. But Johnnie Sr. is careful also to distance himself from his son. He says the two of them have little in common. Certainly, he says, not the anger. About the only similarity between them, he laughs, is that they both skipped school. "He had some devil in him. Like his brothers and sisters. They all about the same, they all had their devilish ways. We all did. We all did childish things. I didn't see nothing unhuman."

To this day, he believes Johnnie would have been fine if the govern-

ment had left the family alone. The whole problem started when Johnnie was placed in foster care, his father says in an interview at Warren
Correctional Institution, a close security prison where he is serving his
time, in a county where prisons are the area's second-largest employer.
Built to hold 680 inmates, Warren holds 1,377 prisoners. For a time,
both Johnnie Jr. and his father were in the same prison. When I
requested permission to interview both father and son in 1998, Johnnie
Jr. was quickly transferred to a nearby prison. Family members are not
permitted to serve time in the same institution.

Before they were separated, Johnnie Sr. says he tried to look out for
his son in prison. He waited for Johnnie in the chow line. They would
eat lunch together. Whenever they had recreation time, they would sit
down and talk, smoke together, walk around, or Johnnie Sr. would watch
his son play basketball. He told Johnnie Jr. which inmates were dangerous. It was the most fatherly he had ever been in Johnnie's life.

But Johnnie Jr. says he tried to avoid his father in jail. He felt something was not right about him and about their past. For the first time,
Johnnie saw his father as different from the person he pretended to be.
Sometimes he was disgusted by his father. At times, the feeling was so
intense, Johnnie felt he would throw up. He turned those feelings away
by steadily persuading himself that he did not care one way or the other
about his father now. He was just another person, not someone who
could influence him, certainly not someone he loved.

But one day, Johnnie says, as more events from his childhood began
emerging from the family's quilt of paranoia, loyalty, and lies, he was
overcome with a searing hatred for his father. The feeling lingers,
although he is confused as to why.

"I don't even know if what I remember is true anymore," Johnnie
says. "Shit, man."

III

What is known about those first years of Johnnie's life is that his early
experiences were powerful influences on his developing brain. There is
little argument today that early environment influences the development of the nervous system, so that even if cognitive memories are not
profound, the legacy of feelings they produce are. Research suggests
that early stress and trauma may even program the nervous system to

make a person more or less reactive to future stress. These influences may alter not only personality, but also brain chemistry. Some child development experts consider birth to three years of age a critical time for children. The brain is shaped dramatically by stimuli during this period, much as experiences shape it later in a child's life. While there is a huge potential for learning in these early years, the brain is also extremely vulnerable to hurt. Repeated "hits" of stress caused by abuse, neglect, and terror cause physical changes to the brain for life.[2]

A certain amount of fear is necessary for survival, but too much fear is threatening and sometimes destructive. Repeated floods of stress chemicals elevate and alert the level of fight-or-flight hormones. The result may be an impulsive and aggressive child, one who is quick to strike out physically, who courts confrontation, and is generally disliked by his peers. The heightened chemical level does not necessarily make a child violent, but it does affect the way he reacts to stress and the feelings stress calls forth.

Even more dangerous, constant exposure to pain and violence can override the stress response system entirely, like a button that has been pushed so often it stops working. This may lead to children with antisocial personalities. Hostile, impulsive aggressors usually feel sorry afterward, but antisocial aggressors do not feel at all. They do not respond to punishment because nothing hurts them. Tests have shown physiological abnormalities in antisocial children. They have low heart rates and impaired emotional sensitivity. Sticking their hands in ice water, for example, does not elevate their heart rate. In most people, the heart rate and metabolism will speed up to warm the hand. But these children tend to show no such metabolic response. Their ability to feel and to react has been dulled to the vanishing point; so too, it seems, has their conscience. With few exceptions, children who kill are not immmoral. Morality is simply not important to them.

2. An April 1999 report by the Bureau of Justice Statistics found a high percentage of the nation's prison and jail inmates had been physically or sexually abused before their incarceration. In the state prison systems, 57 percent of female inmates and 16 percent of male inmates reported having been physically or sexually abused, 37 percent and 14 percent, respectively, before the age of 18. When prior convictions were included, the percentage was higher. More than 75 percent of male prisoners and almost half of female prisoners who reported being abused had been convicted of a violent crime. ("Prior Abuse Reported by Inmates and Probationers," by Caroline Wolf Harlow.)

Antisocial children lack empathy and a general sensitivity to the world around them. Many such children also abuse animals. Kip Kinkel, the fifteen-year-old in Springfield, Oregon, who killed his parents and shot twenty-five schoolmates in May 1998, tortured animals. So did sixteen-year-old Luke Woodham, who killed his mother and two schoolmates and wounded seven at his Pearl, Mississippi, high school in October 1997. In fact, several of the school yard murderers who exploded on the country's consciousness in recent years had inflicted their anger and rage on animals at some point in their childhood.

Neglect has less graphic effects on a child's threshold for anger and violence, but for a vulnerable baby, neglect is no less tragic. Dr. Bruce Perry, a neurobiologist and psychiatrist at Baylor College of Medicine, has found that neglect impairs the development of the brain's cortex, which controls feelings of belonging and attachment. If these feelings are underdeveloped, children can have difficulty empathizing with others. They tend to be passive and see themselves as victims. This appears to be the case with the seven-year-old boy in Flint, Michigan, accused of shooting to death a six-year-old classmate. He sat passively before detectives, showing little understanding of what he had done and no regret. His mother was later found guilty of neglect after it was discovered that she left her son and his older brother alone for long periods of time in a house with guns and drugs. Similarly, Andrew Golden, who was eleven when he and thirteen-year-old Mitchell Johnson shot to death four girls and a teacher in a Jonesboro, Arkansas, school, felt emotionally abandoned after he lost his father to divorce and was left to his grandparents while his mother worked.

There are no known genetic abnormalities associated specifically with violent crime, though many genetic theories have been entertained throughout history and in modern times, particularly in the 1970s. What has been proven through brain imaging is that brain damage may alter a person's behavior. Damage to certain parts of the brain may lead to paranoid misperceptions, impulsiveness, and extremes of emotion, especially rage. Brain-damaged murderers often cannot stop once set on a course of action, leading to what has been called "overkill."

Lesions on the frontal lobe, often caused by physical trauma, can distort judgment and emotion. In studying fifty murderers, psychiatrist Daniel Amen has found that the cingulate gyrus, which curves through the center of the brain, was hyperactive in these killers. This part of the brain acts as a transmission, shifting from one thought to another. When it fails to function, the individual becomes fixed on one thought, such as vengeance or murder. Amen also found that the prefrontal cortex, which manages the brain, reacts slower than normal in murderers he studied. Damage to the cortex can result from head injury as well as exposure to toxic substances such as alcohol during gestation. Johnnie Jordan, Jr. suffered on both counts.[3]

There is evidence to suggest that, even without brain damage, children's and adolescents' brains operate differently from adults'. Using brain imaging, one National Institute of Mental Health study found both the frontal lobe and the corpus callosum, the cable nerves connecting the left and right sides of the brain, underdeveloped in adolescents. The study's researchers surmise that until the brain is fully matured, this contributes to a greater impulsiveness and more frequent mood swings.

Scientists are only beginning to understand brain chemistry and the effects of specific neurotransmitters on behavior. Research has suggested that people prone to violence may have abnormal levels of certain hormones in brain chemicals. Neurotransmitters are chemical messengers that transmit impulses from one cell to the next. Norepinephrine, dopamine, and serotonin are neurotransmitters believed to hold some clues to violent behavior. Lowering the serotonin levels in animals, for example, makes them more aggressive. But the level of brain chemicals like serotonin is not determined by genes alone. Experience has some effect. Certain types of stress, such as pain and fear, can decrease brain serotonin levels and thereby change behavior. Dr. Perry

3. More recently, a controversial study partly funded by the National Institute of Mental Health, and published in the *Archives of General Psychiatry*, reported a correlation between violence and a specific deficit in uninjured brains. Smaller than average amounts of grey matter in the prefrontal area of the brain may predispose violent anti-social behavior, according to the study's coauthor, Adrian Raine of the University of Southern California. The prefrontal area is thought by many scientists to integrate input from different neural systems and has a large role in determining behavior and weighing the consequences of possible actions. Among other roles, it apparently inhibits impulses that originate elsewhere in the brain and is thus involved in the development of conscience, says Raine, or at least to social "fear conditioning," in which people learn to avoid certain behavior because of punishment.

found that minor stresses administered to rats in their infancy permanently changed their neurotransmitter receptors.

The work of Perry and other neurobiologists demonstrates that trauma can also affect the brain much more than previously thought. Trauma is not a more extreme version of stress. Particularly in young children, traumatic experiences such as witnessing or experiencing violence can alter a developing brain's anatomy and chemistry in ways that interfere with learning, focus and concentration, attachment, and even empathy. Brain imaging and medical research have shown that trauma, which is stored in the brain separate from ordinary memories, leaves scars on the brain and central nervous system.

Posttraumatic stress disorder (PTSD) is a relatively new field of study, especially when applied to child development. Only since 1980 has PTSD been included in the American Psychiatric Association's *Diagnostic and Statistical Manual of Mental Disorders*. And in the years since, research has focused almost exclusively on adults. Today, however, psychiatrists see posttraumatic stress far more in "veterans of childhood" than they do among the war veterans in whom the disorder was originally found. Abused children, Perry found, have much in common with Vietnam veterans neurobiologically. Whether they have been victims of physical violence or witnessed it, their symptoms were the same as these war veterans, including high resting heart rates and increased startle response. In short, they had the physiology of permanent fear.

The traumatized brain stores sensory memories of horror with the neurochemical reactions they triggered. Sights, sounds, and smells associated with danger trigger the fear reaction, before rational thought can intervene. The smell of cooking chicken or the thought of rejection can spur a reaction before understanding or even recognizing the triggering memory.

"I don't let things go," Johnnie Jordan, Jr. says. "I don't forget the moment something happens against me. I might let it slip, but it's going to come back and I don't know what brings it back. It's not like I think something, it's just like something in my mind goes with a taste or smell or something. And whoever is there just happens to be the victim."

There is much debate among trauma researchers over how long

changes last and why so many children can navigate extreme horrors virtually unscathed while others cannot. What kinds of violence, witnessed at what ages, and how they vary depending on the genetic makeup and environment of the child all need to be investigated further. The answers seem to be rooted in a combination of fields, including psychiatry, criminology, and child development, whose overlap and interrelationship are only now being recognized.[4]

Certainly one specific condition, whether it is trauma, brain damage, or a chemical imbalance, is not sufficient to cause infants to become violent adolescents or adults. But they do hold clues. Most empty, emotionally detached children do not become violent, but those who do are usually children whose problems are ignored or neglected—as were the Jordan children's were and as were the children who have committed the fourteen school-yard massacres in the United States between 1997 and 2000. Juvenile homicide is twice as common today as it was in the mid-1980s, but not because children are born with different brains than half a generation ago. Some children do have neurological vulnerability, as children of all generations have had. What may be newer and more common is today's tendency to turn a blind eye to bad parenting: repeated rejection, displacement, and bullying of children; a generally terrifying environment in which children have little to begin with and nothing to fear losing; and perhaps in part the glorification of violence in music, video games, and the media. This confluence of culture, environment, and biology was most apparent in the Columbine High School massacre, in which eighteen-year-old Eric Harris and seventeen-year-old Dylan Klebold murdered thirteen people and wounded twenty-three others. Harris and Klebold clearly liked violent movies and video games, felt socially ostracized by the Columbine High School culture, embraced Goth esthetics, had access to weapons, and used the Internet to learn how to wire the thirty propane-tank and pipe bombs they planted in the school—all for the purpose of venting their rage.

Children have always been a product of their culture, to some extent. At least, as Erik Erikson's work points out, there is a vital relationship between culture and personality. The impressive works of James Q. Wil-

4. Trauma research is still in its infancy. The National Institute of Mental Health has increased its research budget in the area of children and violence 60 percent over the past five years.

son, as well as those of Robert Coles, independently explore the importance of raising children with morality and conscience.[5] These critical
values, which must be taught during child development, especially during the first twelve years, appear to have been neglected or even ignored
in dangerous youths today.

For behavior is the result not just of the brain and its chemicals, but
its interaction with experiences. In her book *The Biology of Violence*,
Debra Niehoff writes that "Although people are born with some biological givens, the brain has many blank pages. From the first moments of
childhood the brain acts as a historian, recording our experiences in the
language of neurochemistry."

Johnnie simply shrugs when I tell him of the various studies and
research. They hold no interest for him. "I don't know why Mrs. Johnson died," he says when I tell him of these findings.

"You killed her," I remind him.

"Yeah," he says quietly, his head down. "I don't know why."

Growing Up

Johnnie does remember when, as an eight-year-old, he found himself in
the cross fire between his parents and Lucas County Children Services
the foster care agency responsible for taking abused, neglected, or
unclaimed children into protective custody. A neighbor of the Jordans'
had called Children Services about Johnnie's two-month-old brother.
Social workers found that the baby was being fed sugar water. The Jordans had sold their furniture for drugs, save for their television set and
two lawn chairs. The seven children slept on two floor mattresses. Caseworkers were shocked by the filthy conditions. Rotting food, cigarette
butts, and other trash cluttered the small apartment. A foul smell hung
in its lifeless air. An uncle and aunt lived with the Jordans at the time.
Johnnie's older sister told a social worker that her parents smoked a

5. Erik Erikson was a prominent American psychoanalyst and author of *Childhood and
Society, Identity and the Lifecycle,* and *Identity: Youth in Crisis.*
James Q. Wilson, a UCLA professor, is a scholar on ethical issues. His books include
Crime and Human Nature (with criminologist Richard J. Hernstein), *Moral Sense,
Moral Judgment,* and *Thinking About Crime.*
Robert Coles, a child psychiatrist associated with Harvard as a clinician and teacher, is
the author of the series *Children of Crisis,* which won a Pulitzer Prize. Among his other
works are *The South Goes North* and *The Moral Life of Children.*

clear pipe, and her mother often acted differently afterward. For several days each month, the only food in the house was water and peanut butter. The children rarely attended school and were failing their classes.

Johnnie and his two sisters were taken to St. Vincent's Medical Center for examination. Doctors found scars on their small bodies, indicative of whippings. The oldest girl, who cared for the other children during their parents' sudden and often prolonged absences, said her parents sometimes beat the children with belts or extension cords. Doctors also found evidence that one of Johnnie's sisters had been sexually abused. A Children Services report called for the three oldest girls to be screened for sexual abuse, but there is no indication that the girls were ever in fact examined.

Family Court ordered Johnnie's parents to submit urine samples for drug tests. After a long delay, they finally complied: Marilyn tested positive for cocaine, but Johnnie Sr.'s sample was mistakenly tested for marijuana instead of cocaine. He refused to submit another sample.

Four days after the social workers' visit, the Jordan children were taken into the county's custody because of neglect and divided among three foster homes. Johnnie remembers that day vividly as the day he was forcibly removed from his parents. He did not understand why the government had shattered his family. He did not see anything wrong with his life. It was as it had always been. His parents were all he had to love. He did not like people coming in to mess with his family. He did not understand why his sisters started telling family secrets. Sure, they went hungry sometimes, but that was because they were poor. Sometimes his mother would take him and his sister to panhandle outside a bar or a shopping center. His second-oldest sister was his parents' favorite. They would take her all the time because she was the cutest. In the beginning, it was an honor to be chosen to go panhandle with them. It meant they thought he was handsome and appealing enough to get money. But more important to Johnnie, it meant that he was pleasing to his parents. As he grew older, he noticed the pitying looks on the faces of strangers passing by as they handed him change, and he felt shame.

"I guess you're worth this," said one child barely older than Johnnie himself, handing him a nickel. From that moment, Johnnie did not like begging for anything, not even for his parents' sake. He swore that he would not ask for anything from anyone. He'd get what he wanted on his own. When he was seven years old, he said, his father taught him how to shoplift and sell drugs on the street. In his world, he was already self-sufficient. But he chose to stay with his family. They needed him. When he got some money, he gave it to his mother, thinking she would buy food with it. She didn't. He learned that lesson quickly, so he would buy the food instead. Without him, Johnnie believed, his parents would probably starve or die in the cold.

Sometimes his parents fought, and he'd run out the door. When his oldest sister, not yet a teenager, stepped in to stop the fighting, she ended up hurt more often than not. She was tired, she told the social workers finally, tired of raising her younger siblings and maintaining her parents. She wanted out, even if it meant foster care.

Johnnie did not like the nosy questions social workers asked him the day they took him from his parents. He felt it was none of their business. He knew that what he told them could get his parents in trouble. Johnnie in particular believed what his father had told the children, that Children Services was just out to get the Jordans and hurt them any way they could. He stuck by the first lesson his father instilled in him: loyalty. He denied being sexually abused, or abusing any of his siblings, but he did confirm a story told by his sisters, that a friend of his parents' had sex with them. They were ten and eleven years old at the time.

Signs of sexual abuse were not hard to find in the Jordan children. A month into their foster care stay, the girls' foster mother became concerned about the children's sexual behavior. She suggested counseling, but Children Services took no action. A second foster mother suspected the children had been abused and were engaging in incestuous sex. The caseworker tried to convince her otherwise. In her notes, the caseworker reported she "tried to explain that I don't really consider that they had intentionally meant to be sexual with each other because of their ages and because kids experiment and play with each other." The foster mother accused the caseworker of making excuses for the girls. Apparently no counceling was set up, no connection was made to the other Jordan children, and there is no later mention of this incident in any case records.

Around the same time, Johnnie's foster mother found Johnnie trying to have oral sex with his younger foster brother. Johnnie admitted to "humping" the three-year-old. When a caseworker asked where he learned this activity, Johnnie said a sixteen-year-old foster boy in the same foster home had taught him. According to the caseworker's records, the "allegation was determined not to be true." Just a few days before, the foster mother had seen Johnnie on top of his younger brother teasing, "I'm going to do it tomorrow." Even so, social workers did not order sexual abuse screens for any of the children. No one followed up on either incident.

Johnnie's foster mother did not want Johnnie to remain in her home because of his sexual behavior. She liked him well enough, but she was seriously concerned about the danger he posed to other children. She knew that Johnnie needed help, and he was not getting it. But she was persuaded to let him stay. The caseworker told her simply to "watch the boys, especially Johnnie, closely," according to Children Services records.

Johnnie's behavior worsened. He lied more frequently. He suffered from involuntary urinating and defecating—both considered signs of abuse. He felt caged and kept. He was ridiculed at school by other children. He desperately wanted to return to his parents and his siblings. He ran away periodically, to check on his parents. He gave them whatever pocket money he found or was given. They took the money hungrily, even though they were also illegally cashing child welfare checks sent to them mistakenly while their children were in foster care. Later, Johnnie would want to go home to take care of his parents. But now he missed home because he didn't understand the world in which he found himself. Only his family, it seemed to him, spoke his language. In this way, he convinced himself that they cared for him. They shared the same understanding of life. Johnnie believed they loved him even when they beat him. At home, Johnnie was left to run free and do as he pleased. If the Jordans lived on a sinking ship, at least he felt his parents were in the boat with him.

Most of the time, he could not help wetting his bed. But sometimes, when he was angry, he would urinate on a sofa or in the corner of a room. This was his way of punishing and rebelling. He knew he couldn't get his way with words. He didn't even know the words to fit his feelings, he says. He dared not fight openly with the adults, but he figured that he could get his foster mother to reject him and he would be sent back to his parents.

His father inspired this thinking. Sometimes his father would appear on a street corner that Johnnie passed on his way to school. He told Johnnie how much he and the family missed him. He told his son not to cooperate with any adults other than his parents.

Even when life was comfortable for Johnnie in a foster home, these chance meetings with his father or glimpses of his mother made him anxious for their safety. He was convinced that the world outside was being unfair to them. He had to fight and rebel, and then the system would give up and the family could be back together again. At age eight, this is what Johnnie believed.

Although his mother failed to attend any counseling sessions, Johnnie's two youngest siblings were returned to her and Johnnie Sr. Two older girls were moved to another foster family, but within only a few days the foster mother demanded their removal. One of the girls was found holding a pillow over the face of a foster baby also in the home; the other had violently seized a tricycle from another child.

Johnnie's ploy worked. His foster mother asked that he be removed from her home because he had become "very disruptive and had damaged" some of her personal possessions after she tried to punish him. Children Services began to allow Johnnie to return to his parents on weekends. On one visit, a caseworker caught him in bed with one of his sisters. The caseworker reviewed "good" and "bad" touches. He promised not to touch his siblings inappropriately again. Johnnie was taken to "sexual offending" counseling. He saw a therapist six times and was told his habit was "inappropriate and why it must stop." Apparently no one reported to the therapist that Johnnie continued to touch his siblings throughout his therapy.

Nonetheless, the foster care agency returned Johnnie to his parents' house because they could not find a family or institution willing to take him, and because Johnnie wanted to go home. The same thing happened to all the other Jordan children. But within twelve days of the reunion, on their first check-up visit, caseworkers found the Jordans again living with no furniture, no stove, and no refrigerator. For electricity, they ran an extension cord to a neighbor's house. Their utilities had been cut off for lack of payment, although they continued to receive Aid to Families with Dependent Children (AFDC) checks from the government. Soon after, Johnnie's little sister was found to have burn marks. A little later, another sister was hospitalized with stitches in her face, and Johnnie's brother was found with burns on his stomach. These incidents were reported to Children Services, but never investigated.

In the midst of these difficulties, family outreach services instigated and commissioned by Children Services abruptly ended, claiming that "all the basic needs were being met." In fact, none of the family's needs were being served in the slightest, let alone met. Counseling for Johnnie's father's, for example, had been "terminated" by the agency contracted to watch and help him because he never showed up. "Drop out without notice and unresponsive client," the agency notified Children Services.

One counselor reported he suspected the Jordans were continuing to use drugs and questioned why the agency did not investigate the recent reports indicating physical abuse of the children. He strongly opposed the family reunification. But his protests were in vain. Children Services did not reconsider their decision to let the family live together again.

Several months later, when caseworkers made a surprise early afternoon visit to the Jordan house, their knock awakened Johnnie's mother. All the children were at home rather than at school, without excuses. The oldest child was caring for the younger ones. The house was filthy, according to their report. Children Services again ordered the Jordans to undergo drug testing. There was no food in the house. One space heater was used to heat the one back room where the entire family of nine slept.

Meantime, Johnnie was finding school increasingly difficult. Children teased him about his family. He was easy to make fun of. He was soft, until he became enraged. They laughed at his dirty clothes and the awful smells. He had not been taught to bathe or wash his clothes. Later in his life he would become almost compulsive about his appearance, ironing both T-shirts and jeans. If he hadn't any clean clothes to wear, he would not dress at all. But now, at age nine, he was confused about why the kids were laughing. His mouth stunk, they said. Getting nowhere with his mother, the school called his stepgrandmother and Children Services to report that Johnnie had gingivitis and badly needed to see a dentist. Nothing was done.

About the same time, another school refused to let Johnnie's older sister attend classes because she had an untreated ringworm infection. All the children had severe diarrhea. In spite of all these conditions, Lucas County Children Services did nothing.

Johnnie's stepgrandmother, Lorraine Saunders, came by the Jordans' various houses and apartments sometimes to take the children to church and to buy them shoes at JC Penney's. She would bring food, but never went into their homes. She would sit in her silver Oldsmobile until the children came down to her. She knew something was going wrong with the children, but she pictured nothing worse than a lazy mother. She saw her stepson, Johnnie Sr., as a father who tried to clean up and do the best that he could. That was all she cared to see, she admits now.

Johnnie agreed to go to church with his stepgrandmother so that he could be with her, and maybe get a McDonald's hamburger and sometimes a new pair of shoes. He liked her very much. But he never understood a word spoken in church. The swaying, the music, the words of the preacher and invocation of "the Lord," he didn't care for or understand. He didn't understand what "saved" meant. He didn't think much about heaven or hell, just as he never recounted the past or dreamed of the future. He only thought of the very minute he was in. And in church, each second was an eternity. He'd bite himself to stay awake.

After a second month, a caseworker paid another visit. They found the children alone again, the home still squalid. No one knew where their parents were. That evening, the Toledo police took Johnnie and his siblings away for the night, returning them the next day after Children Services provided vouchers for food and the electricity bill. The foster care agency asked the Neighborhood Improvement Foundation of Toledo to remove the trash strewn on the Jordans' yard. The agency also provided another refrigerator and stove. Again, CSB officials told the parents to get urine tests for drugs. Again, the utilities were turned off. And again, with no explanation, the agency ended its supervision of the family, leaving the Jordans to fail their children further.

Just four months later, at the beginning of a new school year, Johnnie's elementary school called Children Services to complain about the Jordan children's dismal attendance record. A teacher who had gone searching for the children found the Jordans' house vacant. School officials also told the agency they were concerned that Johnnie's fourteen-

year-old sister was prostituting herself. A Children Services investigator confirmed that the house was empty, the utilities again cut off for
lack of payment. Social workers and teachers saw Johnnie's mother pan-
handling with Johnnie and his sister. One of Johnnie's sisters had fresh
burn marks. Flea and mosquito bites covered the children's legs.

The children were immediately taken away and divided among four
emergency foster homes. A judge awarded Children Services custody of
the seven Jordan children, again on the grounds of neglect. This time,
the family's separation would be permanent, and Johnnie sensed it.

His return to foster care was a free fall into grief. A grief of terrifying, endless confusion. He had lost his parents and family, but he could
not mourn their loss because they were still alive and around town. If
he didn't see them from a car window passing through his old neigh-
borhoods, he heard about them from classmates. He was supposed to act
as if they were dead or unimportant. He wasn't supposed to care for
them because of the abuse and neglect. But he needed to believe someone loved him and cared for him. To Johnnie, everyone else was a
stranger.

Very few psychological studies have focused on children who have
lost both their parents and their siblings to death. No studies deal with
children's loss of parents and family who are still alive but forcibly separated by the government for the children's sake. Taken from parents
who are all they have known, even if only through cruelty, the children's grief is profound. Few receive any counseling. They cannot
understand their loss. For most children in foster care, losing their abusive parents is not considered a loss at all by Children Services, and children are left to cope in their confusing world with angry and sad
emotions on their own. Absorbing this trauma in their lives has a more
lasting effect than anything they may have experienced before.

Once again in the custody of Children Services, Johnnie's old behavior pattern emerged. He ran away from his foster homes several times to
find his father. Once, his father returned him to the foster home. More
often, the police had to pick him up and take him back. He sold drugs
with his father, even while in foster care. Caseworkers took no action.

Children Services officials warned the Jordans that the children
would not be returned to them unless the parents graduated from a
substance abuse rehab program. Rather than graduate, however, both

were thrown out for nonattendance and failure to cooperate with the counselors. Johnnie Sr. even tested positive for cocaine in a scheduled screening while still enrolled in substance abuse classes.

When Johnnie was ten, he was placed in a therapeutic group home for sexual offenders. During that time, he also received group therapy with his younger brothers and sisters. His older sisters were supposed to attend as well, but after two sessions, they refused. They had been "involved in illicit activities" on the streets, apparently prostitution and drug dealing, for a few years and were already lost, a therapist reported.

But Johnnie was not yet lost. He was receptive and warm, the therapist, Dr. Barbara Baker, noted. He liked to be hugged. He was needy, the neediest of the children. The rest of the Jordan children did marvelously when Johnnie was with them, she found. Johnnie was hopeful and happy during these sessions, and his outlook was contagious among his siblings. He minded his manners, and theirs. He played gently and laughed a great deal, reveling in their company. Without him, the children reverted to bad form.

Dr. Baker was patient and caring, and in turn, the children began to open up to her. On weekends, on her own time, she would gather the Jordan children from their various placements so they could be together.

Though Johnnie was known to have "episodes of fighting, sexual acting out, and malicious destruction of property" during this period, Dr. Baker wrote that she believed "his prognosis is good if he remains in a therapeutic setting over a long enough period of time to insure that he is in control." Unfortunately his therapeutic home closed soon after she filed her report, and Johnnie was cast into yet another haphazardly run family foster care home.

While Johnnie generally pleased Dr. Baker, she saw increasing signs of danger. Johnnie "is a very angry young man with an identity crisis," she wrote in a report buried deep in one of Johnnie's Children Services files. "Johnny [sic] must be protected from himself as well as others."

Dr. Barbara Baker

Dr. Barbara Baker shakes her head when she is reminded of the report. Her soft cream blouse and faux pearl necklace shudder beneath her stiff pink suit. She turns away to discreetly run a finger under her candy-red-rimmed glasses.

"I missed the mark with Johnnie," she says, her voice trembling slightly. After a moment, she looks up into my eyes, which must show surprise. Her report had foreshadowed Johnnie's future, it seemed to me. Suddenly her pressed suit jacket crumples and her smile dissolves into free-flowing tears. It takes a few moments before she can continue.

"I've seen some really rough kids, and Johnnie was never that. He was so tender and warm. I was so surprised that he could do that. And to a little woman," she says, referring to Mrs. Johnson "and her crying out in pain."

Dr. Baker takes off her glasses and wipes her eyes for Mrs. Johnson, then composes herself with an empty sigh. "I knew Johnnie was hurting. But I didn't think he was capable of that. I never saw that violence. Never knew that was a part of him. But he was ten or eleven then," she reminds herself. "Now I look back and it was just so predictable."

Since 1989, Dr. Baker has been the principal of Lincoln Elementary School on Detroit Avenue, in the once black-middle-class neighborhood where she grew up in Toledo. The neighborhood is a much tougher place these days. Witnessing the destruction of so many children's lives, she opened a private practice as a psychologist a year later. She has since largely given up the practice, mainly because of the paperwork required by CSB and managed-care firms. For every hour she spent with the children, she says, she would waste another on paperwork. There simply was not enough time to help all the children in need, so she agreed to counsel children free of charge and free of paperwork.

Dr. Baker has never been a traditional therapist. She broke rules by taking her hungry young clients to McDonald's, buying sanitary napkins for young girls who could not afford them, and spent her own time seeking out and collecting children whose parents or foster parents failed to bring them to her sessions. For her work with the Jordans, Dr. Baker, who was single at the time, bought a minivan to gather all the children from their various homes.

Several times, CSB caseworkers advised her not to get too involved with the children. The warning still irks her. "How can you help these children without getting too involved?" she asks. "Their problem is that no one is involved in the first place."

To a great extent her approach worked with Johnnie, even though she feels she failed him. Dr. Baker is one of perhaps three people, he says, who had a positive influence on him. He does not remember most of the twenty-one adults who foster-parented him from the time he was eight until his arrest at fifteen, nor the two dozen more whom he encountered in the social work and juvenile justice systems. Only Dr. Baker; J. R. Robinson, his group home counselor, who grew up in the same neighborhood as Dr. Baker; and Ron Wingate, one of Johnnie's attorneys. They were the only people he feels ever truly cared, even if only for a short time.

The mention of Dr. Baker's name briefly lights up Johnnie's eyes in prison, before he reconsiders and anticipates rejection.

"Has she forgot me by now?" he asks dully.

"No."

"Does she hate me?" he asks, now leaning forward.

"No."

"Then why don't she come visit me?" he says, crossing his arms with a jutting jaw. Johnnie demands attention with a child's words, but a man's rough voice. He still feels he is owed loyalty and affection. At nineteen years old, he still does not recognize that such emotions are cultivated and earned.

"She cared about us one time," Johnnie remembers. "That's why I'd do anything I could to be at her sessions and be honest with her. She was the only doctor I ever opened up to like that. The rest, *psheww,* they just trying to get you for something."

Dr. Baker had heard of the Jordans before Children Services brought their case to her. Teachers and social workers often spoke of a family that lived in an empty house with only candles for light and warmth. When the Jordan children came to her, they were so hungry for affection and comfort that they glowed in appreciation of her company. The older two girls were different. They had already hardened. But the younger ones were still fresh to life.

Her memories of the case are vividly refreshed by the young faces she sees in her school daily. By four-forty in the afternoon, Dr. Baker's lunch from Wendy's has long since gone cold. She rarely finds time to eat before nightfall. As a psychologist who was under contract to Children Services, and now periodically works with the agency, she speaks on the record at considerable risk. She does so because she says John-nie's story is important to tell, that it reaches beyond just one boy.

Each day, she watches dozens of children line up before the school sec-retary for their Ritalin and other psychotropic drugs, which, she finds, curb their energy as well as dull their learning. Most of these children are supposedly suffering from attention deficit hyperactivity disorder, but Dr. Baker is skeptical of this diagnosis, which has spread through schools in epidemic numbers. She knows the drill too well. A teacher feels a child is unruly or uninterested in their work so he calls the school counselor, who tells a parent to call a particular pediatrician or psychiatrist who liberally prescribes drugs over the phone. Most of these children don't even see a doctor. The basic problem is not brain chemistry, Baker believes. With what most of these children deal with every day, with what they have gone through, is it any wonder they are restless, anxious, cannot concen-trate on school, or are depressed? But some teachers just look at what is before them that hour of that day and how they can get through their classes more easily. Behavior modification drugs such as Ritalin, Dexedrine, Tofranil, Zoloft, and Paxil are a quick and dangerous fix for children already vulnerable to the plethora of illicit drugs dominating their neighborhood. Too many teachers just want to make the children more docile, and the parents, not knowing better or themselves exhausted, do exactly what the teachers say.[6] Then there are the children with no one at all to look out for their interests, so the school counselor, who does not even know the child, calls the doctor for the absent parent. Johnnie Jor-dan was one of these kids. There are so many Johnnie Jordans, Baker says, children so needy and with such tragic backgrounds. No one knows what to do with them, so the overburdened school system simply does what it can to dull their behavior and ignore their pain. These children are drugged or shuffled from one home to another until they explode. Lots of kids like Johnnie are created by foster care, she says, or find their way into that system because no one knows how to handle them.

6. The use of stimulants such as Ritalin and antipsychotic drugs, which include major tranquilizers such as Thorazine, on children almost tripled from 1991 to 1995, according to a study by Julie Magno Zito of the University of Maryland School of Pharmacy, pub-lished in the *Journal of the American Medical Association*. The number reflecting the increase include children age two to four, though most of these drugs have not been approved by the FDA for children under six. Not much is known about the long-term effects of these drugs on the developing brains of children.

"It's unconscionable to take a hurt kid and put him in foster care homes where he gets hurt more," Dr. Baker says. "What kids have to do to survive a foster home," she marvels. That's what makes a Johnnie Jordan. It is not solely the abuse in the family that destroys children, she contends, though it certainly weakens them, but the prolonged abuse in foster care where the troubled, angry youths cannot or will not bond with their caregivers and few people really try to help. "They are the ones who turn into bombs."

After almost a year of counseling, a foster care family applied to adopt the Jordans. The children liked Cassandra and William Quinn. And the Quinns knew how to deal with children. It seemed a solution better than CSB would have hoped for. While the younger Jordan children were reported in CSB files to be "cute," "attractive," and "adoptable," the older ones were more difficult to place. When Johnnie entered the permanent custody of Children Services, his intake report deemed "it questionable whether Johnnie will be considered adoptable." Furthermore, while the Quinns asked to adopt the entire family, Children Services determined their stepgrandmother's commitment to the children "questionable." Nonetheless, the agency awarded custody to Lorraine Saunders, their stepgrandmother, because she was related to the children even though she was an elderly woman who struggled to care for them. Mrs. Quinn is still heartbroken by the decision. She believes that adopting the children then could have made all the difference.[7] In failing health, Lorraine Saunders was unable to take the children to their therapy sessions.

Dr. Baker campaigned for the foster care parents' adoption but was unsuccessful. Giving custody to Mrs. Saunders "was a critical mistake," Dr. Baker says, shaking her head. "*The* critical mistake." With the Jordans entering adolescence, and with the likelihood that their stepgrandmother would allow them to spend time with their birth parents again, she felt the children would be lost. And they were. They were scattered among institutions, group homes, and foster homes again after only a few months with Mrs. Saunders.

Dr. Baker heard little of the Jordans after that until four years later,

---

7. Mrs. Quinn agreed to an interview, but she soon began to cry, and left before she could be questioned at length.

when she was watching the news on television and saw Johnnie's tired and worn face. It was nothing like the smiling child who played so carefully with his siblings and fought so readily on their behalf. She still cannot call what happened to Mrs. Johnson a murder. "That incident occurred because Johnnie was so deeply hurt," she says, trying to find some rationale for the killing. "He was so desperate and hopeless, he did it without thinking."

Dr. Baker believes the system, much as it failed Johnnie Jordan, fails to deal properly with the scores of Johnnie Jordans now floating through her stone and brick school. Paper cutouts of snowflakes decorate its windows and cheerful construction paper warms its safe hallways. The school can lock out the neighborhood behind its tall walls for five hours of the day, when every visitor must be buzzed in. But it is not enough. Not nearly enough. In the young eyes parading before her, she sees hundreds of softer, younger Johnnies who still fight to be held and who glow in the slightest praise and attention.

As soon as school ends, the children return to the streets, to the trash that fills empty lots near the school, to a house next to the school whose porch has caved in, its windowed eyes smashed and broken. Only a few neighborhood houses survive the heavy weight of life in this neighborhood. A few struggle to maintain the dignity of their past. But many of the wooden houses tumble to the ground like sticks and cardboard.

This is where Johnnie spent most of his early life with his parents. A generation ago, the same neighborhood raised Dr. Baker to be strong and caring. Now it is lost to the gun and drug culture, and along with it, the new generation.

The Destinie store directly across from her school uses plastic yellow banners to advertise cheap cell phones and beepers with no credit checks; its billboard pushes Newport cigarettes. Next door stands the gas station where Johnnie's parents wiped windshields and pumped gas for change. Up the street, at the Swaynfield Shopping Center, Johnnie panhandled with his parents in front of the Payless shoe store. And beyond it all, just past the Interstate 75 overpass, is the burned-out factory in which Johnnie played and sold drugs.

Dr. Baker's husband ministers to prison inmates. She has accompanied him many times to prisons. But still she cannot face Johnnie behind bars.

"Those eyes," she says. She faces them almost every day in her thoughts and blinks them away with hope. "I don't want to see those eyes in a murderer." She stops and thinks for a moment. "I don't want to see a murderer's eyes in Johnnie."

If she does, she might not be able to face her kids in school. "If Johnnie could do this, and he wasn't even one of the more dangerous ones, what hope is there?" she asks, looking beyond me, not expecting an answer.

III

Johnnie passed through nineteen foster care placements between the ages of ten and fifteen. To most of his foster parents, Johnnie appeared a confused and sad child who rarely shimmered with a warm, hopeful smile. Generally each set of foster parents became more disturbed by his temper and behavior. In three homes, Johnnie's foster parents remember him stealing butcher knives from their kitchens and hiding them under his mattress. For protection, he said.

He was not alone in his distrust and fear, and perhaps learned this method of protection from an adult who was supposed to care for him. One of his foster parents told me she also takes measures to protect herself from her foster children. "I took a knife from my kitchen, wrapped it up, and had it in the washing machine" she recalls of the time she took Johnnie in. "[The children] don't know anything, but I feel safer."

Another foster mother later likened Johnnie to a stray dog. A scrappy, pathetic, and ultimately dangerous creature, she said, who needed a good home but whose hunger runs so deep it could not be touched by any show of love or goodness. Sitting across from him at the kitchen table the second morning he spent in her house, she remembers thinking that "he would never be tame." Like all of his foster parents, she asked that her name not be used because Lucas County Children Services has warned each one that they could be liable for violating child privacy laws by disclosing details of Johnnie's life. More significantly, perhaps, she is afraid of Johnnie, of what he could do if he were ever released from prison. She is afraid precisely because she did not see the extreme danger which must have been present in him when he lived with her. When he looked at her with anger, was her own murder on his mind? She is sure it must have been.

She still takes children into her home, mostly for the money she is paid by the foster care system, she admits. She couldn't survive without the money she is paid for taking in unwanted children. After Johnnie, she wouldn't take another child if she didn't need to, she says. She tries to take only children under the age of nine. But even then, she does not feel safe.

"I've had eleven-year-old kids who could do worse things than Johnnie did," she says. "There's nothing we can do. All of foster care is full of Johnnie Jordans and worse."

Most of the children who stay in her house are wild, she says. "They got that same stray-dog look about them, with sharp teeth and angry eyes. I sometimes sit here and think they are Johnnie's eyes haunting me."

III

While he was still under Dr. Baker's care, Lucas County Children Services placed Johnnie at the River Road Group Home. He was ten. After his bouts of fighting, sexual misconduct, and truancy, Children Services decided he needed a more structured placement, under almost constant supervision. This frightened Johnnie, who knew from the streets that a "structured placement" meant an institution. Johnnie ran away from his foster home the night before he was supposed to move to River Road. The next morning, police found him and placed him behind bars for the first time in the Child Study Institute, the juvenile jail downtown, a stark and virtually windowless detention center.

Johnnie had been threatened with prison many times. But only after he experienced time behind bars did he realize that jail was not a place he wanted to be, no matter how much it elevated his standing on the street. He was scared and lonely. Outside, when things got rough, when there were things he did not like, he could run. He knew how to run better than most kids his age. He knew how to hitchhike, and he had a good sense of direction. Locked away, Johnnie realized he had no control. He did not know what to do, except to wait, as he would get used to doing until something else happened.

That is when J. R. Robinson came into his life.

III

J. R. Robinson is a large man in both stature and dignity. He's tough.
He earns respect, especially from kids. He doesn't play mind games. He
demands a lot. But it is the warmth in his eyes which reaches even the
meanest kids. He can also be cold with anger, but his eyes never hold
the chill of irrational violence that is sometimes visible in Johnnie.

By the time he met Johnnie, J.R. had counseled troubled children in
juvenile jails and other places for thirteen years, and never lost hope
that he could help even the roughest kids. His idealism flourished in the
River Road Group Home, which had recently opened in Toledo, thanks
to a wealthy family. River Road was to be, in J.R.'s mind, revolutionary.
Ten boys would live there along with four house counselors, including
J.R. They would parent the children in a beautiful, affluent neighborhood, forming a family that would supplant the families from which the
children had been taken. River Road would instill family values in children who had been denied exposure to commitment, respect and love
from birth. But the children had to cooperate, they had to be engaged, if
the program was to work for them.

Johnnie brightens as he recalls clearly the day he met J.R.

"I was locked up for running away again when he came to see me. I
guess they didn't know what to do with me, so they were just keeping
me there until someone would take me," he says. J.R. looked like a line-
backer to him, someone you didn't want to mess with. But there was
something about J.R. that Johnnie says he understood and liked, though
he tried not to.

"I wasn't about to trust nobody then," he says.

J.R. sat down with Johnnie in a small room in the juvenile jail, with
no staff or guards. He told Johnnie about River Road, about himself, and
about Debbie and Jim Lynch, who ran the group home.

"I want you to come down and visit," J.R. told Johnnie. "If you don't
like it, you don't have to stay. Now, I just want you to understand this is
not a locked facility. We care about people there. You'll see that our staff
is a family-oriented nature. We care about you, and we care about the
rest of the kids there, and that's why we're here." [sic]

Johnnie sat, arms crossed, leaning coolly back on his chair. Only toward the end of J.R.'s talk did Johnnie unbend a little. His face became a little soft, revealing his fear.

J.R. knew he was getting to Johnnie, but he also knew that Johnnie, out of pride, wasn't likely to give in even if he wanted to see what the group home looked like.

"At least you'll be out of here," J.R. said with a shrug. "You want to come with me?

"Noo," Johnnie said defiantly, but unconvincingly.

"Okay then. That's your prerogative."

J.R. stood up and began to walk away. Four steps later, Johnnie called out in a voice chilled with desperation: "Wait!"

That voice touched J.R.'s heart. He would be able to hear it years later. He turned around and saw a scared and tired boy before him, looking for a way out of the world he was born into.

Johnnie did not see any of that. He just knew that he didn't want J.R. to leave. But when asked why he felt so close to J.R., he shrugged.

"I guess I was there so long I got attached to him," he said of his time at River Road. Johnnie stayed with J.R. in the group home, which grew to include eight other boys, for two years, his longest stay in one place, except for prison.

III

Johnnie's small body sprang up like a Muppet when J.R. stopped his van on the round driveway, just before the great stone house of River Road Group Home. His eyes gazed over the broad, leafy neighborhood with grand houses and kids riding bicycles on the brick sidewalks. Julia Bates, the lead prosecutor against Johnnie in his murder trial four years later, lived with her husband, an elected Toledo judge, and their children just blocks away. On her walks through the neighborhood, she would pass Johnnie and the other boys raking leaves in the front yard and smile at them. Her son would play with Johnnie's housemates. But that was well before a future neither she nor Johnnie could anticipate in the security of their beautiful neighborhood.

Johnnie called River Road Group Home "the mansion." Each boy had his own room, with a half bath. But what impressed Johnnie was the small basketball court outside. And a pool, with a water slide.

"You going to stay?" J.R. asked at the end of the day.

"I guess I'll give you a chance," Johnnie said, and smiled.

"From that point on," J.R. said later, "we were close friends."

Johnnie's transition was not always smooth, but J.R. never expected it to be. Johnnie was withdrawn. He had an extremely hard time accepting and owning his history, J.R. recalls. He was gentle and loyal. But he got into fights quickly, and could become extraordinarily angry and violent. His particular target was a white boy from a rural area who was nicknamed Bugaboo by the staff and other kids because he took pride in needling people. Bugaboo kept his hands in his pockets, wore thick glasses, and in every way seemed like a nerd. He used words as his primary weapon. Even the staff found themselves having to call their own time-out in dealing with Bugaboo. With the other kids, Bugaboo could start fights with a couple of sharp remarks. With Johnnie, on his second day, Bugaboo needed only one stinging comment about Johnnie's mom and dad. Bugaboo still has not forgotten the rage with which Johnnie lunged at him, and today, after years in both juvenile and adult prisons, he has never again seen the intense anger with which Johnnie attacked him.

"He was out of control," J.R. remembers. "It took me all I had to hold him down."

J.R., four times Johnnie's size, folded the boy in a huglike grip and wrestled him to the ground, where they struggled for what seemed like fifteen minutes.

"Let me up!" Johnnie shouted.

"I'm not letting you up until you demonstrate some self-control," J.R. told him.

"What do you mean?" Johnnie raged.

In the midst of the struggle, J.R. explained. "You have to get a handle on your emotions," he said. "You got to answer without fighting."

"Okay," Johnnie finally said, almost calmly, after staying still for a moment. "You can let me up now."

"You're not going to hurt anybody?"

"I didn't say that," Johnnie yelled back. "I just said you could let me up now!"

His honesty tickled J.R. Eventually his laughter infected Johnnie, though Johnnie was not sure why he was laughing. All he knew was that J.R. was not laughing at him. It never seemed like J.R. laughed at people, he just laughed. They wrestled a little longer, but it was almost as if, J.R. believed, Johnnie didn't want to be released from his embrace or attention. Finally they found their feet.

Bugaboo still was not easy after that. He continued to have his moments of sharpness. But Johnnie grew attached and loyal to him as he did to all the boys at the group home. After a few weeks, Johnnie looked out for Bugaboo at their public elementary school, a grand Gothic building on a hilltop that overlooked a winding brown river. Johnnie even became protective of him. More than once, J.R. saw Johnnie defend Bugaboo at school against other kids.

Together, Johnnie and Bugaboo would wait outside the school for J.R. to drive them home. Johnnie would run to J.R. with a smile. As much as he liked school now, he liked J.R. better. He was working toward the privilege of walking home. The group home boys had to earn this right, because the staff was careful to avoid any opportunity for one of their children to get in trouble with a neighborhood kid. Residents had been dubious enough about allowing the group home into their area.

Johnnie loved the clean, spacious neighborhood as well as his school, which seemed pristine, free of all the people of his past and their name-calling. Harvard Elementary was the only school he attended that was not marred by graffiti. To fit in, he took newfound pride in his grooming. He cleaned and ironed his clothes regularly. He found dignity in the new skills and habits River Road taught him. He liked school almost as much as he did the group home. The home's eight other boys made up his family now. They had their confrontations, he says, but basically, "we were like a family."

He never felt alien to this new world of an upper-middle-class neighborhood and school, though he says he stood out. "Me and another dude from the home were the only black people there, man!" he says, still disbelieving of his school experience. "Everywhere I had ever been there were no white people."

But Johnnie has never put much stock in race. He doesn't care much about color, except to notice it, or the lack of it. He never felt unwanted at Harvard. In prison years later, he said he never in his life felt discriminated against, though he knows other people who have been. He does not understand why people make such a big deal about race.

Recently, Johnnie shared a cell with a member of the Aryan Brotherhood, a white supremacist gang which, in Ohio, has claimed responsibility for more than a few fatal prison stabbings of inmates based solely on race.

"I told him I get along with everyone, man," Johnnie explained. But his cellmate moved out. Johnnie does not understand why.

III

Every week, the River Road staff would gather the boys for discussions about self-control, machismo, manners, and any other subject that came up during the week. In those discussion groups, as well as in the privacy of their early mornings together, J.R. found Johnnie asking him a lot about anger.

One morning, after an episode with another boy which left J.R. tense with anger, Johnnie asked: "How you deal with that? I know you get real mad."

"Sure," J.R. remembers telling him. "And I've got mad at you. But I won't hurt you, because I care about you and I respect you as a human being."

"Well, how do you do that if you're angry?" Johnnie persisted.

J.R. had no easy answer. He had come to believe that Johnnie lacked a fundamental understanding of emotions. Johnnie could not separate his feelings from his actions. To Johnnie, the only expression of anger was violence.

Johnnie understood he had a problem. But he thought his problem was that he could not stop his violent behavior once started, that he could not throw just one punch. As he grew older, he found that he would "go off," not recognizing how hurt his adversary was. Neither blood nor cries from his victim would stop Johnnie from hitting or kicking.

J.R. saw that vicious tendency evolve in Johnnie over the years. After he was moved from River Road, Johnnie rarely vocalized his anger. But when he acted it out, his violent eruptions came more quickly, were meaner and less rational.

In his own way, J.R. says quietly now, he understood the rage in Johnnie.

"I've been working on my temper for forty-eight years," he admits, almost ashamed. "Johnnie has the kind of temper that goes to a red spot. It goes to a point of no return with him. So much pain and anger there.

There's a lot of pain and anger in my life—that's how I relate to him, that's how I know. I have a real bad temper. I know how all-consuming anger can control you."

Before J.R. was ten years old, he had lost both of his parents in an accident. He and his three siblings were raised by his maternal grand-mother, his extended family, and the neighborhood. For blocks around his home, he says, men took it upon themselves to help father him.

When Johnnie asked why he works as a counselor, J.R. replied that people looked out for him when he needed it, and now he's giving back. "Whatever you do with your life, Johnnie, when you get old enough, I want you to help one person," Johnnie remembers J.R. telling him. "You don't have to save the world, just save one person, and then we'll give back what we owe and come out ahead."

J.R. lost not only his parents, but also his closest sibling, his older brother, who had served in the Vietnam War, earning a Purple Heart. "He went to put me in college," he says.

After the war, a drunk driver killed him.

"I literally wanted to kill the guy who did this," J.R. says of the driv-er, who had a wife and four children but at the time of the accident was with his seventeen-year-old mistress. "Nobody was going to talk me out of it. My uncle was the only one that really made sense. He said, 'You know, you can do this if you like. It's going to destroy your life. It's going to destroy your kid's life. You need to understand that God always has a plan, and because you don't always understand what His plan is, that's okay. There are going to be some stumbling blocks in your life, and you're going to have to deal with them.' That's the same thing I used to try to tell Johnnie."

J.R.'s words never made sense to Johnnie. Though he had come from the same neighborhood, he hadn't come from J.R.'s world. Johnnie could understand J.R.'s pain, his love for his family, but not the concept of reason or of God. Johnnie did not always want a reason or even fair-ness.

J.R. remembers walking Johnnie home from school just after Chil-dren Services decided to split up the Jordan children and keep them from their parents permanently. J.R. explained the agency's decision to take permanent custody of him. He would never go back to his parents.

"J.R., what do they think they can do?" Johnnie asked plaintively.

"They can never make me stop loving my family. I know what they think. They think they can stop making me love my family? They can *never* do that!"

All J.R. could do was wrap Johnnie in a hug and reassure him that no one would stop him from loving his family. "When you get to be eighteen, you can be with your family as much as you want," J.R. told him. Then he would graduate out of the system. As an adult, he would be free of Children Services. Only he had to grow up without his family.

From then on, Johnnie couldn't wait until he was eighteen. Even when he forgot why he wanted to be eighteen, the number stood out as magical for him. For weeks before his eighteenth birthday, he phoned telling me how he looked forward to that day. When I asked why, he became confused. He didn't know why. He didn't want to get old, he said. He wanted to stay young.

In fact, he had very good reason for his Peter Pan thoughts. At eighteen, Johnnie would be transferred from his juvenile block in prison to the harsher world of older, bigger, more predatory inmates. He knew enough of what went on in adult prisons to be frightened. But still, he could not wait for his eighteenth birthday. It was as if he believed that day would bring a miracle.

On his eighteenth birthday, he called, disappointed.

"I'm eighteen and I don't feel no different."

"Did you think you would?"

"I don't know, man," he said, annoyed at me for not understanding. "I just thought eighteen was something special."

And then it came back to him.

"I remember now," he said. "I thought I would be free [of CS]. Now I'm just locked up and won't get out until I'm fifty!"

Johnnie randomly chose fifty as a number representing fathomless old age. I couldn't tell him he was in for a lot longer than that. Three years after the crime, Johnnie might have been able to comprehend his punishment. But at that moment of his eighteenth birthday, I could not bring myself to explain it to him.

III

J.R. had a nickname for all the kids at River Road. Johnnie's was Melon because in cutting his hair, J.R. found that Johnnie's head was round like a melon. Johnnie enjoyed J.R.'s gentle teasing. From anyone else, Johnnie might erupt, but from J.R., he glowed.

Johnnie thirsted for positive attention from anyone, but especially from J.R. He worked hard for it. Aside from hearing news of his parents or siblings, nothing upset him more than disappointing J.R. On his first report card day at River Road, Johnnie was angry at the F's staring out from most of the boxes.

"I can't believe they gave me F's, man," Johnnie said, kicking his sneakered feet under the kitchen table where he sat with J.R. "I show up to school every day on time, I can't believe they be giving me F's," he said, crossing his arms over his chest.

"What's wrong with you?" J.R. shot back. "You *earned* all F's! You got to *achieve* to get higher grades. You got to work to learn." Johnnie was stunned. He had thought school grades were based on attendance and behavior.

Johnnie's behavior in school had improved dramatically. He rarely fought, and avoided suspensions. In the previous year at Nathan Hale Elementary, he had been suspended 120 times. While living at River Road, he was suspended only once, when he found out that his favorite teacher was leaving the school because she was getting married. His jealousy came rushing back to his fists.

Recognizing that Johnnie may have been ready to invest in school, J.R. met with Johnnie's teachers. After some testing, they found that Johnnie's mental ability lay somewhere between "learning disabled" and "developmentally handicapped." J.R. insisted that the school place Johnnie in classes for the developmentally handicapped, and there he flourished. He was eager to learn, particularly because it pleased J.R. Each weekday morning, Johnnie would listen for J.R.'s footsteps, sometimes before 5 A.M., when he rose to prepare River Road for the day. Johnnie would rush downstairs to have J.R. quiz him on his multiplication tables. When Johnnie got all A's except one B on his report card, he came running home to J.R. with the broadest grin J.R. would ever see on him.

"You didn't think I could do it, did you, J.R.?" Johnnie teased in the midst of his gasping breaths. "You thought I was dumb."

"Yeah, I thought you were a dumb ass," J.R. played along. "No, son," he told Johnnie more seriously. "You wouldn't be my son if you were dumb. No son of mine is dumb."

Later, J.R. would say that Johnnie is "not smart in the traditional sense, academically. But when it comes to reading people, he's extremely bright, gifted. He's had to be all his life, not just for himself, but for his sibs too."

He was smart enough not to confess to the cops, J.R. adds. But he did.

"I taught him and all the kids at River Road, you don't say nothing to the cops till I get there. Ohio law states that a juvenile doesn't have to say anything unless his lawyer or his parents are there. Johnnie and kids like him don't have parents, so they just go ahead and spill the beans, and they're the ones who get in trouble. The kids with parents and lawyers, they go free. Johnnie knew not to talk, but he did anyway, I still don't know why."

In part, Johnnie confessed because he is honest. While he might fib, on the basic truths, he is generally honest, J.R. contends. His memory is splotchy and sometimes confused by fantasy, but he does not lie on big matters. J.R. was certain of this.

Once, when J.R. went out of town, his sixteen-year-old son took his car and went joyriding with some friends, then lied about it to his father. "He stole my car," J.R. says, still incredulous about his son, who was president of the student government, starred on the school basketball and football teams, sang in the choir, and earned very good grades. When J.R. told Johnnie the story, he got the response J.R. expected.

"He didn't trust you?" Johnnie asked. "Oooh, man, we need to sit him down."

J.R. brought his son to Johnnie, who was five years younger and a good deal smaller.

"How come you didn't tell your dad the truth?" he lectured, standing with hands on hips before the boy who was almost twice his size.

"Well, I guess because I knew he was mad at me."

"*Pshhh*," Johnnie expelled his disbelief. "Sooo? He's always mad at me, but I still got to tell him the truth."

At River Road, Johnnie began to get a rein on his anger, sometimes by walking around the block. Rather than staying aloof, he seemed genuinely interested in discussions about behavior, sitting forward during group meetings on subjects like respect, anger management, community, manners, violence, conflict resolution, and abuse. Johnnie was eager to understand. Sometimes he caught on quickly. Other times, it was difficult. In one discussion, the subject was conscience.

"Is it like a little voice?" Johnnie asked.

"Yeah, I guess it could be like a voice," one of the staff answered.

"Like 'That's right,' and 'No, that's wrong'?"

"Maybe."

Conscience is a learned behavior, J.R. thought. How do you explain it as experience? Johnnie and the boys around him were raised with none of the moral framework most children are given from birth. Suddenly, at age twelve verging on thirteen, Johnnie was trying to understand values already ingrained in other children. Conscience was a strange concept for him.

"Like a little cartoon? An angel and a devil?" Johnnie asked. "The angel pop up on one side and the devil on the other side?"

To Johnnie, these voices, these cartoons, this conscience, were not internal. They came from outside, not from his mind or heart. The devil, dressed in a red cape with a pitchfork, was always trying to get him in trouble. The blond angel in a white flowing gown tried only to stop him from acting on the devil's whispered suggestions.

But before they could address conscience and morals, J.R. and the River Road staff recognized that their first task should be to help Johnnie cope with his anger. In conflicts, Johnnie would often say he wanted to kill somebody.

"You don't want to *kill* them," J.R. would say, trying to get Johnnie to understand his feelings and better control them. "You want to hurt them."

"No, I don't want to hurt him," Johnnie would insist. "I want to *kill them*!"

"No," J.R. would try to reason. And finally, Johnnie would agree and even back off. "No," he said quietly, "I don't even want to hurt them."

Johnnie was handicapped emotionally and academically, J.R. says, because his mind was never free enough of his past to concentrate on learning and understanding feelings. Johnnie had never experienced a nurturing environment.

"He's a system's kid," J.R. says simply. "The reality is that he was thrown into a system which has a bureaucracy. Whenever there's a bureaucracy, everything is conditional on things like how you perform, how you behave, what you do. There has to be accountability. But with a family, it's not that way. When you screw up, they might punish you, but they still love you. The system doesn't; it's harsh. It doesn't know how to nurture. It doesn't love or support in general. It doesn't know unconditional anything."

Johnnie flourished in the structured environment of River Road and J.R.'s love and patience. He began calling J.R. "Dad," and J.R. often called him "son." Johnnie not only liked going to school; he liked working hard. He was usually first to finish his chores around the house, and often he would ask the staff for more. He glowed in the affirmation and positive attention he received in their smiles and praise. Though he received an allowance from River Road, he volunteered for some of the most menial, low paying jobs at the group home. He saved enough money to buy a blue bicycle with a banana seat.

"Of all the kids that I had, he was the one that I thought would be the greatest success story, because he had the heart and he tried so hard," J.R. says. "Johnnie was the flower with thorns. I believed that sooner or later he would bloom. He was just beginning to at River Road."

III

Johnnie thought he would never move from River Road, and he was almost happy in his belief. He thought he had finally found a home. But one night after dinner, the staff announced that River Road would be closing.[8] Johnnie was scared. Where would he go? Who would take care of him? He asked J.R. to adopt him, but J.R. explained that it would not be fair for him to adopt one boy over the rest. Johnnie said he understood. To this day, J.R. regrets his decision.

That night, a few days before the group home finally closed by financial stress and the boys were dispersed into foster homes, Johnnie ran away with a housemate. Together, he thought, they would stick together like a real family. Taking charge of a future on the streets was better than being shuffled among people who did not care about him. It was his first truancy in a long time.

---

8. Financial pressures were forcing River Road's closure. Private group homes such as River Road allow staff greater freedom from CSB to handle children. They are not, for example, forced to house more children than they can care for. But too many, like River Road, eventually succumb to the whimsical backing of sponsors, many of whom do not or cannot follow through with the money they have pledged. The house had been donated by a family. But River Road was unable to keep up with the costs of raising the boys.

The boys were caught the next day. Johnnie was placed in a foster home where he knew no one. At first, though he tried to fit into the home, he felt cut off and alone. His new bike, which he had bought with money he earned from extra chores at River Road, was stolen. He phoned and paged J.R. frequently. J.R. hesitated to return Johnnie's calls. He wanted Johnnie to bond with his new household rather than continue to rely on him for support. But as Johnnie saw it, the system had taken away J.R., as they had his parents and family.

One night, Johnnie ran away to find J.R. In the dark, he crossed fifteen miles of town to reach J.R.'s home. Not wanting to wake the family, Johnnie crawled into the back seat of one of the Robinsons' cars and fell asleep. The next morning, Gayle, J.R.'s wife, was leaving for her job as a social worker when she noticed a fluffy blue nylon lump. At first, she thought it was her stepson's sleeping bag. As she reached out to touch it, she noticed two small feet sticking out of the lump. Awakened suddenly, Johnnie jumped up. Gayle screamed. When she collected her wits, she ordered Johnnie out of the car, marched him inside, and called J.R., who was already at work.

"You need to come home," Gayle told her husband. "You've got an emergency."

In retrospect, Gayle finds the same humor in this story that J.R. does. But at the time, she did not see anything funny. Johnnie had crossed the Robinsons' front yard, in the process making friends with their overly protective dog. His small footprints in the snow marked his path from the fence to the garage and the car, with the dog's footprints right alongside.

J.R. spent the day with Johnnie. He explained that Johnnie needed to form friendships and bonds with other people now. Johnnie tried to understand, even as he returned to his latest foster home. But he did not. Instead, he ran again.

After that escape, Johnnie was placed in St. Anthony's Villa, a stricter foster care institution. There he was restrained twelve times for assaulting other children, assaulting staff members, threatening staff and children, attempting to cut himself with a knife, cutting himself with a spoon, biting staff as well as himself, and choking himself. He was judged to be depressed, suicidal, and violent. He was also placed in a sex offender treatment program, where he made only "poor" progress. He ran away yet again. This time he got into big trouble.

III

Johnnie stood at a city bus stop with a group he called "his boys" from the neighborhood. That morning, he had received upsetting news.

An aunt had phoned his foster home to tell him that his father was probably going to jail. "If he goes to prison," she said, "they'll kill him. The other inmates will kill him because of him abusing children with the sex and all."

The bus glided past the group, though the boys tried to wave it down. They chased after it, and when it stopped several feet beyond, all were angry at the bus driver for making them run. None was more furious than Johnnie. To him, it appeared that the driver was even laughing at him. For the next thirty-five minutes of the ride, he seethed quietly while the other boys complained loudly to one another in threatening tones heavy with bravado. At their stop, Johnnie waited patiently for those ahead to disembark. When it came his turn, he moved sharply without warning and smashed his fist into the driver's face, then walked slowly off. His friends scattered. Johnnie turned back to see blood running from the driver's face. After a few minutes, he ran too.

The police soon caught him. One of his friends identified Johnnie as the assailant and gave them his address. He was arrested and charged with felonious assault, specifically, assault with a deadly weapon. The bus driver's eyeglasses, which tore a long and deep gash in his face that required nine stitches, were considered the weapon.

J.R. was in juvenile court with another boy when a caseworker mentioned that Johnnie was next door at the juvenile jail. He rushed over. The Johnnie who sat before him threw J.R. off balance. He seemed to have grown several mean years older in the months since J.R. had last seen him. Johnnie was angry and lost, cold even.

III

"I ain't talking to you," he blurted out at J.R. "I quit."

"What?" J.R. asked. He had never before heard Johnnie use the word.

"I ain't talking to you, I quit," Johnnie repeated, turning away with folded arms.

"Look, Melon," J.R. said, trying to placate the boy with his nickname.

"Naw, naw, you can't talk me into doing anything like you used to do. Naw, uh-uh," he told J.R. "I quit."

"What do you mean, you quit?"

"I quit on life."

"No," J.R. said firmly. "No, son, no. You're just fourteen, you're not quitting on life. I'm not going to let you. You got your whole life ahead of you. You're smart. You're a hard worker. You're not quitting on life.

"But if I'm gonna stay in contact with you," J.R. added, "you're gonna make some changes. You're going back to the Johnnie I know. You hear me, son? You're going back to the Johnnie I know."

Johnnie melted when J.R. called him "son." He turned to J.R. afresh, softness returning to his face, which moments before had looked numb.

Johnnie was charged, found guilty, and sentenced to a year in Cuyahoga Hills Boys School, a detention center. Under stricter observation, his self-destructive behavior again became obvious. During that time, the foster care system had Johnnie psychiatrically evaluated because of his self-mutilation, his suicide attempts, and depression. Somehow that evaluation did not qualify him for special treatment or therapy. In jail, his record shows that he was supposed to receive "victim awareness/empathy counseling," but there is no record that he ever did.

Neither the staff at Cuyahoga Hills nor his parole officer recommended early release. "He expressed no remorse for his assault and injury to the bus driver," his parole officer explained in a report. But mysteriously, Johnnie was released a month early, his records indicate, "for good behavior."

To this day, Johnnie is not sorry he attacked the bus driver. His paranoid thoughts of the bus driver laughing gave him reason, he believes, to strike.

III

Despite his sexual offenses, and the recommendation of several psychologists that he not live with other children except under the strictest supervision, upon Johnnie's release from juvenile detention he was placed in a loosely structured foster home with three children, ages three, nine, and sixteen. Johnnie tried to make this foster home work. He did not want to disappoint J.R., who had visited him at Cuyahoga. Nor did he want to return to juvenile detention. But life in his new foster home gave him too much freedom. Children Services failed to register him in school for almost three months. The excuse was that they did not know how long Johnnie would stay in this foster home. Eventually, Johnnie's caseworker enrolled him in a day program with Vinnie Riccardi.

Riccardi ran a residential program in Toledo for kids who had been suspended or expelled from school or, as in Johnnie's case, had not been registered at all. He is a certified criminal justice specialist as well as a licensed schoolteacher with a master's degree in education. He taught Johnnie and one younger boy using books checked out of a neighborhood library. He was impressed that Johnnie tried to help his only classmate and completed his assignments on time, if not early. Johnnie liked reading books on spiders and birds to prepare his required oral and written reports. He seemed even eager.

It wasn't school or learning that interested him, it was having somewhere to go and something to keep his mind occupied. Johnnie's thoughts troubled him. He often lay awake in his foster care bed most of the night. At eight-thirty every morning, a half hour before the program started, Johnnie would knock on Riccardi's door. Exhausted by worry, and usually virtually sleepless, he rushed Riccardi into the day. After three o'clock, class work ended and the recreational part of the program began. Johnnie stayed on, often until eight in the evening. He would go with Riccardi to the YMCA to swim, lift weights, or box. Sometimes he would go to Riccardi's home to play basketball because Riccardi had a full court in his back yard.

Only once did Riccardi see Johnnie's anger flare beyond control. Another youth made a joke about Johnnie's dad or mom, and Johnnie jumped him.

"You know I'm going to whup you," he told the larger boy.

Riccardi intervened, telling Johnnie in an even voice that he was out of line.

"Well, out of respect, I will just drop the issue," Johnnie said, releasing the boy. To Riccardi, whom Johnnie both liked and respected, Johnnie appeared to be controlling his anger.

But his behavior in the foster home continued to deteriorate. He talked back to his foster mother. He picked fights with other kids. He was the star of a church basketball team, but attacked his own teammates when they missed shots. Still, they had a winning team, until the final game, when Johnnie did not play. He had run away again.

Dazed by concern and anger about his family, Johnnie had forgotten the championship game. If he had remembered, he would have run away after the game, he says. He's still mad he missed it. He returned to his foster home three days later.

III

Johnnie found an acceptable outlet for the emotions building inside him by boxing in Riccardi's after-school program. It was an activity he liked, and one in which he was thought to have a raw, vague talent.

Johnnie was not big, and he was not particularly fast. In the ring, he often took a pummeling. But just as the coach appeared ready to step forward to stop the bout, Johnnie would explode. It wasn't only fury that drove Johnnie's fists. He was tenacious. He would take a beating until his opponent became tired or vulnerable. Then, in a flash, Johnnie would attack. No matter how he hurt, he would not admit defeat. If his eyes were bloody, he'd fight through the veil of red. He says he felt no pain, only fury and rage when he boxed. Nothing was clear in Johnnie's mind when he caught the fury. His mind flew to a place he felt free, too free.

The coach saw talent in Johnnie, not danger. He told Johnnie he had the tenacity, strength, and patience to be a winner, that he could be a Mike Tyson, Johnnie recalls. Johnnie heard him. But he wasn't sure. He never admitted to the coach that he did not like becoming so enraged in the ring, because he felt it meant there was something wrong inside of him. He knew his anger was different. Beyond a certain point of red, it was black. Sometimes they had to drag him off opponents. He realized he didn't know how to stop. Sometimes he could not even remember the winning blow. At those times, he felt no pain either. He didn't hear or see or know. It felt good, especially at the end.

But Johnnie quit boxing, not because of any qualms or fears, but because of the workouts. He had been smoking weed several times a day since he was released from Cuyahoga. He liked the way it exhausted him and shut him down. Anger melted away and left him in peace. He felt like he could fit in better then, without all the thoughts that churned his stomach and drove him mad all the time.

He wouldn't have minded making it big as a boxer. It would be alright, all that money. First thing he'd do is hire some big lawyers to get his father and mother out of jail. He'd buy them a house and put them in it. He wouldn't live there with them though. At fourteen, he was too old for that. He'd buy lots of street shoes. Nikes. The fashions changed every week, it seemed, and even when his business selling weed and rock was brisk, he couldn't keep up. Maybe he'd buy some cars. It didn't matter that he wasn't old enough to drive. The cops don't bother people with money, and if they do, the lawyers would get him off. Girlfriends come with money. But he didn't care about that. He already had lots of girlfriends, any girl he wanted, he bragged, and it wasn't far from the truth. Girls seemed attracted to his tough, remote ways, and the touch of kindness in him. They'd come up to him and give him their numbers. He didn't respect them for doing that. But he did them anyway, when he felt like it, and sometimes even when he didn't. Once his family was set up, maybe he'd get out of town, to New York or Detroit, where the gangs and rap artists were. Money can't buy love, he'd heard people say. But what was the difference? If people hung around you because you had money, so what? At least they'd hang around.

But none of these vague dreams encouraged him to put up with the workouts, especially the running. He didn't see what running had to do with fighting anyway. He'd start running and the weed would kick in. He had to make a choice. He chose the weed.

Only the weed left him with the same problem he always had when he wasn't angry. Boredom. Johnnie needed thoughts to fill his mind and activities to fill his days. Otherwise, when he got angry, when he didn't have weed, he couldn't think of anything to divert himself. He'd get so mad he couldn't reason and he just felt like hitting something—a chair, a car, a person. In Cuyahoga Hills, he hit the cinder-block walls with his fists until the guards stopped him. So he started cutting himself in hidden places with a razor or a knife, a piece of glass or plastic he busted from a ceiling light fixture. It released some poison inside of him when he bled. He didn't feel pain, really. All he could say about it was that it helped.

Now, outside Cuyahoga Hills, Johnnie found nothing worked as well as weed. Weed stopped the voices. It emptied his head. Johnnie didn't use other drugs he sold. Never crack or ecstasy or heroin. He saw what they did to his parents and other people's older sisters, uncles, brothers, and parents. It tore them into pitiful creatures, fragments of themselves, made them weak and stupid. He tried methamphetamine once, but he didn't like the drug. It gave him more fire, more energy, but that is what he wanted to get away from. He just wanted to empty his head, and if that meant he was tired all the time, that was okay.

Often there was no immediate trigger to his anger. It wasn't always what someone said or did that made him mad. He might just wake up with a churning stomach and a feeling that he had to do something. He'd pace. His hands would close into fists. He couldn't think or read, not even comic books. The frames jumped around. TV sometimes calmed him, but more often he couldn't focus on it long enough to figure out what was going on. Quickly he'd become bored and then furious.

That's when the voices came, telling him to hit something, or some-one, good and hard. It was a man's voice that spoke to him. Sometimes he'd pause before hitting anyone. What would J.R. think? He'd be disap-pointed. And Johnnie would stop himself, and maybe cut himself instead, and watch his blood run hard and free. But now that he was mad at J.R. for not visiting and calling more, he told himself he didn't care about anything. He didn't care about obeying or not obeying, about getting in trouble, about punishment, about the juvenile jails that threatened to claim him again. He didn't care what anyone thought. He persuaded himself that he didn't care about anything.

Johnnie does not get angry about things. He gets angry at them. He wasn't crazy enough to tell anyone that sometimes voices told him to kill. Sometimes he wasn't even angry when he got these voices in his head. He didn't want anyone to think he was crazy. Whatever happened, no one should think he was crazy.

III

In October, social workers applied for a placement for Johnnie at a stricter foster group home called Parmadale, where his anger could be monitored and he would be supervised constantly. When Donna Lewis, the Jordan family caseworker, arrived to take Johnnie for his interview at the institution, he shrugged. He was used to these kinds of surprises. His personal caseworker, Tamara Cusack, had not told him that he would be going for an intake interview at Parmadale. She had not even alerted his current foster mother. Children Services had decided that he needed to leave his new placement, and that the next one should be out of town, away from his family and their troubles that were so upsetting to him. Because Cusack was out that day, Lewis was called to fill in for her.

It did not occur to Johnnie that he could refuse to go to the interview. He was accustomed to having little say in these matters. Besides, he liked Donna Lewis. On his eleventh birthday, she had gathered his brothers and sisters and taken them all out for pizza to celebrate. She even brought a cake with candles. It was the only birthday party Johnnie remembers, and the only cake especially for him.

On the long ride to Parmadale, Johnnie asked questions about the institution. Lewis, because she was not his primary caseworker and had not set up the meeting, could not answer them. She suggested he ask the interviewer. Johnnie was quiet for some time after that, and fell into a light sleep for the rest of the trip.

On the Parmadale campus, it took Lewis some time to find the person Johnnie was to meet. He became nervous as they walked around. The campus looked alright to him, but he was confused and anxious. Finally they found the interviewer. As Johnnie waited, staff members asked Lewis some basic questions, including Johnnie's IQ. She did not know the answers. She was also asked about Johnnie's past sexual-offending behavior.

Moments after a Parmadale staff member led Johnnie to the interview room, Lewis was invited to observe from behind a double mirror. She had not yet sat down when Johnnie began yelling in a crazed and frantic fury.

"Motherfucker!" he shouted and jumped to his feet. "Just watch me, m-fuckers!" He stormed out of the room. Lewis's jaw dropped.

"Johnnie verbally went off," she later reported, still incredulous. He had been in the room no more than a few minutes.

She found Johnnie in the waiting area, his arms crossed, his body rigid. "What happened?" she asked.

"Those m-fers said I was in DYS [Department of Youth Services] for raping one of my sisters!" he fumed.

Before she could answer, another Parmadale staff member walked

over and asked Lewis if Johnnie would be returning to the interview
room.

"*No!*" Johnnie answered for himself.

Lewis tried to calm him. She suggested that he explain why he had
been placed in juvenile detention, for assaulting the bus driver. But he
refused.

On the car ride back to Toledo, Johnnie considered the life to which
he was returning. He admitted that Parmadale was not that bad after all.
Maybe he would give it a chance, he told Lewis. He did not recognize
that he had blown it.

Years later, he thinks the Parmadale interviewer was testing him.
She knew that he had never been arrested for raping anyone, let alone
one of his sisters. She was just looking to see how deep the darkness was
inside him. It was very deep, and getting deeper. He could have told her
that, he says. "She didn't have to play no games."

III

Johnnie began to "flip out," J.R. says, the day the *Toledo Blade* carried a
front-page article on his father's child abuse trial. Frankie Cooper, Johnnie's foster mother, phoned J.R. immediately. "Don't worry about it,"
J.R. told Ms. Cooper. "Johnnie doesn't read the newspaper."

But one of Johnnie's paternal aunts, whom he knew as Aunt Gail,
read the article, and immediately called him. He did not know what to
think, or what to do. Halfway through the morning, he found himself
walking out of school. As far as he remembers, his feet just carried him
to the downtown jail where his father was being held.

Johnnie had been asking J.R. to take him to the courthouse for his
father's trial.

"It's police court," J.R. made up a quick excuse. "You can't go there."
He wanted to keep Johnnie away from his father. He also lied about the
possibility of visiting Johnnie Sr. in jail.

"Besides," he told Johnnie, "I don't want you down there, son."

When Johnnie reached the courthouse, he walked around the great
structure the entire day, trying to figure a way to get in. He could have
simply walked through the front door, but that did not occur to him.
Some police officers, recognizing Johnnie, called J.R. When he arrived,
Johnnie appeared dazed and agitated. J.R. explained to Johnnie that if his

father was not guilty, a jury would set him free. Johnnie said he knew his father would end up going to jail for a long time.

As J.R. drove Johnnie back to his foster home, he felt that something in Johnnie had changed. Over the next weeks, Johnnie began drinking and using more marijuana. He also started hanging out again on a rough street corner he had avoided since River Road. Johnnie felt off balance. He had a vague sense that things were not going right inside of him. But that was all. He did not notice his behavior change, or his thoughts. He thought he was himself.

In school again, without Vinnie Riccardi's more familiar oversight, Johnnie's behavior grew more erratic and difficult. After breaking parole by running away again, Ed Pendleton, his probation officer, recommended that Johnnie be returned to a detention center overseen by the Department of Youth Services. Pendleton explained his decision to J.R.

"You're too close to talk sense to him, J.R.," Pendleton said. "We have to incarcerate him now before he loses control and does something bad."

To Pendleton's surprise, J.R. agreed that it would be best to lock Johnnie up for a spell, until he regained control. Johnnie had been calling J.R. every day. He would talk rationally, but J.R. sensed he was edging toward disaster.

"He was to the point of being mean with other people," J.R. recalls. "Johnnie wasn't like that. Not the real Johnnie. He was very, very, very upset. He couldn't get his father out of his mind. He blocked out everything else. He was being disrespectful, doing little things, not major things. He was basically losing control."

Johnnie even began hassling J.R. He'd look threatening until J.R. invited him to fight.

"Look, you want some of this? Come on," J.R. teased, affecting a boxer's stance, throwing Johnnie off balance. "You want a piece of this meat?"

Johnnie stepped back, looked at J.R.'s greying temples, and the small smile spreading across J.R.'s lips, revealing the slight gap between his front teeth. Together they laughed.

"No, you won't try to hurt me," J.R. said. "No, son, we love each other. You don't hurt people you love."

"But someday I probably might," Johnnie told him, a reply that stuck in J.R.'s mind. He believed Johnnie would never hurt him. But he also heard that Johnnie didn't know or trust himself.

To put Johnnie in the juvenile detention center again, Pendleton and Johnnie's caseworker were required to appear before a juvenile court judge. Children Services had agreed with Pendleton that Johnnie should be detained until his behavior improved. But on the appointed court date, Johnnie's primary caseworker, Tamara Cusack, failed to show up. By law, the motion to put Johnnie in juvenile jail was dismissed. Johnnie was dangerous, and free.

III

Supported by state funds, Pendleton asked J.R. to keep in close touch with Johnnie. In the weeks following, Johnnie began to talk more honestly with J.R. about abuse. Pendleton tried to persuade himself that Johnnie might get better. It was a slim hope. His instincts, well seasoned with experience, told him Johnnie was dangerous and should be locked up. But there was nothing he could do until Johnnie broke his probation again, or committed a crime.

III

Frankie Cooper, Johnnie's eighteenth foster mother, had not been told of Pendleton's anxiety nor of Children Services' difficulties with Johnnie, but she too became increasingly concerned about his behavior over the few weeks he stayed with her. She did not usually notice those things. She is somewhat hardened and cold about foster children. She has had some of the worst of kids, she says, but if she saw the worst *in* them, she could not continue foster-parenting. The boys she gets—and she prefers boys because she worries less about them when they stay out late or are promiscuous—are almost always troubled. Generally she thinks she can handle them. She inherited a philosophy from her father: "Everybody has some goodness in them. Even the biggest liar tells the truth sometimes."

To that she adds her own truism: "The worst child can be loved."

Ms. Cooper is hard on outsiders. But to her boys, as she calls her foster children, she is often a compassionate and caring woman. Because she is a grandmother, most of her boys call her Nana. Some of them she likes better than others. She liked Johnnie. He had charm. He had a smile. He was respectful. Even his toughness she liked. The two of them knew their way around the world they lived in better than others did, she says.

She does not go for all the psychobabble CSB caseworkers throw at her, she says, or even for all their rules. When Johnnie was placed in her home as a way of providing him short-term emergency shelter—which by negligence and default turned into a stay that lasted more than three months—Johnnie's caseworker reported that Ms. Cooper "doesn't fully understand the complexity of Johnnie or other children in her care. [She] understands only the surface personality and deals with that."

It seems clear from other reports that if Children Services could have placed Johnnie with some other foster parent, they would have done so. But no one else would take Johnnie. He was already into the lowest rung of foster parents, the foster parents least inquisitive about the children who were entrusted to them. Sometimes these foster parents were the most giving of people. But usually they were just eager for the money. Ms. Cooper claims she takes foster children in not for the money, but because no one else will. She kept Johnnie for longer than the ninety-day limit she is licensed for. She accepted Johnnie because she made it a point to ignore the talk circulating among other foster parents and social workers.

Ms. Cooper also ignored the warning of fourteen-year-old Anthony Thomas, who, together with Johnnie and one other boy, Marcus Watson, made up her foster family at the time. Anthony came from the same mean world as Johnnie. He grew up like Johnnie, in the same housing project, then shuttled from home to foster care placements and back and forth again. He did not scare easily. But he became scared when he heard Johnnie talking to Marcus about a plot to kill Frankie Cooper.

According to the plan, Johnnie would hit her over the head. That was the point of the crime, the part that excited Johnnie most, hitting her over the head. He figured that might make her dead, he didn't know or really seem to care. Then they would take her car and run away. They would need money, so they would take what they could from her purse.

If she recovered from the blows, they would get arrested. So they would then kill Cooper and dump her body in the country. They would use knives, if necessary. Johnnie said he had already taken a knife from the kitchen and hidden it between his mattress and bed frame.[9] He told Marcus to steal a knife too. The talk got bigger and bigger.

Perhaps hitting Ms. Cooper over the head was simply the physical

---

9. Ms. Cooper later found the knife, which had been missing since the summer.

manifestation of his rage that excited him most, a psychologist later suggested. But no one knows, not even Johnnie, who had not recognized the similarities between the crime he planned to commit and his actual murder of Mrs. Johnson. "I never really thought about that," he said later in prison when I asked Johnnie why he chose that method of violence. "Hitting her over the head is just what I thought about doing. Maybe from cartoons or something."

Thomas had heard talk before, and this wasn't just talk. He was so sure that the plan would be followed through that he broke all the foster care rules of survival and told Ms. Cooper of the plan.

"They're going to kill you," he whispered at breakfast while the two other boys were still upstairs. She laughed and shook her head.

Ms. Cooper still does not believe Johnnie intended to kill her, despite the murder of Mrs. Johnson. Boys like to talk, she says. Rather, she says she was annoyed at Anthony's tattling.

"Johnnie was *my* boy," she says now, fiercely. "Some boys you don't get attached to. But some boys, you feel the frustration and hurt inside of them. Those are my boys. Johnnie was *my* boy and I never give up on *my* kids."

Frankie Cooper refused to speak with me about Johnnie for a year. Children Services had ordered all their foster care parents not to discuss Johnnie's case. But always independent, Cooper had her own reasons for speaking and, after many false starts, finally agreed to talk. She believed Johnnie should be paid for this book. When I told her that I would not pay Johnnie or her, she told me to ask Johnnie to phone her. After several calls and a letter from Johnnie specifically giving her permission to talk to me, she did so reluctantly. She began by telling me that if I were African-American, I would understand her better. She would trust me more too.

"I don't believe Johnnie would ever hurt me," she says. "Maybe I don't want to face it. You have to distinguish between truth and lie. I don't believe in my heart that he would ever hurt me. I heard about it afterwards from the police too. Maybe I don't want to believe it, but that's the way I feel."

Johnnie and Marcus, in any case, never made an attempt on her life. Anthony says Marcus backed out, but he also claims credit for talking Johnnie out of the murder plan. Although Johnnie agreed not to kill Ms. Cooper, Anthony says, Johnnie made another threat: he swore he would kill his next foster mother if she did not treat him right. That was four months before Johnnie bludgeoned Mrs. Johnson with the hatchet.

Johnnie acknowledges plotting to kill Frankie Cooper, but brushes it off as bluster.

"That was different," he says. "That was just talk. I wasn't really going to do it. I never thought I had the guts to do nothing like that. I was all talk."

Yet the plan was eerily similar to the murder he later committed.

Johnnie pauses when reminded about this. "It would have happened someday, to tell you the truth," he says finally. "I still feel that anger. It's getting worser by the minute."

III

Despite her affection for him, Ms. Cooper eventually kicked Johnnie out of her home because she thought Johnnie might be harboring a gun. Another foster mother in the neighborhood told Ms. Cooper that Johnnie had shown her foster child a gun he owned. Without hesitation, Ms. Cooper called the police. Guns are one thing that Ms. Cooper does not tolerate. She is not afraid for her own safety, it's the children she worries about. Too many boys in the neighborhood have been killed by guns.

The police searched Johnnie, his locker at school, and his foster home. They found no gun, but Johnnie's parole officer, Ed Pendleton, filed a warrant for his arrest. He would not serve it now, but he held it so he could arrest and hold Johnnie whenever he was suspected of a crime. Pendleton thought the time was coming. This was the most he could do.

Johnnie in fact had two guns. The day the police searched, he had "rented" his revolver to a friend, and his semiautomatic was buried near a fence outside Ms. Cooper's house.

III

Johnnie understood why Frankie Cooper kicked him out. He was not angry or disappointed that she called the police about the guns; he understood her rules. If there was any foster parent he liked, it was Frankie Cooper.

But when Johnnie found that Children Services planned to move him outside of the city limits, he was upset. He was a city kid. He wanted to be in Toledo, near his sisters and brothers and "associates" on

the street. But the agency wanted to keep Johnnie far away from his
family and his street buddies. It was also desperate. Toledo foster families knew of Johnnie and would not take him. None of his former foster
parents would accept him back.

Only the Johnsons in Spencer Township agreed to take him into
their home, and only for a few nights. They knew nothing of Johnnie
but nonetheless were reluctant because social workers had been sending
increasingly troubled and difficult children. But because the caseworker
was desperate, and because of their sympathy for an unwanted child,
they decided to take Johnnie on the condition that he would stay for
only a brief spell. Children Services extended those few days to more
than five weeks.

Distance did not keep news of his father from reaching Johnnie in
Spencer Township, however, and with each bit of information he gathered, he grew more anxious about his family. He felt cut off, alone,
angry, and scared. Anxiety led to nightmares he carried through the
day. He broke curfew intentionally. Jeanette Johnson told Children Services caseworkers she was concerned about Johnnie, that he was restless
and agitated. Still, the agency never warned the Johnsons that Johnnie
could be dangerous, that he had been found guilty of felonious assault
and served time for attacking the bus driver. Nor did they reveal that
Johnnie, while he was living in their home, had been rejected by the
strict institutional boys' home of Parmadale for his profane outburst.
The Johnsons had no idea that Johnnie was prone to abuse and violence.
But they sensed that something was not right.

On December 12, 1995, a month before her murder, Mrs. Johnson
again complained to caseworkers about Johnnie's restlessness and his
temper. She thought Johnnie should be enrolled in school. Children
Services refused to respond. The foster care agency's file says only that
"Johnnie initially tried to sabotage the placement due to the rural
nature of the area," and that Tamara Cusack, Johnnie's caseworker, told
him to "chill out until we can get things set up."

Eight days later, Cusack dropped off two bags of his clothes. Though
the visit came well into the afternoon, Mrs. Johnson had to wake Johnnie. He asked if he could spend Christmas with his brothers and sisters at
his stepgrandmother's. Johnnie loved how his family came together on
Christmas Day. No matter what was happening in their lives, everyone

gathered for the Christmas dinner of sweet ham and juicy turkey his stepgrandmother spent weeks preparing. It was the one day he could eat as many yams and candied sweet potatoes and collards as he wanted. "My grandma cooks like thirty cakes and pies," he remembers with a young smile. "I never could eat none of them because I ate too much dinner." But the food is not the only thing that drew him to the table. It was his brothers and sisters. For that one day, they could be a happy family.

His chances of being at his grandmother's Christmas dinner did not look good this year. Cusack said his visitation probably would not be possible because the court had ordered that he be supervised when he was with his family, and that transportation all the way from the county outskirts into the heart of the city could also be difficult. But Johnnie was determined. He arranged for his grandmother to invite the Johnsons for Christmas. The Johnsons canceled their own plans, for Johnnie's sake. They spent their Christmas at Johnnie's grandmother's home, sitting quietly on the couch, sipping iced tea but declining to intrude at the family's dinner table.

Johnnie quietly appreciated the Johnsons' effort to accommodate him, though he never told them so. He began to like the Johnsons. He felt happy and warm playing checkers with Mr. Johnson and bantering with him about cheating. They laughed about Johnnie's attempt to catch a wild turkey. He liked Mrs. Johnson's cooking. They made a nice family, he thought.

Still, Johnnie could not relax. He paged and phoned J. R. Robinson almost daily, and J.R. responded, often driving out to Spencer to talk, or play basketball with Johnnie. He tried to get Johnnie to become friends with other children, even though he was not enrolled in school.

Johnnie was afraid. "I don't want anyone to hurt my feelings ever again," he told J.R. sullenly.

Johnnie had few people to hang with in Spencer Township. J.R. urged social workers to enroll him in a trade school, if not regular school, anything to give his days some structure and focus. Johnnie was at loose ends. Sometimes he would walk a mile from the Johnsons' home to Oak Terrace, the public housing development known in Spencer as "the projects." There he would find some boys his own age.

Johnnie's only real friend was the stray dog that followed him home one day. Johnnie's face still lights up when he remembers the dog, though he never gave it a name and always called it stupid. The dog dashed inside one day, and Mrs. Johnson and Johnnie gave chase until they fell to laughter. Mud was everywhere. At night, Johnnie would sneak food to the dog. Sometimes, he says, he struck the dog to keep it from jumping on him and following him. But the dog stuck close to Johnnie anyway, and Johnnie liked that. When his caseworker, Tamara Cusack, visited, she took the dog away, at Mrs. Johnson's request. Johnnie is angry at the Johnsons for this, but shrugs at the memory, saying he didn't really care, the dog was stupid anyway. Still, from prison, he asks if I can find the dog and make sure it's okay.

Though he liked the Johnsons, Johnnie still depended almost entirely on J. R. Robinson, whom Ed Pendleton, Johnnie's parole officer, paid with DYS funds to look in on Johnnie. But J.R. could not keep up with Johnnie's many and increasing demands. Even if he had been the only child in J.R.'s caseload, it would have been difficult to meet Johnnie's many needs during this critical time. The drive from Toledo took almost an hour. J.R. did his best to hold Johnnie together. He believed that if he could manage to get Johnnie through the next few days until he could be put in a better placement with trained professionals, as the caseworkers had promised, Johnnie would be okay. Once, J.R. rounded up most of the boys from the River Road Group Home and drove them out to play basketball with Johnnie. For that afternoon, Johnnie was his old self, his father and family forgotten for a time.

Johnnie told Tamara Cusack that he wanted to stay with the Johnsons and enroll in the local public school or a nearby trade school. She told Johnnie that Children Services had a different plan, that she was trying to place him at Bury Road Group Home. He had already been rejected from Parmadale twice—and she had just received word from St. Anthony's Villa, a therapeutic institution where Johnnie had spent several weeks a few years ago, that they would not take Johnnie again. His problems were too great. He was too dangerous. Even though he had not yet been accepted, Cusack told the Johnsons that Johnnie would be transferred to Bury Road Group Home soon. She did not tell them that both Parmadale and St. Anthony's Villa had rejected Johnnie while he was living in their home. No one did.

Mrs. Johnson told Cusack that Johnnie did not want to go to a group home and was "attempting to cajole them into maintaining him in their home," according to the caseworker's files. She reassured Mrs. Johnson that he was slated to enter a group home within the week. She told the Johnsons only that "due to Johnnie's runaway behavior and adjustment problems in foster care, the case plan is designed to address Johnnie's unstable placement history, advocating an environment which would hopefully give the structure and discipline he needs." Nothing about his many rejections and dangerous behavior.

When Cusack scheduled a time for Johnnie to visit Bury Road, she asked J.R. for help. Johnnie did not want to go to Bury. It was too strict, he said, and he didn't like the other kids. She wanted J.R. to persuade Johnnie that it was for the best, that he would have to leave town and that he had no control over where he would end up. Even though J.R. tried to change his mind, Johnnie would not budge. He wanted to stay with the Johnsons.

The Johnsons felt differently. They became increasingly anxious and fearful of his presence. Because they believed Johnnie would be placed in a group home the next week, however, they agreed to allow Johnnie to stay for a few more days. But the days stretched into several more weeks, because in truth, Children Services still had no other place to put Johnnie and was still looking for a solution. In the meantime, Cusack took Johnnie for yet another interview at an institutional home. Johnnie blew this interview too. Again, he was judged to be too dangerous. Johnnie didn't care. He wanted to stay with the Johnsons.

When Johnnie found out that Mrs. Johnson had asked that he be moved, he became angry. He said he wanted to go to live with Vinnie Riccardi, who ran the school program for troubled boys in Toledo and sometimes took in foster children. Impossible, his caseworker said. He wanted to choose whom he lived with, he said. But he did not have much of a say in that matter, he was told.

On January 19, the Johnsons again called Cusack. Johnnie's behavior had deteriorated even more. He was now disrespectful; he was using profanity. Johnnie was beyond their control, they said. But Children Services didn't accept their warnings. On the other end of the phone, his caseworker assessed the Johnsons as overly religious people who simply did not like Johnnie swearing.[10]

10. According to Children Services memo of January 20.

After his probation officer's visit, during which Pendleton played checkers with Johnnie and convinced him to call the DYS psychiatrist, Johnnie again erupted. Johnnie made the appointment by phone while Pendleton watched, but had already made up his mind to ditch the psychiatrist after Pendleton left. When Mr. Johnson, who was also in the room when Johnnie made the appointment, tried to encourage him to see the psychiatrist, even offering to drive Johnnie himself, Johnnie burst out cursing.

"No one is going to tell me what to do. I don't have to do what people say!" Johnnie yelled.

On January 26, the Johnsons called Children Services yet again. The agency staff member who took their call left this message, written in bold print on a bright pink message pad, for his caseworker: "Johnnie is blowing his placement. [The Johnsons] will try to hold together for the weekend (if he doesn't end up in CSI!)" The exclamation quivered with warning that Johnnie was heading toward a crime that would put him in the Lucas County juvenile jail, the Child Study Institute.

The CS staff member told the Johnsons that someone would call them back. She also made a notation that since Johnnie's caseworker, Cusack, would be off Monday, another social worker should return the Johnsons' call. "I told X to tell foster parent to call police if he is violent and to notify Ed Pendleton," the social worker wrote in Johnnie's file.[11]

No one returned the Johnsons' call. No one told them to call the police.

"Call Bury Road about placement!" was the last notation in Johnnie's file.

Johnnie knew the anger inside him was growing out of control.

"I'm going to do something stupid," Johnnie warned J.R. on Friday, the last time they met before the murder. "I'm going to do something stupid, J.R."

J.R. thought Johnnie meant he might run away again.

"Just chill out," J.R. told him. J.R.'s nerves were fraying from the stress and intensity of his workload. He had worked eighteen-hour days for two weeks straight. "We'll work on it, son."

Johnnie paged J.R. again and again from the Johnsons' while J.R.

---

11. The name of the person she directed to call the Johnsons was blanked out of the document.

drove home that Friday. J.R. returned the calls from a pay phone, then again when he arrived home.

But J.R. desperately needed time away from Toledo and his work. This weekend he planned to go to Cleveland and to watch the Super Bowl with some of his old fraternity brothers. Everything just had to wait until Monday. Just this once, he thought, they could all wait.

"I'm going to do something bad, J.R.," Johnnie warned again on the phone.

"Hold on, son. Hold on until I get back. You can hold on until then."

III

As dawn broke Monday, the day of the murder, the Johnsons again phoned Children Services in a panic, begging the foster care agency to take Johnnie from their home.

They called twice more that day. Each time, staff members put the Johnsons off. First, they simply said that Johnnie's caseworker was not working that day. The next time, they told the Johnsons just to wait.

III

The house was smoke-filled and a strong odor of kerosene was present. The victim's body appeared to be burned over 90%. The victim also appeared to have two gashes on the right side of her head.

—Detective's report

That evening, J.R. returned from his weekend in Cleveland. Two hours after he opened his front door, just as he began changing his baby daughter's diaper, he got a call from Marilyn Young, a friend who was also Ed Pendleton's supervisor at the Ohio Department of Youth Services.

She cried when she told him of Johnnie's arrest for murder.

"Johnnie?" J.R. said. "No, not Johnnie. Not my Johnnie. No, he wouldn't do that. Johnnie?!"

He raced down to the juvenile jail in downtown Toledo, taking three steps at a time to the floor where Johnnie was being detained.

Johnnie looked at him and dissolved into tears.

"I don't know why I did it, J.R.," Johnnie blurted out before J.R.

could say a word. His hot tears fell on the back of J.R.'s neck as J.R. embraced him. It was the last human touch Johnnie would have for weeks, save for the guards' rubber-gloved hands when they put metal cuffs on him. "She was a nice lady, she never did nothing to me. I was so angry, I couldn't figure out what for. When I hit her, I realized I was really messed up. Then I just wanted her to die."

"No, son." J.R. shook his head in disbelief. "No." He wanted to believe that Johnnie had blanked out during the murder, or at least that there was some clear provocation. Only Johnnie could persuade him otherwise.

"J.R., you know I wouldn't lie to you," Johnnie said, looking directly into J.R.'s eyes. Even then, J.R. didn't want to believe any of this was true. But it was too late. Everything was too late.

"I know you wouldn't lie, son," J.R. said finally.

"Yeah, it was hard for me. Extremely hard, because I knew Mrs. Johnson," J.R. says now. "I thought she was the sweetest lady I had ever met in my life. She was so sweet. So was Mr. Johnson. They were just endearing kinds of people. That's why people were so enraged and angry. That's why they can't understand. But the thing is, it wasn't about them at all."

III

If there was reason behind the killing, J.R. thinks that it was only because Mrs. Johnson was a woman. Johnnie harbored more anger toward women than men, J.R. believes, because Johnnie told him his mother sexually abused him and prostituted him in the crack house for drugs. His father may also have done so, but Johnnie blamed his mother more, J.R. says. She rejected him more often. It was a mother's love he was searching for, J.R. thinks. And Johnnie knew Mrs. Johnson, a surrogate mother, had rejected him too.

Hearing J.R.'s explanation, Johnnie shakes his head.

"She was a good lady," he says again of Mrs. Johnson. "I don't know why I did it to her."

J.R. feels guilty that he was not in Toledo when Johnnie needed him. If he had just known how to talk to Johnnie about anger, he thinks, if he had adopted Johnnie as the boy had asked, Johnnie wouldn't have committed murder. Johnnie was righting himself during the brief time J.R.

had him under his wing at River Road, maybe the best time of his life. He was learning to hope.

There was no best time of his life, Johnnie counters. But if there was any period that was okay, he says with a shrug, it was at River Road with J.R. "He's not responsible for what I did though," Johnnie adds swiftly. "People made me the way I am today, but not J.R."

J.R. takes little comfort from Johnnie's words. In his heart, he feels the heavy weight of Johnnie's murder, though in his mind, he knows he is not responsible.

"There were two sides to Johnnie Jordan," J.R. says firmly, blinking away the pain in his eyes. "If there's just one thing I want to get across to you today it's that there were two sides to Johnnie Jordan. One really wanted to achieve and be good. There was a time when that side was winning out. I thought he would blossom into a flower, and for a time, he did. He blossomed under structure, when he finally got it. He even weathered the storm for a while. But then, all of a sudden, no one watered him."

12

The Johnsons were beautiful people. Um-hum, oh Lord. What happened to Johnnie? Killing, kids raping, children doing evil things. Never heard such things in my whole life, and I'm 55. Now that's all we think about. Who's going to be next?

—Margaret Campbell, foster parent

In the Child Study Institute, a juvenile jail where he would await trial, Johnnie sat on the edge of his metal cot, head bowed, forearms resting heavily on his thighs, hands clasped ahead of him. He was not thinking or feeling much of anything. A hollowness filled his mind, a grey emptiness that brought him closest to peace. He did not rethink the effects of his confession. He sat and waited, not caring or wondering what came next. Things like this just happen. So he waited, figuring that whatever happened to him next he probably deserved.

Few people came to visit over the next several months, as the prosecutor petitioned a juvenile court judge to move Johnnie's case to adult court. By law, only his family and attorney were allowed to see him. But what remained of Johnnie's family did not attempt to visit, not because they were appalled by his crime, but because the ties that bound the family were never as strong as Johnnie had imagined, and because they had their own problems. Johnnie Sr. was in jail awaiting trial on charges of physically and sexually abusing his children. Marilyn, Johnnie's mother, was also in jail waiting to be tried as accessory to her husband. One of Johnnie's older sisters was locked in a juvenile detention center out of town. Another sister failed to visit him because she repeatedly said she had too much housework to do. Children Services decided that his younger siblings, all of whom were in its custody and under its guardianship, were too young to visit a jail or comprehend what was happening. Agency staff neglected to explain the reason for Johnnie's arrest to his younger siblings. What they learned of Johnnie's crime, they gathered mostly from talk on the streets.

Ed Pendleton, Johnnie's parole officer, visited Johnnie once after his confession. His job did not require it, or even suggest it. But because he met Johnnie almost immediately after the murder, and because the confession spilled from his prompting, he felt an uneasy responsibility. The image of Johnnie alone in his cell, with no visitors and no one caring, burned in Pendleton's head. The angry reaction from people reading about Johnnie and his crime in the *Toledo Blade* struck Pendleton as harsh. They were right to be outraged, but they didn't know who Johnnie was, whom he had been. They also didn't know that there were hundreds of kids passing through his department who clearly were more dangerous than Johnnie.

In early February, confidential memos began circulating in the juvenile justice system about Johnnie's history and character. Johnnie was "a seriously abused youth who was very angry, withdrawn, uncooperative, and certain no one cared for him," the Parole Department determined. This was no revelation to Pendleton. He knew the same could be said for almost every child in his agency's files. But Pendleton saw a plain truth behind those children's angry eyes, the same thing he saw in Johnnie's. At his core, Johnnie was just a kid. Like any kid, Johnnie feared, he cried, he hurt, even if he didn't understand his emotions or the reasons for them. If Pendleton couldn't explain this disconnect in Johnnie to himself, how could he explain it to those people brimming with fury and outrage, calling for Johnnie's execution?

Pendleton did not know what to say to Johnnie on his second visit. Johnnie didn't know either. Johnnie was not angry with Pendleton, though, nor was he grateful. He simply did not harbor any feelings toward Pendleton at all, except to recognize him. Pendleton felt lost without a reaction from Johnnie. He wanted to defend himself, for encouraging the confession. But Johnnie did not blame him. Pendleton badly wanted to see Johnnie relieved and unburdened by the confession, but Johnnie showed no visible change. In fact, Johnnie says he felt no different. Clearly, Johnnie's grasp of the seriousness of this incident in his past, as he considered the murder, was as faint as his idea of what lay in front of him. Pendleton knew, though he could not bring himself

to bridge the gap of knowledge between them. The meeting was so awkward that Pendleton decided to cut off contact with Johnnie, realizing it
would do no good for either of them.

III

Pendleton did give Johnnie one thing before he let go of the case, something that he had to work around the system to accomplish. Through
Pendleton's authority, J. R. Robinson was allowed to visit Johnnie.
Everyone credited J. R.'s influence for Johnnie's brief improvement at
River Road Group Home. But because J.R. was not related to Johnnie,
even though he was more a real father, friend, and kin to Johnnie than
anyone in Johnnie's life, he was technically barred from contacting
Johnnie until Pendleton pulled some strings and gained approval for
visits.

On his first visit, J.R. found that Johnnie wanted to talk about the
night he had murdered Mrs. Johnson and the weekend leading up to it.
But J.R. could not allow himself to hear it. As much as he wanted to
know what happened, and to help Johnnie, he knew that as part of the
juvenile welfare system, he could be ordered to testify on behalf of the
prosecution. He wanted to do his best for Johnnie, as he had always
promised Johnnie he would. But he was caught between his knowledge
of what was best for the child and his job. The system that employed
him decided his role.

"I think I need help, J.R." were Johnnie's last words on that visit.
They burn in J.R.'s memory. Johnnie had always felt a need to hide the
shame that he was falling apart inside. This was the first time Johnnie
had ever admitted need, the first time he was really open to help. But it
was too late.

Everyone who spoke to Johnnie in jail, except for his lawyers, had
allegiance to the government—Children Services or the juvenile justice
system—and would testify for the prosecution. Children Services
required the caseworkers who visited Johnnie to write up reports of
their meetings, and those reports would be subpoenaed. The only psychiatrists to see Johnnie would be sent by the court to evaluate him for
the purposes of the murder trial.

Instead of Johnnie, J.R.'s anger focused on Pendleton, one of the few
people Johnnie trusted. How could he do it? J.R. wondered. How could

he suggest to Johnnie that he confess without an attorney or anyone else present to protect him? At the very least, an attorney could have brokered a deal to get Johnnie some psychiatric help during the long months he awaited trail. Johnnie was just a kid, but he was treated as a smart and educated adult. To J.R., none of this was fair.

As the months passed, J.R. came to recognize Pendleton's position, though he could never fully accept it. Pendleton did what he thought he had to do, J.R. decided. He had understood and respected Pendleton up to that point. The two had a close working relationship and shared a similar outlook on their work. Both began their careers as young African-American men motivated to contribute to their community. J.R. believed he had inspired Pendleton to go into parole work long ago, when Pendleton first came to Toledo and J.R. became something of a mentor to him. Now, after Johnnie's case, J.R. and Pendleton no longer meet as friends. J.R. still respects Pendleton, except for how he handled Johnnie's case. The most he will concede is that Pendleton did what he thought was his job when he counseled Johnnie to confess.

III

In the months leading up to his trial, Johnnie's world behind bars stood still. Mrs. Johnson appeared to him at night, when he felt quiet and alone. Not thoughts of her brutal murder, but fresh memories of her smiling or telling him not to feed scraps to the stray dog. Sad thoughts of Mr. Johnson hit him too. Mr. Johnson was alone now, and that upset Johnnie.

After one of J.R.'s visits, Johnnie decided that he wanted to die. He took a life, so he figured he should give up his life. He didn't want to kill again, but he knew if he didn't get help, he probably would. He resolved to wait for a while for the help Pendleton promised, but if it didn't work, he would take his own life.[1]

In the meantime, time passed slowly for Johnnie. Boredom seeped through, and annoyed him. He did not like being bored, he complained as though the adults around him should have learned this lesson. Rather than feeling sorry for the Johnsons, his daytime thoughts grew agitated and mean, with nothing to take his mind off his situation or

---

1. Studies show young prisoners are more likely to commit suicide than adults.

away from his parents, who were awaiting their own court dates. He did not worry so much about himself. He assumed he would be back on the streets soon enough. It did not matter when: days, months, or even a few years; time all felt the same to him. Only, he wished his court date would come fast. He was getting tired of this.

Then overnight, it seemed to Johnnie, his patience spiraled away. He couldn't control his thoughts any more than he could his environment, and this made him furious. He began to shout and curse at the guards. He did not want to go to sleep, he would yell, he was tired of this place. He was put into solitary confinement for twenty-four hours. Once out, he was accused of making gang signs to other prisoners, a strict violation of the rules. He was sent back to "solitary." Johnnie blamed the staff; some of them didn't like him. "They're always watching me, waiting for me to mess up," he complained to a social worker.

He soon trained himself not to react to solitary confinement. He conditioned himself to pretend that he in fact wanted the punishment. For almost a year, it worked. He also manipulated his memories, and found that by doing so, he could also manipulate his life. Solitary only meant that he was not allowed off his floor, which he shared with other youths in detention. Meals came to him; he was not allowed to go to the cafeteria. Although his social interaction with other inmates and visitors was restricted, he claimed it didn't bother him a bit. He was not permitted to attend classes, because school was held on another floor. He claimed not to miss that either, but given the opportunity, he acknowledged he would have liked to go to school to ward off the boredom. In fact, he would take part in just about any activity available to him, except for religious services, because they annoyed him.[2]

On television and sometimes in the newspaper, he would see snippets about his parents' trials. He asked his caseworkers questions about his father and mother. These inquiries spurred John Weglian, the prose-

2. Just after his hearing in juvenile court, Johnnie received a Bible with no note, no return address. Donna Lewis, the Jordan family caseworker, had taken up a collection at work and purchased the Bible for Johnnie. He left it in his cell when he was moved. He says he doesn't know how to use it or how it can do anything for him. He doesn't understand when preachers talk religion, so how, he asks, can he figure it out by reading it.

A second-grade teacher of Johnnie's also visited him once in jail. He didn't recognize her by name or face. She had seen an article about him in the newspaper. For thirty minutes, she tried to proselytize Johnnie. He didn't understand why she came or what she was talking about.

cutor in Johnnie Sr.'s case, to ask Johnnie's court-appointed lawyer if Johnnie would agree to testify against his father in the abuse case.

"If they'd have asked me directly, I would have gone off on them," Johnnie paced as he shouted at his family caseworker, Donna Lewis. He was enraged at the notion of being disloyal. "My attorney told them no," he added more calmly, his anger turning to sadness. "I'd be really upset if my dad goes to prison."

Johnnie was not even certain about the nature of his father's charges. Lewis didn't know either. He had written his mother soon after his arrest, but she never responded. He thought that the detention center was keeping letters from him. But his mother simply decided not to reply. When he later asked about her, he was told she had been found guilty of two counts of child endangerment and, by way of a plea bargain after claiming a religious awakening, had been sentenced to a year in prison.

"That's not bad," Johnnie said of the sentence.

Johnnie still felt that he himself was getting the punishment he deserved, but the feeling was wearing thin. When Lewis advised him to behave in court, he again erupted.

"I'm not going to kiss a judge's butt!" he said furiously. He believed that judges were his family's ultimate enemy.

He was proud when he learned that his girlfriend, Katrina, was pregnant, from the night of the murder. But it got him to thinking about how he was missing out on life on the outside, and he worried that he would be forgotten soon.

"I'm going to lose track of my sibs," he complained. "I'll be gone six years and won't know where they are."

It still did not occur to him that he could stay behind bars beyond the age of twenty-one. Six years was a lifetime to him. The thought of losing touch with those he cared about depressed him. He told Lewis he didn't care about anything or anyone. It would be okay to die, he said. "There's nothing anymore."

He tried three times to kill himself, he says. But they were halfhearted attempts. Twice he stopped eating, but no one seemed to notice. He doesn't know what made him start eating again. The third time, he wrapped a sheet around his neck and tried to choke himself. He stopped when he felt faint and heard footsteps.

He no longer asked for his siblings or parents to visit him. He didn't

want to know when his baby would be born or to see pictures of Pebbles, as he called Katrina, or their child. The photos would make him
mad that he was stuck in the prison, and when he got mad, he'd hurt
someone. He didn't want that.

Johnnie began to worry about other things. He feared he was losing
his memory. Lewis tried to reassure him, saying that he was probably
just distracted, that jail was not a good environment for remembering
things. But he felt that memories of his earlier life were fading. He
couldn't remember places, or names. He had no true recollections of his
parents, only pieces of dreams. Perhaps they were not real, he thought.

He grew lonely, but still he didn't ask to see his family. Instead, he
asked his caseworker about the dog that had followed him around for
several days at the Johnsons'. He told her again how stinky the dog was
and how he used to sneak food to the dog while it slept in the snow outside the house waiting for him. And he expressed pleasant memories of
Mrs. Johnson, as if the rest didn't really exist, though he knew, when
asked, that he had killed her.

The disjuncture between his gentle thoughts of Mrs. Johnson and
the reality that he killed her intensified through the days and nights.
Thoughts of Mr. Johnson alone, of Mrs. Johnson dead, confused him. He
would try to distract himself, but the contradictory thoughts would
emerge when he was least aware, when he was alone, when he was
bored. Thoughts, half memories, were being stirred up. His reaction was
to become angry, even furious, which saved him from thinking. His
attention span frayed. His guilt lessened as his anger grew. Each time he
was slapped back into solitary fed his anger.

III

On April 1, two months after the confession, Cusack visited. She asked
Johnnie if he had heard about his father's trial. No, he said, though he
had. He didn't know if what he had heard was true.

"Your dad was found guilty of twelve priors," she told him. Johnnie
knew this included rape and felonious assault.

Johnnie hung his head. He never cried before anyone but J.R. He
asked if his father was out on bail. Cusack assumed so because he had
not yet been sentenced. Johnnie asked about his mother. Unaware that
Marilyn Jordan's case had already been disposed of, Cusack said his

mother would be sentenced the following week. There was no more talk of family, only silence. Cusack suggested that he write his feelings and thoughts in a journal. But Johnnie didn't want to. He thought that whatever he wrote could make him look weak, or worse, crazy.

That night, Johnnie attacked another inmate on his floor. When guards stopped the fight, he hit the heavy steel walls with his fists until they were bloodied and swollen. When he was injured during a basketball game, the prison doctor sewed him back up with nine stitches. Two days later, alone in his cell, he pulled them out one at a time, taking blood and skin tissue with them. "It didn't feel like nothing," he says with a shrug. He claimed not to feel pain anymore. Not physical pain, or emotional pain.

A series of solitary confinements followed. For fighting. For verbal aggression. For turning on the TV when it was not allowed. For "acting out" and yelling. For ignoring direction. Once, in his rage, he broke the glass cover on his ceiling light. It was the only thing he could find to destroy.

Johnnie blamed everyone else for his behavior, claiming that in every instance he was provoked, even when he slammed a new boy who was quietly passing by into a wall. Asked if he was responsible for his actions, he admitted he was but said he did not care.

The world was closing in on him and he fought to keep his space. Even the air he breathed was dangerous, he felt. He was convinced the air was filled with nastiness and tried to breathe only through his nose, and never through his mouth. This was difficult when struck by colds. He would force himself to stay awake, so that air would not enter his mouth.

III

In March, the court had ordered Dr. Gregory Forgac, a psychologist who consulted for the Court Diagnostic and Treatment Center, to evaluate Johnnie and determine whether he could be tried and sentenced as an adult. Forgac would determine whether Johnnie was "amenable to care and rehabilitation in any facility designed for the care, supervision and rehabilitation of delinquent children [or] whether the safety of the community may require the child be placed under legal restraint including, if necessary, for the period extending beyond his majority," or after he turned twenty-one.

The evaluation would prove critical in the court's deliberation.

Though his attorney told him it would be important, Johnnie believed only that the psychologist was sent to help him understand his crime and recover. Without hesitation, he signed the standards of confidentiality form, which warned that the information gained by the doctor could be included in court testimony and made available to the prosecutor as well as to Johnnie's defense attorney.

To Dr. Forgac, Johnnie "appeared a relatively neat and clean fifteen-year-old." At first, Johnnie was hesitant, even guarded. But with time, he relaxed. On the psychologist's second visit, Johnnie stayed attentive and cooperative. He was forthcoming, almost eager to talk. He seemed "well oriented." He knew the name of the president, but not the governor of Ohio nor the mayor of Toledo. He admitted that at times he felt something crawling on him, even when nothing was there, but the doctor found he had no other unusual experiences or signs or symptoms of mental illness. Johnnie had quickly volunteered that he never felt that he was mentally sick or that he needed psychiatric hospitalization.

At first, the doctor annoyed Johnnie with persistent questions about his family. He never could understand why counselors and psychologists pried so much about them. Why didn't they just move on to him or whatever the incident he had done? Focusing on the past, and particularly whether his parents messed with him, was beside the point and nosy.

Johnnie told Dr. Forgac that there were seven children in his family—three boys and four girls. He said he felt close to all of his siblings but did not have much contact with them. One sister ran away, one was in a group home, one lived on her own with her baby; the other children were with his grandma. He also told Forgac that his relationship with his parents was "alright. Both are locked up for raping us when we was little. Don't know how long locked up." But Johnnie denied that his parents sexually abused him or his siblings. He also said they were not physically abusive. He was getting angry at these questions. After looking through hundreds of pages of Johnnie's medical and social services reports, Dr. Forgac concluded that Johnnie had a distorted recollection of his childhood, or else was consciously diminishing the horrendous situation in which he had grown up.

Johnnie did not object so much to the next line of questioning. No, he didn't set fires as a child. No, he never tortured animals. Yes, he had a problem with bed-wetting up until the age of thirteen. And yes, he did have extreme temper tantrums. He got into a lot of fights, he said, because "people used to mess with me in school." He admitted having lost control of his temper in the past, but shrugged it off, saying he'd always been that way. He denied doing anything just to be mean, except "if someone deserves it."

His last school grade was ninth. He thought that he had flunked that grade twice. "I used to get good grades if I go to school," he said. "When I do the work, I always get A's and stuff."

On the Ammons Quick Test, which measures verbal intelligence, Johnnie scored an estimated IQ of 58, which falls in the range of Mild Mental Retardation. His mental age, according to this score, was seven and a half. But the doctor noted that in earlier tests in school, Johnnie scored 84 on Performance IQ and 81 on a Full-Scale IQ. These results put him in the range between low-average and borderline for his capacity to function intellectually.

"Although this individual does have some intellectual limitations," Forgac wrote in a report, "he does not appear to be mentally retarded. It does, however, appear that Johnnie is functioning within the range of borderline intelligence."

Johnnie told the psychologist he had a problem with discipline. He was expelled from school the last four years in a row for fighting. For the last three years, he had been a member of the East Coast Crips gang. He joined because his older sister was a member, and when one of the Bloods messed with her, he joined a carload of gang members who were planning to shoot a girl belonging to the Bloods. When Forgac asked why he joined the gang, Johnnie told him he did not know.

Yes, he owned guns, he said. A .25-caliber, a .38, and a .22.

"Revolvers?" the doctor asked.

"Yes," Johnnie said. "No bigger than a .38," he added.

He claimed that the Bloods had shot at him many times, and that he needed the guns for protection. But shooting was a game to Johnnie. When rage gripped him, he rarely thought of using a gun unless he had one with him. He wanted to hit people, bang them on the head, stab them with a knife maybe, tear things up. With guns, you shot at other people to set them straight, or to kill them. It didn't really matter. They were just a quick way to get a job done. They were less personal. They made killing a lot easier. They were like a game, he said later. He didn't tell the psychologist this.

Moving on, Johnnie said his health was not good.

"Why?" Forgac asked.

"I smoke too much weed." Until his arrest, he had smoked marijuana every day since he was eleven, he said. "One time, I got paranoid." He started drinking when he was eleven, he told the doctor, and since then he had a drink every once in a while, but it was never a problem. He had gotten drunk maybe three or four times in his life. He smoked about a pack of cigarettes a day. Weed was the problem, Johnnie said.

"How's your appetite?"

"Sometimes it's good," he said with a shrug, "but I usually don't eat that much."

Johnnie usually ate two pieces of toast at breakfast, no lunch, and some dinner. He didn't count the Little Debbies and candy he snacked on during the day. Johnnie never looked skinny. His 149 pounds filled out his five-foot-six frame.

He often had a hard time going to sleep, he said. But he told the doctor he did not suffer from nightmares.

He wasn't a nervous person, he told the doctor. But he was depressed. "I've been sad ever since I've been away from my parents. I don't like listening to nobody who isn't my mom and dad. That is why I end up getting kicked out" of foster care placements.

He recounted that he was nine years old when first placed in foster care. Afterward, he had to run away to see his parents. When he got word that one of them was in trouble, he would run to them. He had seen his father only five or six times since he was nine, and his mother only once in four years. He thought his parents had divorced while he was in foster care; in fact, they had not.

To Johnnie's relief, the doctor finally asked him why he was in the juvenile detention center. This was what Johnnie wanted to get to. This is what he felt he needed help with.

"I killed somebody, foster mom. Had been with her for a month," he said. It seemed casual to the doctor. To Johnnie, it was factual.

"What was your relationship with her?"

"We're getting along. It happened in the afternoon. I didn't go to school. I felt like somebody was telling me something inside of my head, like a little voice telling me to do it, one telling me don't. Two times, I sat back down. The voice told me to kill her."

"Did you like her?"

"Yeah, her husband left," Johnnie said. "Got along with him alright. The third time I got up, I had picked it [the hatchet] up before, that's when I got up. Went into the kitchen. She was washing dishes. I didn't say anything to her. She didn't say anything to me. I hit her once. She jumped back and was looking at me. I just looked back. I was surprised I did it. I didn't know what to do. About five seconds after that I hit her, hit her about twelve times.

"Went over to my girlfriend's house and started kicking it with her." The doctor noted that Johnnie smiled at this point, knowing that the phrase would confound him.

"You were talking with her?"

"We weren't talking, had sex, didn't tell her what I had done," Johnnie said.

He paused for a moment. "I guess she died there," he said of Mrs. Johnson. "I don't know. She was old, but she looked young. She looked thirty," he said. From Johnnie, this was a tribute. He thought women liked to look young.

"I feel bad about it," he added.

"Why did you do it?"

"No idea why I did it," he said, slowly shaking his head. He looked to the doctor to give him an answer. The doctor just wrote something down and turned away.

Forgac also administered an MMPI-A test (Minnesota Multiphasic Personality Inventory). The configuration results, he wrote in language favored by psychiatrists, were "similar to that found with adolescents who have family problems centering around angry feelings that they are unable to express and feel intensely guilty about. They have feelings of social inadequacy, worry and depression. These individuals are unlikely to be frank and open in discussing their problems. They have a tendency to over-react to minor problems and substance abuse might be present. These males are usually verbally hostile, dependent and highly immature. They have difficulty in maintaining control over their impulses and conduct. After acting out in a socially unacceptable manner, they typically feel guilt, though this concern may reflect situational difficulties, for example, being caught rather than guilt from internalized conflict. Future acting out is likely to recur in a cyclic pattern."[3]

After taking the psychiatric tests, Johnnie denied that he had attempted to commit suicide in jail, although he had tried three times earlier in detention. Once, before his arrest, he had threatened to jump off a bridge if Children Services didn't reunite his family. He believes he would have done so if caseworkers had not agreed to allow him to visit his family.

Johnnie did admit to thinking about suicide, however.

"When I came up here, I thought about killing myself," he said, referring to the jail. "Because I took someone else's life, I should have took mine."

Johnnie stopped for a moment, then continued, talking more to himself than his listener.

"To tell you the truth, I don't care if I live or die. Ain't nothing to live for. Not like I'm happy or nothing, I don't think I'll ever see my parents again. I wouldn't want to see my sisters and brothers after four or five years. I don't want to see them like that. I call Grandma, I'd tell her I was out of town."

"Do you have thoughts of murder?"

"No," Johnnie told him. There was quiet for a moment.

Then Johnnie said, "I've got a feeling I ain't going to live long."

III

Dr. Forgac concluded, based on tests and observation, that Johnnie had a "personality pathology" formed by long-standing patterns of "maladaptive behaviors" and abuse. The test results, he reported, did not

---

3. The tests, Forgac declared in his report, were valid for interpretation. "Two of the basic Clinical Scales exceeded normal limits. Three more scores were moderately elevated within the normal range. Elevations on the Content Scores are similar to those found with individuals who report general symptoms of anxiety. They find life to be a strain and have difficulty making decisions. They have significant depressive thoughts and low opinions of themselves. They hold many negative attitudes about themselves. Elevation on the Subscales were similar to those found with individuals who feel unhappy or depressed. They lack energy to cope with problems of everyday life and have difficulties with concentration, attention, and memory. They may feel that life is no longer worthwhile. They feel uncomfortable and often are not in good health. They feel alienated, isolated, and estranged. They believe that other people do not understand them and feel they are getting a raw deal from life. They see other people as selfish, dishonest, and opportunistic, and because of these perceptions feel justified in behaving in similar ways."

suggest a thought disorder or loss of contact with reality. Johnnie came from an extremely chaotic, abusive, and neglectful family, the doctor gleaned from reports. It appeared to him that Johnnie was physically abused as a child, and very likely exposed to sexual behavior at a young age. Although Johnnie would be turning sixteen in less than a month, he seemed to be functioning more at the level of a twelve-year-old. Taking into consideration the results of the evaluation, as well as Johnnie's age, physical and mental health, his prior record, efforts previously made to treat or rehabilitate him, his family environment and school records, the doctor was not optimistic about Johnnie's future.

"His history," the psychologist wrote, "is replete with risk factors for future violence . . . Johnnie Jordan is not amenable to care or rehabilitation in any facility designed for the care, supervision and rehabilitation of delinquent children."

Furthermore, "it is quite likely that even if he were to receive long-term treatment, he would still present a threat to the safety of the community . . ."

His conclusion was plain: "Johnnie Jordan should not remain in the juvenile system and should be transferred to the adult system for criminal prosecution."

III
JUSTICE

13

On April 18, at nine twenty-five in the morning, the first of Johnnie Jordan's many days in court got under way. In Lucas County's juvenile court, Judge James Ray would decide whether Johnnie, at age fifteen, should be certified and tried as an adult. Ohio law at the time required two steps for certification. First, the prosecution had to show that Johnnie probably committed the murder. In light of Johnnie's confession, this stage was waived. Second, the prosecution had to persuade Judge Ray that Johnnie would not benefit from, nor be receptive to, rehabilitation and correction in the juvenile system.

While law spells out clearly under what circumstances a child should be treated as an adult, science and philosophy find no such rigid definitions. Knowing right from wrong is presumed the indicator of legal maturity, a standard that is likewise applied to determine if adults are sane enough to be held criminally responsible. The court simply looks at whether the individual has a conscience.

But in children, science treats conscience as a developing state. Children may know something is not right, but not yet fully understand the meaning of their actions. They may know that it is wrong to kill, but not comprehend entirely that murder ends life, and even destroys life beyond that of the victim. Nonetheless, current criminal law, reinforced by public outrage, is simple.

"You do adult crime," says Lucas County's prosecutor Julia Bates, "you get adult time. It might not always be right, but that's the way the system operates."

In most states, accusations of homicide or rape automatically merit an adult court trial with adult punishments, regardless of age. Public anger and frustration that have boiled over in response to the increasingly violent acts of young people has pushed lawmakers in twenty states to allow children of any age to be tried as adults, and children as young as thirteen to be given the death penalty.[1]

In Ohio, Johnnie escaped death by three months. He was fifteen years and nine months old when he murdered. Had he been sixteen, he likely would have been sentenced to death. Few people familiar with the Jordan case and the outrage it stirred could have expected a twelve-person jury to show clemency, let alone sympathy, toward him. Partly in response, the state of Ohio lowered the minimum age for the death penalty to fourteen soon after Johnnie's case.

The first day of pretrial hearings in juvenile court, there was little doubt that Johnnie's case would be transferred to the adult criminal system. The murder was horrendous and frightening. Johnnie had confessed. Outsiders would see the certification process for Johnnie as merely a formality. But Judge Ray and attorneys for both sides prepared thoroughly, as if the outcome was not certain. For almost three months, attorneys had waded through eight large boxes of Children Services files and memos on Johnnie, his parole and probation records, his medical records, and his family history. Everything was documented, giving a greater wealth of clues to, and evidence of, what went wrong in Johnnie Jordan's life than they would have had for a child raised in the privacy of an ordinary home.

But both sides soon discovered that the files provided a maze of conflicting facts and information. Johnnie's name was often spelled incorrectly. His birth date was sometimes wrong, as was his grade level in school. There were differing IQ test scores. Contradictions flooded the files. Half notes, unintelligible script, and scraps of memos filled the boxes. Making the lawyers' work even more difficult, Johnnie had a

---

1. The U.S. Supreme Court upheld the constitutionality of the death penalty for juveniles by one vote in 1989. By 2000, in part as a reaction to the sharp escalation of juvenile crime in the mid-1990s, twenty-three of the thirty-eight states that have the death penalty permitted the execution of juvenile offenders. Eighty children in the United States were in prisons awaiting execution of their death sentences in 2000. That same year, five juveniles who committed murder were put to death, more than any other year since 1954. The execution of children for any reason is banned under the International Convention on Civil and Political Rights, which the U.S. Senate voted to ratify in 1992 while retaining the right to execute juveniles. According to the U.S. State Department, Amnesty International, and the United Nations High Commission on Human Rights, only six other countries have executed children since 1990: Iran, Yemen, Nigeria, Pakistan, Saudi Arabia, and the Congo. Since then, fourteen juveniles in the United States have been put to death, more than the other countries combined.

younger brother who had been given the same name by their parents. It was not clear whether reports on one Johnnie had been misplaced in the files of the other child. Worst of all, there were records of plans and intentions that may or may not ever have been actually implemented. The files read like the beginnings of short stories that were missing a plot.

Johnnie's juvenile court defense attorney assumed that all pertinent files had been given to him. But the attorneys who would later represent Johnnie suspected that Children Services tried to hide some documents which suggested the agency had ignored or moved slowly in response to reports of child abuse in the Jordan household and, more significantly, had ignored fearful complaints and pleas for help from foster parents about Johnnie's behavior, warning signs that should have led to his treatment and even restraint. Arguing that it was protecting Johnnie's privacy, Children Services in fact did attempt to withhold files. The judge tried to coax, but eventually had to threaten the agency before it relinquished all files.

III

This was not the first time Judge Ray had confronted Johnnie in his courtroom. He had come across Johnnie before on minor charges and saw him then as just another juvenile delinquent, one who had not committed crimes as attention-getting as others. Those kids sometimes haunted him with uncertainty, but Johnnie never haunted him. Johnnie did not stand out enough for the judge to remember him well.

For twenty-two years, Ray had dealt with troubled children, first as a juvenile court referee and then as an elected judge. Over the years, he learned that the greatest predictor of delinquency, the trait shared by all mean and dangerous children, was that adults had betrayed them during their childhood. The betrayal may have been sexual or physical abuse, or neglect. In any form, it was betrayal which caused the most damage—permanent damage—in children who could not articulate or even identify their feelings.

But Ray also knew there were abused children who never murdered, never even threw a punch. So the judge, who is also an ordained minister, made an effort to look more deeply into Johnnie's case than the superficial history proffered by the Children Services files. He was surprised by what he found. He knew Johnnie "was a pretty damaged kid," he says, but not how profoundly he had been damaged. Ray learned during the initial hearing about the neglect, but he had no idea, until the second day of the juvenile hearing, the degree to which Johnnie had been abused and even tortured. Johnnie's parents had failed in every respect, Ray concluded, and foster care had failed miserably to parent him as well. Together, they had turned Johnnie's childhood into a nightmare.

Judge Ray believes that kids like Johnnie can be saved if they are rescued by age two or three. After that, he says, their odds plummet. His reading on juvenile crime research indicates that in rare circumstances adolescent children can start over. He hopes that is so. But he believes only children who are preverbal, who have not yet come to accept betrayal as "normal," can be saved. The child is lost unless he or she can articulate feelings about betrayal. Otherwise, the anger remains inside and builds until it explodes.

The juvenile justice system is not designed to deal with children who explode as violently as Johnnie Jordan. Thank goodness, Judge Ray thinks, or else he would be handling every child who comes before him with iron gloves. Hard cases make bad law. And from the onset, Judge Ray knew that Johnnie's would be a hard case. Not an unclear case, or a particularly challenging one in legal terms. But a child who murdered his foster mother out of rage from betrayal was not a case that would end in good justice.

He deliberated for only a day. But the case still lingers with him. It recalls in full the sadness of all children ruined by violence, who go on to destroy others. For them, there is no appropriate remedy, no appropriate justice.

III

At the hearing, Assistant Prosecuting Attorney Jennifer Bainbridge presented the state's argument for trying Johnnie Jordan as an adult. Johnnie would turn sixteen in only a few weeks. He was not physically handicapped. Nor was he mentally handicapped, she said, promising to present psychiatric testimony to that effect.

For Johnnie to be transferred to adult court, the state was required to show that he functioned as an adult. The study of intellectual development has struggled for centuries to answer the question of when a child becomes an adult. The modern consensus is that adolescence ends in the mid-twenties, even later than age twenty-one, when the law bestows upon citizens many of the rights and responsibilities of adulthood. In terms of crime, many states, including Ohio, have arbitrarily set the minimum age at which a child can be tried as an adult as low as thirteen. In those states, the law presumes that a child younger than thirteen is not cognizant of the repercussions of committing a murder. Tests showed Johnnie was functioning at the intellectual level of a twelve-year-old and some even suggested he operated as a child five years younger. But his biological age was the only age that really mattered in the courtroom. The test scores did not interfere with Bainbridge's argument; she did not have to address them.

Johnnie knew murder was wrong and that he could be sent to prison, she declared. He knew enough to run from his crime. "His aggressive behavior, his disruptive behavior, and his sexual inappropriateness," she said in her opening statement, "highlight Johnnie's school, probation, and foster care situations."

Bainbridge recited Johnnie's litany of transgressions. At age eight, he was placed in an institution in an effort to correct his sexual misconduct. When he was eleven, he was put on probation for unruly behavior, a probation he repeatedly violated. At fourteen, he was convicted of felonious assault and jailed for a year. Along the way, through nineteen foster homes in the last six years, he lied, he stole, he ran away. He was a member of a gang. He used and sold drugs. He owned guns.

It wasn't that the prosecutor was shocked or even surprised by Johnnie's previous crimes. "Johnnie's prior record is not outrageous, as far as some of the people we see down here," Bainbridge conceded, although "his reported conduct and placement at the school and county is and has been outrageous throughout."

His home life was "a nightmare of epic proportions," she acknowledged. Never in his fifteen years had he known a place to call home. Nowhere did he receive a family's love. "He has never had anything that we can even come close to calling a family environment," she said. She had read the reports about his abusive home life twice to appreciate the depravity of his parents, she assured the court. To a jury, Johnnie's horrendous past might make him appear pathetic and evoke sympathy.

But Bainbridge knew that to a juvenile court judge who saw each day how such early and constant damage irrevocably scarred and changed children for the remainder of their lives, this would only buttress her argument that Johnnie's childhood environment made it impossible for him to fit back into society.

She contended that the foster care and juvenile justice systems had done their best to help Johnnie and set him on the right track, but he posed an impossible task. He did not want treatment, and he refused to accept it when it was prescribed. Rehabilitation, the goal of the juvenile courts, would not work now. Certainly there was no hope that Johnnie could be "fixed" by the time he turned twenty-one, five years' time, when the law would be required to set him free from the juvenile system. The safety of the community, not Johnnie's dim prospects for rehabilitation, must be the concern of the court, she maintained.

Then she turned to the horrendous and emotional nature of the crime.

"Jeanette Johnson was sixty-two years old," she reminded the court softly. "She was a wife, a mother, a grandmother, and a foster mother.[2] Jeanette Johnson reached out to Johnnie. She opened her home to him and she is dead. She was attacked while she did dishes at her kitchen sink.

"The coroner's report said she was killed by twelve chop wounds to the head. Her eye was destroyed, her nose—and as she laid on her kitchen floor dying, she was set on fire."

As Bainbridge addressed the judge, Johnnie sat stoically at a table in the courtroom. His expression did not change during the entire proceedings. Hard lines cut his face, across his forehead and spread diagonally from the inner corners of his eyes down to his slack jaw. His hair strayed into an unkempt Afro. Only out of boredom did he bow his head. Otherwise, he looked unshaken and aloof. As he had done throughout his life when confusion, fear, and all the emotions inside him became so muddled together he could not understand himself or anyone or anything going on around him, he removed himself from his body and fled to the ceiling, where he watched the proceedings unfold

2. Bainbridge was mistaken. Mrs. Johnson did not have any biological children or grandchildren, though she did have a grown stepdaughter whom she rarely saw.

beneath him. This way, it was no longer him on trial. He was away. It would all just happen, like life usually did; he had no control. They'd do what they wanted to him. His lawyer was there and his caseworkers and probation officers. They'd decide. It didn't matter, he told himself. He didn't care what happened. A numbness seeped through him. He simply watched, even as Bainbridge described the hatchet chops to Mrs. Johnson's head, and her destroyed face.

"This is one of the most horrific crimes our community has seen . . . and there is no question that the crime deserves to be treated in an adult court, as does Johnnie. It doesn't get any more violent than this crime," she concluded. "Johnnie is clearly dangerous."

Johnnie still did not flinch or budge or react in any visible way. Reporters saw "coldness" in Johnnie's demeanor. He was apparently "remorseless."

Judge Ray was not surprised by Johnnie's detached manner, however. He calls it the "flat effect," common in damaged children. Unable to cope, they don't try. The result looks bizarre. The blank faces, sometimes even a strange smile. The emotions do not fit the scene and the gravity of their condition.

Bainbridge argued that, for the sake of community safety, Johnnie should be bound by adult laws that could lock him up for a long, long time. He was dangerous, she repeated. He extinguished Mrs. Johnson's life with a hatchet "and has no idea why he did it. None. He tells Dr. Forgac, 'I have no idea why I did it,'" Bainbridge said incredulously. "He even acknowledges that he got along with Mrs. Johnson, and there's no question that that's very scary."

Bainbridge ended by quoting from Dr. Forgac's assessment report which, even though couched mostly in psychological terms, left a chilling impression: "His history is replete with risk factors for future violence."

III

James Popil, Johnnie's court-appointed attorney, used his opening statement to echo many of the same arguments laid out by the prosecution, but his aim was to evoke sympathy for Johnnie. It was a long-shot attempt, but the only one Popil had.

Johnnie had spent nearly half of his life—seven of his fifteen years—living in foster care and juvenile detention centers, Popil began. Until the murder, his criminal record consisted of a single felony charge and conviction. In arguing that Johnnie could benefit from rehabilitation and therapy, Popil noted that Johnnie had behaved reasonably well in very structured placements like juvenile jails and group homes, better than in foster care, where he was often forced to fend for himself. But Popil stopped short of arguing that if Johnnie had been given a proper home he would not have murdered Mrs. Johnson. Mrs. Johnson's was a good home. And even at River Road, his best placement, prosecutor Bainbridge had pointed out, Johnnie had gotten into some trouble. Though his difficulties were early on in his stay at River Road, and in the later part of his stay he was reported only for running away, the court would still view his transgressions as troubled behavior.

Because of his rough past, Johnnie developed "behavior deficits" both in terms of communication and socialization, Popil said. He functions more like a twelve-year-old than a fifteen- or sixteen-year-old. Johnnie was still a very young child. He was also full of remorse about Mrs. Johnson, Popil claimed, although Johnnie's blank stare did not support the words.

Popil hadn't much to go on, but he liked Johnnie. He found him polite, respectful, and candid. Popil had represented about ten children charged with rape or murder in the past decade. Johnnie was different. He did not display the same anger and hostility as his other clients.

Popil called as witnesses seven people closest to Johnnie, those who he thought would give the most positive testimony. Their words came across as raw and confused, however, as if they wished to help him but were still shaken by the crime. All worked for the foster care system in one capacity or another. To make sense of a murderer of any age is almost impossible. To look at a kid they liked and knew well was even more difficult. Their answers were honest and stark, struggling to describe the Johnnie they knew but unable to reconcile him with Johnnie the killer.

First was Vincent Riccardi, the criminal justice specialist who ran a day program for kids suspended or expelled from school, or who, like Johnnie, were not enrolled at all at the time. Children Services had failed to enroll Johnnie in a school for three months after he was released from the Cuyahoga Hills Detention Center. Riccardi testified that Johnnie had obeyed his rules and "did actually quite well within the program." Johnnie was respectful, he worked well with younger children, he was artistically gifted.

On cross-examination, Riccardi was asked if Johnnie could tell the difference between right and wrong.

"Yes," he answered.

"Did you do everything you could in your ability or in your capacity for Johnnie at the time that he was with you?"

"Yes."

The prosecutor had nothing further.

III

Dr. Gregory Forgac, the psychologist sent by the court to evaluate Johnnie, was the next witness for the defense. His report to the court was evidence Popil could not avoid, no matter how he would have liked to. Before the hearing, Johnnie's defense attorney had called for a second psychiatric opinion, to which the court had agreed. But the second expert only echoed Forgac's conclusions. Rather than introduce the second confirming opinion, Popil focused on the primary report and tried to soften its import when Forgac took the stand.

Nothing in the psychological tests indicated a psychosis, a mental illness that would indicate lost contact with reality and perhaps provide a legal excuse for Johnnie's crime, the report said. So Popil briskly moved to Johnnie's IQ results. Johnnie functioned at the level of a twelve-year-old child, Dr. Forgac found. While many twelve-year-olds follow adult rules and conform to adult standards, the psychologist said, "it's normal to expect some immaturity and the inability to really perceive situations and to process as many variants as adults do." Johnnie was "on the brink, the border between moving into full adult thinking, full—normal, operational thinking—and so you would expect an individual to display traits of adolescents, not necessarily always following the rules." As a child, he had a "relatively long-standing pattern" of "maladaptive behavior." For example, Johnnie never accepted the fact that he would not be reunited with his parents. Instead, he continued to believe that if he wished for something hard enough, it would come true. And he tried to minimize and even deny his "horrendous situation at home."

Was Johnnie depressed? Popil asked. Did he have a substance abuse problem?

"Yes," the doctor answered to both. "He certainly did not appear to be a happy adolescent," Dr. Forgac said in an understatement. "He certainly was not happy. He talked about, you know, that there's not really a whole lot of reasons to live."

Forgac also reported that Johnnie had expressed concern about getting caught and that he made sure Mrs. Johnson was dead because he was afraid she might recover and report him. That alone showed Johnnie was able to reason to some extent; it also highlighted the cold self-preservation in his antisocial behavior. Then there was the way he felt about Mrs. Johnson, Forgac added. Ironically, he liked her. Forgac found "significant" that Johnnie could be so cruel to someone he cared for, but added he was disturbed when Johnnie said he "wasn't sure why he did this, that he just felt that he needed to do this."

"He did talk about some anger," Forgac went on. "But anger about basically his life situation, and feeling that is where his anger comes from in situations like this."

Had he done well in detention? Popil asked. Not necessarily, Forgac said. His behavior exceeded some expectations but not all.

What did Johnnie need?

A great deal of structure, the doctor replied. "A lot of attention towards promoting an adaptive functioning."

Work on thinking errors, Forgac continued, vocational rehabilitation so that he could perform tasks that made him feel good about himself, emphasis on self-control training, alternative-thinking training, "a lot of things I think would be necessary . . . And this would have to continue for a long period of time."

How long?

" . . . probably as long as possible," the doctor answered.

Finally, Popil asked Dr. Forgac to explain his report's damaging conclusion that "Johnnie's history is replete with risk factors for future violence."

The inconsistent childhood, the exposure to violence within the family home, Forgac enumerated dryly. Gang involvement, particularly because three years of gang involvement in a fifteen-year-old's life is "significant." The availability of weapons. And poverty. "There tends to be greater violence associated with poverty. So there are just a number of factors that suggest, you know, the risk of future violence," he repeated.

On cross-examination, Bainbridge emphasized the key points Forgac had made. But she went a step further.

"When we are talking about rehabilitation, we're talking about taking someone and making them normal again. Do you think this is possible with Johnnie Jordan?"

"He hasn't lived a normal life," Forgac replied. "There has been incredible inconsistencies . . . when you move from different parent figures to different parent figures in foster home placement . . . He was exposed to just a terrible situation with abuse and neglect . . . it was just a very, very difficult situation: physical, sexual, emotional abuse, deprivation. "It's not as though there's a trauma that lasted for six months or a different situation that lasted for a few weeks. We're talking about a lifetime," Forgac said.

The implication was obvious: Johnnie could never be normal.

"And is it your opinion that he is a danger to the community?" Bainbridge asked.

"Yes, it is."

III

J. R. Robinson was Johnnie's best hope. If anyone could testify that there were redemptive qualities inside the young murderer who sat before the court, it was this man, who had dedicated his life to helping high-risk kids survive and stay out of trouble, and who had called Johnnie Jordan "son."

J.R. had known Johnnie for almost six years, ever since he had entered the River Road Group Home. Johnnie, he testified, gets very attached to people, and doesn't let go. "He's one of the most loyal people I have ever met in my life. And once he's established himself with a family, with people, he's set up, he's concrete. He has aspirations. He is a very caring and concerned young man." Johnnie wants to please, J.R. added. When River Road provided Johnnie with stability, he thrived. When the group home closed, Johnnie started down a precipitous course that ended in tragedy at the Johnsons'.

J.R. testified that when Johnnie first moved into the Johnsons' home,

Johnnie told him: "I'm not going to do well and I don't care anymore because no one cares about me." J.R. said later that he intended this testimony to win sympathy for Johnnie, but it sounded ominous instead.

Johnnie had rejected or shied away from offers of psychological help before, J.R. said, but he was ready to accept therapy now. If Johnnie could just receive some treatment, some help, he would benefit greatly, J.R. promised. "Johnnie is a very feeling person. I want everyone to be aware that he is a very feeling person," he almost pleaded. "We were very close . . . He is a good young man."

Under Bainbridge's cross-examination, however, J.R.'s efforts to help Johnnie became blurred. Had J.R. done everything he could to help Johnnie? Yes, he had. You've helped many other kids who also were scarred by horrific childhoods, but none have been accused of a crime so violent as this one, she pointed out. And couldn't Johnnie's emphasis on loyalty be misplaced? Couldn't he show loyalty to a gang?

"He could," J.R. replied. "But to be honest with you, I think the loyalty . . . would apply more to a specific individual in a gang rather than the gang itself." All in all, it did not sound good.

J.R. hurt for days—and even years—after his testimony. He had been honest. The avenues to the good truths about Johnnie did not open on the stand that day, he says. He replays his testimony often even today. He had answered the questions put to him as fairly as he could. Only they were just part of an entire truth that wasn't heard that day, he says, painfully shaking his head above his broad, hunched shoulders.

III

Ed Pendleton was no longer serving as a parole officer for Toledo's juvenile criminals when he was called to the stand. He had been promoted to lead case manager and a representative to a large area of northwestern Ohio. He had met Johnnie two years earlier, after Johnnie had slugged the bus driver in the face and was committed to the Ohio Department of Youth Services. When Johnnie was in that detention facility, he had been "meeting expectations," Pendleton testified, and even avoided trouble in some instances. His last report card at River Road carried all A's except for one B, Pendleton pointed out. He had been reported for behavioral infractions five times, but they were minor complaints, Pendleton said, like horseplay and talking during quiet time. Even after

River Road closed, Johnnie did pretty well. For the first month and a half, he lived in a foster home where he grew so comfortable that he asked his foster mother to adopt him.

But soon after, Pendleton acknowledged, Johnnie's behavior nose-dived when news of his father's child abuse trial hit the papers and the streets. He ran away, acted unruly, and violated his parole four times. He went to jail for a month, and then violated his parole again.

Pendleton told the court he tried other ways to bring Johnnie under control. One was to enroll him in an "Alternatives to Violence" counsel-ing program. Another was to arrange for him to visit a state psycho-logist regularly; yet another was to sign Johnnie up for anger management therapy. But because the Johnsons lived outside Toledo, it was difficult for Johnnie to attend. He could have taken a bus, but John-nie lacked the motivation. When he did see the psychologist, his progress was "very inconsistent," Pendleton admitted.

"Is it true that you wanted Johnnie returned to [the Department of Youth Services] . . . that you believed that he needed further institu-tionalization?" Popil asked.

"Yes," Pendleton answered.

"Why wasn't it done?" Popil asked.

Pendleton gave a haunting answer. Tamara Cusack, Johnnie's case-worker, had failed to attend the meeting that had been called to discuss putting Johnnie back in the detention center. If this meeting had gone as planned, if Johnnie's caseworker had simply showed up, Johnnie would have been locked up in an institution at the time he killed Mrs. Johnson. But like traffic court, when a ticket for speeding is dismissed because an officer fails to appear, Pendleton's request to put Johnnie in a detention center was not acted upon because Cusack was not present.

Popil concluded by asking Pendleton if he felt Johnnie stood a chance at rehabilitation within the juvenile system. Pendleton sidestepped the question twice. Instead, he listed the services that Johnnie would receive if he remained in juvenile custody for the next five years, until he turned twenty-one, when he would be released. "Whether he will fol-low through on them, I don't know," Pendleton said finally. "I can't make that judgment call."

The implied answer was no. Neither J.R. nor Pendleton could stand up unequivocally on Johnnie's behalf. None of his character wit-

nesses—the closest he had to allies and mentors—could do so. None
had anticipated that Johnnie could murder anyone, and none could
explain why he had done so. Without an explanation, they could not
provide reassurance that Johnnie could be rehabilitated.

"At this time, do you feel he is a danger to our community?" Bainbridge asked Pendleton.

Pendleton paused. He knew he had told Johnnie that if he confessed,
he would receive help. But he also knew he had sworn to tell the truth.

"Yes."

III

Johnnie's first probation officer, John Thomas, was the next witness.
Thomas had liked Johnnie, almost too much, he said, in the two years he
had supervised Johnnie's case. Johnnie was eleven years old when they
met, and his behavior was not always good, Thomas testified. He could
be unruly at school but didn't cause any "major" problems.

Johnnie behaved best, without a doubt, when J.R. counseled him,
Thomas said. "Johnnie and J.R. were very, very close. At a point, I think I
fell in there with J.R. and I pulled myself back . . . Johnnie is the type of
person that will pull you in . . . He accepts you and he is so likable that
you have to really be careful and realize where you're at with him."

When it was her turn to examine the witness, Bainbridge had no
questions. Thomas had already largely negated J.R.'s favorable testimony by suggesting that J.R. was not objective about Johnnie.

III

Tamara Cusack, Johnnie's caseworker for four years, next took the
stand. She described how Lucas County Children Services had hoped
someone would adopt Johnnie when he came into their custody at age
eight. But after four years of shuffling him among temporary homes,
they decided he had little chance for adoption and made plans to keep
him in long-term foster care, a category designed "for a teenager or for
a child that is not adoptable," Cusack said. Johnnie was to remain in foster care until he turned eighteen, when he would be on his own.

Cusack echoed much of the other witnesses' testimony but could
recount few specific details. She said Johnnie's progress had been

"inconsistent" but that he had done well when he received consistent therapy or lived in a strict, institutional setting.

Popil, Johnnie's attorney, then asked Cusack about a meeting in which she, Pendleton, and J.R. agreed that Johnnie should receive anger management counseling. Popil wanted to know: Did any of the counseling ever take place?

"I don't recall," Cusack replied. Convenient to her testimony, she did not bring Johnnie's files, which included her case notes that would contain the precise answers. "I know that that was something that Parole was going to set up."

This was the first of several finger-pointing episodes that occurred during the hearing. As Johnnie's caseworker, Cusack was at least partly responsible for making sure that Johnnie received counseling for his anger—an increasingly apparent problem. Instead, the failure to get Johnnie help in this instance was one of several times in which Johnnie fell between the cracks of overlapping bureaucracies that failed to coordinate with each other or to take charge of a situation.

Cusack applied for an even more structured, stricter foster care setting, an institutional placement, for Johnnie. He was rejected. She tried to enroll him in another group home, Parmadale. Again, he was rejected.

Popil asked why. Had the Parmadale staff asked him about his abusive past, about things "he still is in a shell about"?

Cusack blamed their concerns on his "poor impulse control," and his "anger management." But in fact, the group home's written explanation, which was provided to CSB, stated that Johnnie had refused to discuss the abuse he had suffered and that, therefore, they did not think they could help him. Cusack instead cited more damning reasons— anger and impulse control—for his rejection.

Popil then asked about a hearing for Johnnie three months before the murder, when he had violated probation by not attending school and missed curfew in his foster home. Cusack said she would have to refer to the hearing in her case notes to answer but testified that she had not attended the meeting. One of her coworkers had attended on her behalf.

Popil moved on to Cusack's next case note entry, when Johnnie told Cusack he was comfortable living with the Johnsons and did not want to be moved to a group home. If he were moved, Johnnie threatened he'd "mess up."

In Johnnie's case record files, which Children Services was reluctant to surrender, even to the court, the Johnsons asked three times that Johnnie be removed from their home. Their last call came the morning of the murder. Cusack said she was not aware of those requests, although one of the notes was written in her hand and signed by her.

Does Johnnie generally react in an angry manner when he hears news about his parents? Popil asked.

"He's not necessarily angry all of the time," Cusack told the court. "I know he has a hard time sometimes hearing that information."

Seeking to show that Johnnie was receptive to rehabilitation, Popil asked if his detention in the Department of Youth Services had made a difference. At first, Cusack testified, she noticed that Johnnie's attitude had became more promising. His self-esteem had improved. It was the most helpful response Popil had been able to wring out of Cusack during her measured and careful testimony. He tried for more.

"Do you, as an individual, as a caseworker, as a social worker, have hope for Johnnie that he will succeed?"

But Cusack gave little. "I hope he can succeed, yes," she said.

III

For the prosecution, Bainbridge easily turned Cusack's testimony to her advantage. She pointed out that even when Johnnie "did well" he still caused serious problems and was hard to control. In one institution, he had been restrained twelve times for assaulting other children, assaulting staff, threatening staff and peers, attempting to cut himself with a knife, cutting himself with a spoon, biting staff, and choking himself.

Finally, Bainbridge revisited Cusack's halfhearted statement in which she said she hoped Johnnie would succeed.

"You said that you have hope for Johnnie. Don't you have hope for every child that you see?" Bainbridge asked.

"Yes, I do," Cusack said, undercutting Johnnie's defense.

III

Popil tried to repair some of the damage from Cusack's testimony by swearing in Donna Lewis. Lewis was also a social worker for Children

Services. But while Cusack's job as Johnnie's caseworker was to focus on what was best for Johnnie alone, Lewis's job as the Jordan family caseworker was to consider the interests of the Jordan family as a whole—Johnnie and all his siblings.

Johnnie's rejection from the first institution Children Services applied to after the River Road Group Home closed left him in a critical emotional state, Lewis testified. He needed to live in a closely supervised group home or institution, or else he might fall apart. But "another caseworker," she said, alluding to Cusack, thought differently, arguing that in a foster care home rather than a group home Johnnie might bond with a parentlike figure and get the one-on-one relationship he desperately needed.

Under questioning from Popil, Lewis reviewed her written file on Johnnie, which she had brought with her to the trial. Three months before the murder, "Johnnie's emotional state is grave," she had noted. Two months before the murder, Pendleton, Johnnie's probation officer, feared that the situation was spiraling out of control and recommended that Johnnie be returned to juvenile jail. Nine days before the murder, Johnnie had been accepted in a group home, but was unable to move in because the Children Services bureaucracy had not sent his school records to the home and it refused to accept him until it received them. On the morning Johnnie murdered, Lewis testified that her supervisor got a call from the Johnson home. Johnnie was "blowing" his placement there, her notes recorded. CS needed to "firm up" the group home plans, presumably meaning to provide the required paperwork.

This was not the testimony Popil hoped for, so he changed direction.

"Tell me some good things about Johnnie," Popil invited, almost in desperation.

He was artistic, Lewis replied, and had a "wonderful, outgoing personality. If he respects you, he will be your friend, and he has been very truthful to me. I have never caught him in a lie . . ." He has wonderful manners, she added, when he chose to use them.

Johnnie smiled at Lewis, the first time he displayed any emotion during the hearing.

"Look at him smile," she responded from the stand. "And he has a beautiful smile. I guess that's the clincher."

But when Popil tried to encourage Lewis further, she balked.

Could he get the services and treatment he needed in the juvenile system?

"I can't answer that," Lewis said.

"What is your hope for him?"

"To get the help he needs and become a well-rounded citizen."

"Do you think he can be a well-rounded citizen?"

"Yes."

"Do you think he can do that before he turns twenty-one?"

Lewis paused.

"No," she admitted quietly, looking down at her lap.

With that, Bainbridge had no need to cross-examine the witness.

III

In his closing statement, Popil focused on the psychological evaluation that everyone knew would be the key to the judge's decision. Johnnie was functioning as a twelve-year-old, he pointed out. He did not have the intellectual capacity or reasoning of an adult. He was still developing. He still had a chance.

Popil asked the judge to give fifteen-year-old Johnnie the opportunity to be rehabilitated in the juvenile system. "I don't believe he should be sharing the same situation as his father . . . I don't believe he should be in the same type of institution as his father," Popil ended his defense lamely.

Bainbridge's rebuttal was short. Everyone had gone the extra mile for Johnnie, but he had only failed them in return. It was "totally unrealistic to think that five years from now he is going to be safe to release to this community. The crime he committed is horrific. And he is a danger to our society, and we owe it to our society to protect it from this man," she concluded.

III

Judge Ray's decision was prompt. Johnnie Jordan would be tried for murder in adult court, he ruled the next day. Ray found that Johnnie had exhausted the rehabilitative services available to him as a juvenile, and that he would still pose a threat to the community after he turned twenty-one, when the juvenile system would set him free. The judge said his primary concern was the safety of the community, no matter how much sympathy he may have felt for Johnnie.

Ray left the courthouse that day with a heavy heart. We need to protect our kids better than we do, he thought; this one, we lost.

III

A day after Judge Ray's ruling, Johnnie received a letter from Lucas County Children Services. Because the judge had decreed that Johnnie was no longer a juvenile, it stated, he was no longer under the agency's guardianship. The letter was filled with stilted legal jargon, but after a few hours, Johnnie figured it out. He was no longer a kid in the eyes of the law, so he did not need parents or social workers to take care of him. There would be no more visits or any contact with Donna Lewis or Tamara Cusack or anyone from Children Services.

For the first time, he knew he was completely alone.

III

Two years later, Johnnie doesn't remember his hearing in the juvenile court. He remembers only that he was "bound over" to adult court. He doesn't remember the name of his attorney, or the prosecutor. He remembers only that the judge was an old man with white hair. Did he respect the judge?

"Nooo," Johnnie says, flipping his head like a defiant horse.

Did the judge make the right decision? Was it fair that he be tried as an adult?

Johnnie is quiet for a moment. His head droops a bit, and so does his voice.

"Yeah," he says in a low voice. "It was fair."

Why?

"I don't know why," he says, annoyed. "It just was. I don't know. I'm the same person now that I was when I was fifteen."

But he's not. He is harder now; meaner, colder, and more demanding.

"Have you talked to Ronnie?" he asks, referring to Ron Wingate, his attorney in adult court. "When you talk to him, tell him I want him to come up and visit me on my birthday."

Johnnie would turn eighteen in ten days. He was restless. He spent more time in solitary confinement than on his regular cellblock because he continued to break rules.

"I want to go to a different camp," he said, meaning a prison. "It don't matter which one. I'm bored here."

While most young prisoners on his block dreaded their eighteenth birthday, when they would be taken from their juvenile block and placed with the adult prison population, Johnnie seemed not to care.[3]

He would go anywhere to get away from where he was now except, he said, to the beginning, where it all began. Even if it meant Lucasville, the strictest prison in Ohio, Johnnie wanted out. There was nothing to keep him anywhere—not love, friendship, or hope.

3. Ohio is one of the few states that segregates juveniles from the adult population in adult prisons. In the juvenile block, young convicts have the opportunity to go to school and earn a GED. They are also safer. At eighteen, however, they are mixed in with the adult population, where they are vulnerable to sexual exploitation and physical brutalization. Not only children's advocates favor separation, so does the American Correctional Association, a professional organization representing prison staff. According to the ACA, juvenile prisoners need to be handled differently from adults. They are more mercurial and have more special needs, such as increased exercise. Put in adult facilities, the ACA argues, juveniles come out worse criminals.

14

Three years after the murder, Johnnie is the only person who believes he is the same person he was when he was fifteen. Three years of prison have been full of ugly experiences, with predictable consequences. People outside have moved forward in time, on with their lives, and away from him as they would from a dreadful incident in their past. Many of those who had been closest to Johnnie now believe they never really knew him because they never saw in Johnnie the brutal murderer, the monster, as he is now defined. Many have shifted their focus to other children in crisis, children who still have a chance. Johnnie recognizes the distance they have put between themselves and him, and he hates it. It makes him mad. He still feels entitled to their care and attention.

Johnnie also realizes now that no one ever really hoped, let alone intended, to rehabilitate him after the murder. He was not aware of this when he awaited trial, during the trial, or even at the sentencing. He has come to recognize that he has no future, or at least nothing to be hopeful about. He has hardened and slipped away. The changes in him seemed to occur suddenly, but in retrospect, over the course of our years of conversations, they have been gradual. His behavior is unpredictable. He can be a child one minute, only to turn into an angry adult the next moment, a furious inmate, a person who presumes that he will soon be dead to the outside world. He says that he knows he will probably kill again, that murder is still inside of him. Sometimes it worries him that he will take another life. Often he doesn't care.

While deadened, Johnnie is not yet dead. Compassion still flickers in him. He worries about his baby daughter, conceived the night of the murder, and his brothers and sisters, even his parents. Sometimes there is concern for me. "You have that little puppy dog in your voice," he says after a particularly disturbing conversation about his life. "You okay?" he asks with a mixture of annoyance and concern.

But these moments have grown increasingly rare. His eruptions occur more often now, more directly in response to an event or a collision of unknown feelings inside of himself. He seldom holds his rage inside, as he did when he was younger. He is provoked more easily, sometimes by my questions pressed too hard and too often, or the rudeness of a guard, or something deep in his mind. His eyes darken, his forehead creases to a scowl. He looks away with folded arms, and he spits out his standard retort: "I don't care!"

"Look at me," I say, trying to head off the rising rage, bracing against the fury in his eyes, which are no longer masked by confusion. His face is more open and honest than usual. He is more alive, more vibrant, and whether by fascination or terror, I cannot look away. I find I have glimpsed something so authentic in him, something impossible to forget. When he does glance at me, I go on.

"Johnnie, it's just one thing. You're feeling it just for this moment. It will pass. Let it go. Don't let it get you so angry you hit something. Don't let it control you."

He tries to talk about something positive, to divert his fury, but it's a temporary fix. The fury returns later, when he's alone, and he strikes the wall with his fist, or another inmate's face. Sometimes his fury breaks almost immediately after our conversation, and he will strike an unsuspecting guard or inmate on his way out of the interview room or just feet from the phone when he hangs up. The violence makes Johnnie feel free. He may express remorse later, but less and less often.

It was during the months when he sat in juvenile jail, as a teenager awaiting trial, that Johnnie began to change. He became known and defined as a murderer. He did not understand at first why other inmates looked at him differently. They backed away. He wanted them to get to know him, but they turned from him.

"How do they look at you?" I ask.

"Like I'm a murderer or something," he says, shifting in his orange plastic prison chair. He is still uneasy with that description, believing it does not fit him. "It made me feel bad 'cuz I know I did wrong and I sorry they look at me the way they do. A lot of people scared of me. I don't like that."

His first night in juvenile jail after the arrest, he told everyone—guards, staff, and other incarcerated children—that he was accused of murder but innocent. He lied, he admits now. He doesn't know why exactly, but he thinks he wanted to hide from his crime. He also has come to realize that in his child's mind, he believed he could change how he felt by what he said. He thought he could even change the truth to the outside world. But night after night, in grey flickering television segments, the local news told the reality of what had happened to all those around him. He was made to be a liar and a murderer. He wanted to stop the programs, as though stopping them would erase all that had happened.

When word of his confession spread through the jail hall, Johnnie denied the truth even more vigorously. It was months before he realized that he could not stop people from knowing the truth about that night, and that he forever would be defined by the murder. Still, he assumed he would be locked up for six years, at most, until the age of twenty-one, when the juvenile justice system would have to free him to start a new life as an adult. He had no family or religion to help him. He had no therapist or counselor.

But over the next year, as he progressed through the justice system, he would change even more.

15

When kids get "shipped across the street" to adult court, says Joe Scalzo, who specializes in juvenile law and is one of only five Toledo attorneys certified to represent children and teenagers in death penalty cases, "they can kiss their butts good-bye. Adult court will show no mercy. They figure if the juvenile court washes their hands of the case, the kid must really be bad. They'll throw the book at them. I just stand there." He shrugs at his imminent defeat in an inevitable process. "Court finds probable cause, then a mandatory transfer [to adult court], then it's all over." A young person's level of intellectual functioning has no bearing or influence on a child's transfer into the adult system or the subsequent punishment. Rehabilitation is not even part of the question.

In 1999, Scalzo represented five murderers in Toledo. All of them were about fifteen years old, Johnnie's age.

"Best I got was fifteen years to life." Scalzo plows through the facts briskly, with the high-octane energy of a determined lawyer. "It tears me up. These kids are going to die in prison. There is nothing you can do as their attorney—just stand there and watch." He pauses briefly. "Now they don't even have to show probable cause that the kid committed the crime to bind him over to the adult system."[1]

Since Johnnie's case, and in response to his crime, the Ohio legislature has passed a law mandating that all youths fifteen years and older who are charged with murder must be tried as adults. Lawmakers also stipulated that at a judge's discretion, children of any age may be tried as adults. The judge no longer must find probable cause, or that the child could not be rehabilitated within the juvenile system.

---

1. The number of juveniles in adult prisons doubled in twelve years, from 3,400 in 1985 to 7,400 in 1997, and has continued to steeply increase. Today one in ten juveniles incarcerated is serving time in adult jails and prisons rather than juvenile facilities.

The laws do not make good sense to Scalzo, but he understands them. Kids are getting tougher and seemingly crueler, and in response, public outrage has forced its way into the driver's seat of the justice system. Scalzo sees exactly what is fueling the popular sentiment almost every day. Since Johnnie's trial and the passage of the new laws, he and other lawyers have represented more, not fewer, juvenile killers.

Moreover, while acknowledging FBI and police statistics that report a decline in the total number of juvenile crimes nationwide, Scalzo sees, as the statistics also show, that the types of crimes committed by children have become meaner, more shocking, and often more bloody. Their crimes hold less and less reason. As abhorrent as Scalzo feels it is to throw away a child, regardless of age, intellect, sanity, or life conditions, he admits he is seeing a newer, more brutal criminal behind the stony eyes of these children. They may squeeze enough water to shed a tear before sentencing in an effort to win sympathy, but Scalzo finds them dead. Dead to true remorse. Dead to life. They scare the public, for good reason, so the community seeks to dispose of them quickly and irretrievably. They are tossed to an adult judicial system not designed for them, and ultimately into the predatory world of grown-up prisons. They do not realize until they enter that world that their life after sentencing can be crueler than death. There is so much they don't understand, Scalzo says, and so many chances adults get with age and reason which children were never given. Their development has been stunted.

They are still kids without an adult's capacity to reason, Scalzo argues. They can't vote, join the military, or drive. If an accused juvenile criminal is found to have the mental capacity of a six-year-old, that child can still be tried as an adult. In contrast, an adult who is tested and found to have the mental capacity of a six-year-old cannot face trial. It seems bizarre to Scalzo, even Dickensian, to effectively end the life of an eleven-, twelve-, thirteen-, fourteen-, or fifteen-year-old because the cruelty inflicted on the child in the past later manifests itself in momentary rage.

For a lawyer, there is little to gain by taking a Johnnie Jordan or any other child killer as a client. Nothing, in fact. If you are lucky, Scalzo says, the case leaves you drained and empty after hours of low-paying, fruitless work that will not mitigate the sentence. If you are unlucky, the tragedy lingers as a personal failure or profound disillusionment with a legal system to which you have committed most of your waking hours. The system does not do justice in your case, or in the next case like it because, the truth is, there is no justice to be done in such cases. At least not in the system as it stands today, he says. Even the Lucas County prosecutor, his proclaimed nemesis, agrees. It is, perhaps, the only thing they agree on.

III

"There are no winners," explains Julia Bates, the lean, blond, and charismatic lead prosecutor in Johnnie's adult court case, who is known for her tough approach in treating juvenile criminals as adults. Not because she believes in this new aspect of criminal law, she says, but because these young people have committed the ultimate crimes. "That's what happens when you do adult crime," she says with a heavy shrug.

A forty-five-year-old attorney with a son Johnnie's age and a husband who is an elected Lucas County judge, Bates long had the ambition to run for: Lucas County Prosecutor. After graduating from the University of Toledo law school, she worked as a legal intern for the Children Services Board and for the juvenile court prosecutor, and then, for two decades, she served as one of several county assistant prosecutors. She has no experience as a defense attorney. But that is an experience that she says she does not want. As Lucas County Prosecutor, she feels confident that she "wears the white hat" most of the time. Her boss, who was elected five times and who wanted to see her succeed him, assigned her Johnnie's case in the middle of her election campaign to gain her added publicity and approval. Bates had to scramble. It was high-profile. The community's eyes were on her, and emotions ran high. It was a sure win. But if she lost, it would cost her career. The voters wanted blood.

"They don't see the whole picture," Bates says of the public. "They see the violence, the danger. This is terrible, this is wrong. The community wants the death penalty. How come this kid didn't get the death penalty? We don't give the death penalty to anyone that's a minor, folks. That's the law of the state. But that was the situation.

"I saw it from a different perspective. I saw him up close," she says of Johnnie. "I saw him in court. I saw him there, breathing. He was crying. I saw him even when the media didn't. It was very sad in a sense, because he didn't have anyone there with him. You know? That catches my heart, because you think, what chance does this kid have? But my job is helping the victims and protecting the public. Doing what you have to do. This kid did a horrible thing and we can't let it happen again."

She dismisses the notion that prosecutors are always out for blood. "Everyone thinks that we're like, 'Alright, we're putting another one of them in jail! Alright, we got another one of them the death penalty!' But it's not like that," she says. "Sometimes, like in this case, you do your job because you have to."

Her public persona as a tough prosecutor clashes with a softer side: Sunday school teacher, gourmet cook, gardener. In her fresh, light-filled office on the second floor of the Lucas County Courthouse, pictures of her children and stepchildren fall in line with a neat arrangement of white irises in a solid crystal vase on her grand desk. Her pantsuit moves sharply and gracefully with her quick but unhurried step and firm handshake. She is direct and confident, but she is not totally at ease with her work on these juvenile crimes. She goes for the jugular, though part of her wonders at the larger picture, where real truth and justice lie.

"There are monstrous crimes," she says. "I'm somewhat of a religious person. I guess I feel that good people can do bad things, and that doesn't necessarily mean that they are an evil person, that they are a devil, that they are totally without redeeming value. Because good people do bad things. I've argued for the death penalty, but that doesn't mean the person on trial isn't worthy of some forgiveness. There is still something there. They're still human."

Bates not only saw that Johnnie was human; she saw the victim in Johnnie.

"Johnnie is still a kid. Absolutely he was a victim," she says. "Because he got born. What choice did he have where he came to? Where he lived? How he was treated? None. My son was lucky enough to come into my womb. He had medical care, friends, opportunities. Johnnie didn't have any of that. My children came to people who loved them. Johnnie Jordan did not have that."

And what about the system that judged Johnnie? Is it fair to try a child in an adult court? Where should the line be drawn on age and reason?

"That's a really hard question," Bates says. "This is all we got. It's a balancing, that's how I rationalize it. All of us are balanced against him. All of us have a right to be safe here. Okay, we've given up a bit in return for our safety in this case, and in other juvenile cases."

Whether it is fair takes second place to the crisis at hand. She looks away, down into the dark hardwood of her shining desk. "The caliber of juvenile criminals is going up," she says. "That's what's really scary to me. The cases we have are more scary. More violent. More dangerous. The kids here have a wanton disregard for life. They can take a gun, shoot you, with no idea of the repercussions. No value of life. This is rage. It's not kids drag racing or skipping school like it used to be. That was excitement, passion almost. This is rage. This is hate. What do we do? We haven't an alternative right now." She looks up again, beyond the photographs of her family and the white irises.

"The sad part is that Johnnie Jordan is just one kid. He's gone now. He's out of my life because he's in prison and his case is off my desk. The tragedy is there's a whole bunch of Johnnie Jordans just out there waiting. Next week, we're going to sentence a kid who shot a lady in the back of the head to see what it felt like. Johnnie's got a thirteen-year-old brother just as bad, but he's too young to certify as an adult, so he'll be in the juvenile system. But he's another one that's just another ticking time bomb. He'll wait there until he kills somebody."

There is no glory in the war on juvenile crime, she says. Everyone is left with a little fragment of themselves broken, as though something ended not quite right, not quite solved. "These cases have no winners," she says. "Johnnie's sure didn't. Everyone does their job well, and we all fail."

III

Attorney Ron Wingate knew all this, or predicted it, when he was asked by Don Cameron, Johnnie's court-appointed lawyer, to be his co-counsel in adult court. It was not a case Wingate wanted. He would have liked to say no.

Cameron is a partner in the successful law firm Konop & Cameron, situated on Michigan Avenue, practically next door to the juvenile court building and across the street from the adult court. From his large windows, Toledo's white marble, domed courthouse looks as spectacular as its American flag whipping in the blue sky. A judge chose Cameron to defend Johnnie, but after Cameron selected Wingate as co-counsel, he recused himself from the case because of a conflict of interest. His law partner, Alan Konop, had agreed to represent Mr. Johnson in a civil lawsuit against the Lucas County Children Services Board. Wingate became Johnnie's lead counsel.

Wingate's office is down the street from Konop & Cameron and the courthouse, in the law firm of two prominent senior African-American attorneys, one of whom was a Toledo city councilman before he was appointed a Toledo municipal judge. Wingate speaks highly of the partners in his firm. They hired him after a scandal which nearly ended his career.

The local papers called it "the Afscam scandal." A grand jury indicted several of Toledo's attorneys for neglecting to return affidavits to the Clerk of Courts office. About twenty lawyers were publicly reprimanded, fined, or suspended. Wingate received the second-harshest punishment—deservedly so, he says, because he had an unusually high number of missing affidavits; the bar association suspended his law license for eight months for improper conduct, obstruction of justice, and "unethical violation." He would be allowed to resume practicing law, the bar ruled, only if he joined a firm that gave him structure and oversight.

Despite the lapse, which he is forthright in discussing, Wingate has earned the respect of colleagues as well as the *Toledo City Paper*, an alternative newspaper, which rated him one of the city's ten best defense lawyers. "He is one of the few attorneys around here who still has heart in his case," says another attorney. "Maybe because he's an underdog who got a second chance. Maybe because he's one of the few African-Americans with stature here. He's had to work hard for that. He won't talk about it, but it's been hard for a black man around here."

Wingate was born in North Carolina to parents who worked in a tobacco factory. He was their eldest child, the first in the family to go to college—Kent State, on a scholarship. Playing basketball one day in high school, he made a pact with his cousin and his best friend that they would all become lawyers and open a firm together. Wingate alone became an attorney. His friend is now a detective in Detroit; his cousin is head of security at a JC Penney store in Wisconsin.

Wingate is tall and fit at fifty-five, with sideburns that have begun to grey, hair lightly slicked back, and a faint, stylish mustache. His dark shirt, rich bright tie, British penny cuff links, and suspenders stand out among the mostly white, conservative courthouse crowd. Maintaining his style has not always been easy in this environment. One judge labeled him as the "peacock of Lucas County Courthouse," because of his flair for dressing. He takes the comment in stride, as he takes almost everything, flashing a great smile that even grumpy courthouse clerks find contagious. He has toned down his dress some, he admits, after another judge called him a "Harlem sissy" when he wore a brick-red Hugo Boss suit to court. His face hardens slightly at the memory.

Some judges have also criticized his habitual tardiness, ruefully applying "Wingate Mountain time" to his estimated time of arrival. He has donated a great deal of money to the Cherry Street Mission and shelters for abused women, not out of benevolence, but for his tardiness. One judge orders him to pay $10 for every minute he is late to court to the charity of his choice. Another threatened to order him to wear a polyester suit. He will not be late to her court again, he promises, shaking his head.

As we walk briskly along a polished courthouse hallway, he swoops down to pick up a four-year-old girl who has taken a tumble while playing with her brother. On one knee, he dusts the girl's pink and white dress down while playfully inquiring whether she thinks she has a concussion or needs surgery. She nods with a serious expression, her quivering lip threatening tears.

"Did he push you?" he asks her, pointing to her brother. "He pushed you, didn't he? He did. Here's my card," he says, taking his business card from a soft leather wallet. "Call me. We can get him on personal injury."

The stunned girl nods again. Focusing on the sharp white card he's handed her, she wipes the tears from her cheeks and smiles in response to Wingate's reassuring grin.

Now almost late for court, he glides into the prosecutor's office to pursue a deal in a case in which his client is clearly guilty, or in Wingate's words, "could be in a better situation."

III

Wingate can be caught whizzing around the office, and back and forth to the courthouse, working off intense energy by chewing bright blue gum. His work week begins around noon on Saturday and ends on Friday evening. As a single parent of a teenage son and daughter, he worries about sacrificing time with his kids in exchange for professional success. He gets anxious when his son accepts collect calls from clients in prison, calls that are intended for him. Johnnie still calls often, and for a while, Wingate's son found it cool to brag to his friends that he knew the infamous Johnnie Jordan.

"You do not know Johnnie Jordan!" Wingate once yelled when he overheard his son boasting that he was friends with the murderer. "You are nothing like him."

He was puzzled by his outburst afterward. He had allowed Johnnie to chat with his son on occasion. Johnnie needed it. And knowing Johnnie as he did, Wingate would have allowed his son to play with Johnnie when they were kids. That would be a different matter now, with so much prison in Johnnie's blood. But his son's comment shook him. His son had touched on something that had drawn Wingate deeply into the case to begin with. But for the grace of God, Wingate once thought while looking at Johnnie, this could be my son.

It is difficult for any defense attorney to explain to people how they can bring themselves to represent criminals. In the face of crimes that stir up passion and outrage, the reasons seem inexplicable or wanting. Wingate himself has been attacked from all sides and in many different ways. There was the time he represented a minister who allegedly had routinely exposed himself to motorists on a busy highway. Wingate became unpopular when he won the case on a technicality because motorists had phoned a local talk show to air their grievances and in the process, it seems, obstructed justice. Soon after, while a guest lecturer at the University of Toledo, he was challenged by a student who questioned how he could be a party to defending black-on-black crime. "Well, I suppose if they murder a white person, that's okay," Wingate argued sarcastically. And then there was the occasion when a grandmother assaulted him from behind with her bag in the courthouse after he defended a man she wanted put away.

His reasons for defending criminals are both complex and gritty. The law is geared more toward setting the accused free than it is toward putting the innocent away, he says. His clients usually cannot afford the most expensive, highly skilled, defense lawyers, but he thinks it is important to give them the same quality defense, regardless of what their money can buy. He handles two or three death penalty cases a year. He does not approve of the death penalty, not because he is opposed to capital punishment itself, but because the practice is not racially or economically neutral.

He is more concerned with society's increasing hostility toward people accused of crimes and the lawyers who defend them. "There are defendants whom I have represented whose crimes have disgusted me. I don't like them in any form or fashion," he told the *City Paper*. But he argued that they still deserve the best defense the law allows.

He defends his clients with a passion that has resulted in contempt-of-court charges three times and landed him in jail once. He deeply resents judges who speak to his clients as if, he says, "they are the scum of the earth." Once, in a neighboring town, he became incensed by a judge's demeaning attitude toward his client and made a questionable decision to fire back. When he challenged the judge, he was held in contempt.

"Fine, but you have to have a trial," Wingate said defiantly.

"I will, Mr. Wingate," the judge told him. "I'll set the date for tomorrow. And since you are from out of town, and I have reason to believe you won't show up, I'm going to hold you in a jail overnight."

When he talks about those hours he waited behind bars, Wingate concedes he was young and out of line, but falls short of saying he was wrong. Everyone deserves the dignity of a fair and respectful trial, he says, regardless of where they come from. But even Wingate has limits. There are two types of cases he will not defend, he half-jokes: "Those involving crimes against children, because I have children. And those against the elderly, because I hope to become elderly one day." At first, the court gave him no choice but to make an exception for Johnnie Jordan. Later he took up the case with unusual dedication and vigor, because, he says, he began to see more clearly a quiet, systematic crime against a child no one wanted to recognize in addition to the crime against the Johnsons.

In all of his experience as a trial lawyer, Johnnie's case was like no other for Wingate. Its effect was profound. He gave Johnnie more than he had ever given any client, and he lost more of himself than any case had taken from him. What it has left him with, what it has made him now, is something that he cannot put into words.

"I don't think I can ever take another case that will compare to Johnnie Jordan," he says, suddenly looking like he has weathered, rather than glided through, his years. "I hope I will never have to. No matter what, it's etched in stone."

16

Johnnie's first impressions of his lawyers, Ron Wingate and Wingate's choice of co-counsel, Rick Meyer, did not go much beyond noticing that one was black, the other white. Word on the street was that it was better for a black man to have a white lawyer because whites had a better "in" with the judge and prosecutors, who were almost all white, and could negotiate better deals for their clients. Johnnie didn't care much. He was screwed anyway, he thought, having to rely on court-appointed lawyers. Judges go easier on defendants who have money for expensive lawyers; if you look poor and black, your life isn't worth much in the court's eyes, he assumed.[1]

From the way people were acting toward him, as if he were untouchable, Johnnie figured he was going to get time. He believed he deserved to be punished—some. He just hoped he would get less than the six years he had left in the juvenile system. Though his attorneys tried to explain the serious punishment he could now face, Johnnie did not real-

---

1. Johnnie's view is well founded, according to *And Justice for Some* (April, 2000. Youth Law Center), a report funded in large part by the U.S. Justice Department and prepared by the National Council on Crime and Delinquency, a juvenile crime think tank. The report finds a great deal of racial and economic bias built into the juvenile justice system. Three in four teanagers and children imprisoned with adults are black, though minorities make up only 15 percent of the population for their age group. Of the juveniles sent to adult courts, 40 percent are black. A full 58 percent of teenagers and children sent to adult prisons are also black. The bias filters down to lesser crimes as well. When charged with the same crime, black children and teenagers with no prior prison record are six times more likely to be locked up than their white peers in the same category. For those charged with violent crimes and who have not been in prison before, black teenagers are nine times more likely to be sentenced to juvenile prison. While critics of the report suggest the numbers could simply mean black teenagers are commiting more crimes or more serious crimes, researchers maintain that many policies discriminate against low-income children and teenagers who are minority, from single-parent homes, or in foster care. The findings were based on national and state statistics compiled by the FBI, the Office of Juvenile Justice and Delinquency Prevention, and the Census Bureau.

ize that since the juvenile court found him fit to be tried as an adult, he could spend the rest of his life behind bars or even face death in an electric chair. His crime did not seem bad enough for all that. It was just one mistake. That's all.

Johnnie did not absorb many of his attorneys' words during their visits to his jail cell. He cooperated, but he didn't offer much in the way of help. Nor did Children's Services, the agency that had been Johnnie's official guardian. Wingate knew nothing about Johnnie's siblings and their lives in foster care, but he had heard courthouse murmurs about Johnnie Jordan Sr.'s sordid abuse trial. Johnnie Jr. never mentioned that he was abused in foster care or by his parents, nor did caseworkers offer this information to his lawyers. Johnnie continued to maintain that he had had a normal past aside from being placed in foster care.

Johnnie did not try to help plan his defense. He had never participated in decisions about his future. It was his lawyers' job to figure things out and do them, he thought. As his case moved forward, and his attorneys repeated the dire possibilities, Johnnie stubbornly remained disconnected and disinterested, even bored, during his lawyers' visits. He scribbled or drew obscene figures on the legal papers before him. At the same time, he was happy that they visited at all because he felt lonely and cut off from the world outside. The lawyers seemed okay, a little distant, like most adults assigned to oversee his childhood. The government paid them to take care of him.

Both Wingate and Meyer had experience with young offenders like Johnnie. In terms of street smarts, these kids have degrees in it, Wingate would say. They are so disillusioned with life, they don't care whether they are free or in jail. You expect nothing from them for their defense. You cannot anticipate their reactions based on how you or anyone you know would react. Often, they will even resist or work at cross-purposes with their defense. These kids come from a different world. A lonely, mean world, where they became emotional mutants.

To Meyer, Johnnie appeared somewhat personable, like his stepsons who sandwiched Johnnie in age. But unlike Wingate, Meyer never imagined his kids could find themselves in Johnnie's situation. They had nothing in common with the youth he saw. He did not think Johnnie was dumb, despite his IQ scores. He seemed "pretty flat-line" to Meyer. Defendants usually ride an emotional roller coaster. Johnnie did not.

With death, or life in prison, in prospect, clients are usually scared.
Johnnie was not. They go into denial. Johnnie denied nothing about his
crime. They get angry at the prosecutor or judge for what is happening
to them, or what, in their minds, the prosecutor and judge are trying to
do to them. Johnnie was not angry at court officials. He was just there,
barely. He cooperated. But he never truly absorbed the enormity of the
fact that he was the person on trial for murder. This detachment makes
cases harder to win but easier to keep at an emotional distance. After all,
this is just another client, regardless of his age.

The kid Ron Wingate saw in Johnnie was hard and a little cold. But
he also saw a flicker of warmth or softness in Johnnie that he couldn't
quite put his finger on. It was something that made you remember
Johnnie was a kid caught in the meanest and starkest of adult worlds. A
kid with no one there for him. It was eerie, the stillness in Johnnie, and
surrounding him. He had no support, no one asking about him or what
was going on with his defense, no prayers said for him, no one to even
give him spending money for a candy bar.

Wingate tried to play some of those roles. He began giving Johnnie
money for soap, and even for shoes when Johnnie outgrew his sneakers
while awaiting trial. Neither Children Services nor the jail considered
clothes for a growing defendant as their responsibility. He pestered
Johnnie about school, telling him to maintain his focus in prison classes,
to treat them as importantly as if he were still outside. They talked
about basketball. A few times, Wingate urged Johnnie to get some religious counseling. He wasn't particularly religious himself, but he felt
Johnnie could benefit by believing in something, by finding some
meaning, at least someone to talk to.

Slowly, their relationship deepened. Eventually, Wingate became
Johnnie's only link to humanity, the only person who cared more than
he was paid to. "Yeah, but me and Ron got a different relationship,"
Johnnie explained later when I asked him if he grew angry at Wingate
like he did with me sometimes. "We tight," he said. "He know."

"You go through those boxes of files from CSB and see if this kid
should rot in hell for the rest of his life," Wingate wanted to tell the
judges and the many people who questioned how he could represent
Johnnie. "Johnnie Jordan is no monster; he's just like us, only he's had
no guidance, built no core. I've been angry, felt like I wanted to kill that

judge or that prosecutor, but I have that internal control that tells me not to. He doesn't have that. That is the difference. That never developed in him, and no one was watching to help that it would."

At bars and on the street, people joked to Wingate about how good it would be to see Johnnie fry. "He's already been in hell," he wanted to shout. Instead, he forced himself to turn away.

"You realize that at this juncture of Johnnie's young life, there was not a thing you can do to help him. All you can do is stand by and watch him and see he gets his constitutional right to a fair trial," Wingate says now, a quiet anger sharpening his eyes. "But in fact, justice to Johnnie Jordan was never, ever done. Bad life, bad situation, give him a trial, put him in jail. That was supposed to be justice."

17

Wingate and Meyer figured they had only one hope of winning Johnnie's case. On July 16, they filed a motion to suppress Johnnie's confession to prevent its being used as evidence.

That confession was the prosecution's cornerstone. Twice, Johnnie had confessed. Once to his parole officer, Ed Pendleton, and then again formally an hour later, to Detectives Lamb and Richardson. The detectives taped the confession at 11 A.M. on January 30. Johnnie was read his Miranda rights. With his signature, he waived his right against self-incrimination on a form intended for adult suspects. He also signed papers designed for juveniles, waiving his right to have a parent or lawyer with him at the time of his confession.

Wingate would argue that, despite the signed papers, Johnnie initially invoked his right to remain silent while in custody, when he first denied killing Mrs. Johnson. Throughout the night of January 29 and the early morning of January 30, Johnnie had kept silent. Only after Pendleton visited him did Johnnie confess. It was not clear whether Pendleton had visited Johnnie as a friend or as an officer of the law, Wingate claimed. Pendleton had not read Johnnie his rights although he appeared to be seeking a confession. When Johnnie confided in him, Pendleton told Johnnie that to get the help he needed, he should confess to the detectives. Pendleton was not acting as a father to Johnnie, Wingate argued, but Johnnie treated him as such a figure, making his confession legally suspect.

Johnnie believed not only that he would get help if he confessed but also that punishment would be lighter. He did not understand the extent to which punishment can hinge on deals between the defense and the prosecution. Johnnie never thought he could avoid punishment altogether. But in fact, he could have.

With the confession as evidence, the state's case was strong. But that was all it had. No other evidence linked Johnnie to the crime. Police found none of Johnnie's fingerprints on the murder weapon. They had not even been able to find the bloody hatchet until Johnnie told them where it was. DNA tests could not match the blood or body fluids on Johnnie's clothes to Mrs. Johnson. There were no witnesses. Without that confession, Johnnie would have stood a good chance of escaping punishment altogether. With a lawyer or parent to counsel him, he almost certainly would have received a lighter punishment at least.

III

Wingate fully expected his objections to the confession—that the child had little understanding of the law—would fail, so he and Meyer searched for holes in the confession itself. They found one in the time element. Johnnie was arrested around 11:30 P.M. At 4:30 A.M., the detectives finally left him alone in his cell to sleep. He was awakened two hours later, at 6:30 A.M., for breakfast at the start of the regular jail routine. He met with Pendleton at 10 A.M. and confessed by 11. Wingate argued that Johnnie was interrogated throughout the night and was sleep-deprived when he confessed.

He also argued that Pendleton had tricked Johnnie, a fifteen-year-old with diminished mental capacity, into confessing. In their motion to suppress the confession, Wingate asserted that in the "inherent coercive atmosphere of the attendant custodial setting, Parole Officer Ed Pendleton, neglecting or refusing to provide the defendant with his Miranda warnings, began to conduct an interrogation of the juvenile defendant." Thirty to forty-five minutes later, Pendleton called the detectives and advised Johnnie to tell them his story "if he wanted to get the help he needed."

Defense lawyers almost always try to have a confession thrown out if their clients make incriminating statements to the police, but they rarely succeed. Still, the prosecutors and detectives worried that the court might agree that Johnnie had not had a normal night's rest before the confession. It was the only concern they had. But it was a real one.

Attorney Meyer had his own concern. "If we get him off on this," Meyer whispered to Wingate as they stood in the courtroom to argue their motion, "we'll have to kill him ourselves."

III

The judge considered the matter of the confession in a pretrial hearing. To show that Johnnie's mind was calm and clear when he confessed, the prosecution called Detective Richardson.

Throughout the interrogation, Richardson testified, Johnnie "seemed pretty unshaken by the whole thing." When detectives told Johnnie that Mrs. Johnson had been murdered, Johnnie did not flinch. He certainly did not seem surprised. His whole demeanor was matter-of-fact and calm, Richardson said. Johnnie asked and was permitted to visit the bathroom. The police asked him if he was hungry; he said he was not.

On the morning of his confession, Richardson said, Johnnie's "demeanor was the same." The detectives interviewed him in the Ping-Pong room of the juvenile jail. There he signed an adult Waiver of Rights form and a Juvenile Waiver of Rights form. He had almost no trouble reading a paragraph of the Miranda form into a tape, which was played for the court. He ate a box lunch while confessing to killing Mrs. Johnson.

"Johnnie, you have the right to refuse to make a statement or to answer questions. If you remain silent, your silence cannot be used against you in a court of law. Do you understand?" Detective Lamb asked in the taped confession.

Johnnie nodded while he chewed.

"Johnnie, you have to say it," Richardson told him.

"Yes."

"Anything you say can be used against you in a court of law. Do you understand?" Lamb continued.

"Yes."

"You have the right to the presence of a lawyer or parents or both during the questioning. If you cannot afford a lawyer, a lawyer will be appointed for you before questioning, if you so desire. Do you understand that?"

"Yes."

"Unless you are willing to give up the above rights, no statement of yours can be accepted and no questions will be asked of you. Do you understand that?"

"Yes."

"The above rights stay with you and may be claimed now or at any time during the questioning. Do you understand that?"

"Yes."

"Okay. At the bottom here, it says, 'I have read the statement.' Please read that and sign it," Lamb told Johnnie.

"Okay. Are you able to read that out loud, this bottom paragraph? Can you read well enough?" Richardson asked Johnnie.

"I have read the statement of my rights shown above," Johnnie read haltingly, yet determined not to appear dumb. "I understand what my rights are. I am willing to answer questions and make a statement. I do not want a lawyer or a parent at this time. I understand and I know what I am doing. No promises or threats have been made to me and no pressure of any kind has been used against me."

Then Johnnie read aloud and signed the Lucas County Juvenile Waiver of Rights.[1]

Wingate objected to the prosecution's intention to continue and play the entire confession for the court, claiming that it was not relevant to the issue of Johnnie's surrendering his rights. His objection was denied. The confession was "totally relevant to his state of mind," the judge ruled.

Meyer believed that the defense lost the entire case on that ruling. As the prosecutors played the tape, Johnnie's voice echoed through the courtroom, calm, firm, solid, and damning.

"Did you tell him he could get the electric chair?" Wingate asked Richardson on cross-examination.

---

1. The waiver reads: "You have the right to refuse to make a statement or to answer questions. If you remain silent, your silence cannot be used against you in a court of law. Anything you do say can be used against you in a court of law.

"You have the right to the presence of a lawyer or parents or both during the questioning. If you cannot afford a lawyer, a lawyer will be appointed for you before the questioning if you so desire.

"Unless you are willing to give up the above rights, no statement of yours can be accepted and no questions will be asked of you.

"The above rights stay with you and may be claimed now or at any time during the questioning.

"I have read the statement of my rights shown above. I understand what my rights are. I am willing to answer questions and make a statement. I do not want a lawyer or parent at this time. I understand and know what I am doing. No promises or threats have been made to me and no pressure of any kind has been used against me."

"No," Richardson said. The law does not require such things to be explained to a defendant in the adult system.

III

On the second day of the pretrial hearing, Wingate called Johnnie to the stand and asked why he had confessed to Pendleton, hoping to lead Johnnie toward the issue of a child's trust.

"Because I figured they would leave me alone," Johnnie answered simply, referring to the detectives instead.

Wingate showed Johnnie the forms he had signed, waiving his Miranda rights, now marked "State's Exhibit 1."

"Do you remember signing this?" Wingate asked.

"Yes."

"Now, do you remember on that evening whether or not you were told that you could refuse to make any statements or answer any questions by either Detective Lamb or Detective Richardson. Do you remember that?"

"I just remembered them reading me something," Johnnie answered. "I don't know exactly, no."

"And looking at the State's Exhibit 1, did you, in fact, sign whatever it was that they read to you?"

"Yes."

"Now, did you understand what they were saying to you at that time?"

"Yes."

It was not the answer Wingate expected, nor was it what Johnnie had told Wingate in the privacy of the jail cell. But Johnnie was embarrassed to admit in open court that he had not understood. Wingate tried to recover by asking how much sleep Johnnie had gotten.

Six hours the night before the murder, Johnnie said. On the night of the murder and his arrest, two hours.

On cross-examination, the prosecutor asked Johnnie if he usually stayed up late.

"Yes," Johnnie replied, negating Wingate's effort to portray him as exhausted at the time.

To prove he was literate, the prosecution introduced Johnnie's report cards from the River Road Group Home. He had earned mostly A's.

By the end of the morning, Wingate and Meyer recognized their strategy was failing and recalled Johnnie to the stand, where he pleaded not guilty by reason of insanity. He waived his right to go to trial within ninety days so his lawyers could prepare their case and ask for a second psychiatric opinion.

Johnnie stared down at his hands. He thought of nothing in particular as the court discussed the possible sentences he faced.

For aggravated murder, he could receive thirty years to life. As a fifteen-year-old, there was some question of whether he could be sentenced to death. If he were an adult, the lawyers and judge agreed, he would certainly be a candidate for the death penalty.

The judge would look into it. At that time, Ohio had recently reinstated the death penalty but would not allow a minor guilty of any crime to be executed.

III

Johnnie's lawyers lost their motion to suppress his confession. His voice on the tape had sounded firm and cold in the courtroom. He could read and write English, so it was presumed he understood his Miranda rights. He had not requested an attorney. He had not asked to use a phone, even to call his family. The judge found that no threats or promises had been made to him. The police had not violated his rights.

Wingate asked for a trial before a three-judge panel instead of the usual twelve-person jury.

"After that confession, and Johnnie's cool and apparently remorseless demeanor in court, Wingate knew a jury would hang Johnnie," Prosecutor Bates said later. "He was right. He had to go before a three-judge panel. Emotions were too high. A jury would have hanged him."

III

When the guards took Johnnie back to his cell that morning, Wingate knew that Johnnie did not understand what had just happened. He tried to be reassuring as they walked away. But he found he couldn't smile. He could hardly nod good-bye.

In the hall, Wingate overheard a conversation among some fellow lawyers. "The law is only as good as your attorney," one joked to the other, repeating a well-worn adage.

Wingate tried to shake himself free of the words. But before he could, a sickening feeling spread through him. He knew that he would have to beg for a child's life. And, he knew, he would be alone in doing so.

18

If Johnnie had understood Wingate's next strategy, he would have objected. He would not have allowed his attorney to file an insanity plea.

Wingate and Meyer painstakingly explained this course of action to Johnnie as the only hope of saving his life. But Johnnie paid no attention. He was used to others managing his life. It did not occur to him to take control now, or even to try to understand what was going on with his defense. Even as the experts and other witnesses dissected his life in front of him in court, he acted like the person on trial was a stranger.

In many ways, this detached and ultimately fatalistic philosophy is typical of Johnnie. "If something is meant to happen to me, it will happen," he told me. "I don't scare easily, probably because I don't really care." There is nothing he can do to change what happens to him. Nothing he does affects life around him. Later, he would come to wish that he had paid attention at his trial. He thinks it might have made some difference.

But, he would not have allowed his attorneys to claim he was insane. Even if that legal defense would have set him free, he still would have refused to allow his lawyers to rely on it, he insists. Johnnie did not understand the definition of an insanity plea. It meant, according to Ohio's Standard of Criminal Responsibility, that "at the time of the offense, he did not know, as the result of a severe mental disorder or defect, the wrongfulness of his act." He only knew he didn't want anyone thinking he was crazy.

III

The court again sent Dr. Forgac to interview Johnnie, the same clinical psychologist who earlier examined him as part of the juvenile court proceeding. This time he was to assess whether Johnnie was sane enough to stand trial as an adult.

Johnnie hardly cared what the doctor found or what the findings meant to his case or his future. He thought each doctor sent to evaluate him was sent to help him. On each of the visits, Johnnie immediately signed, without reading, a disclaimer form the doctor handed him, acknowledging the limits of confidentiality. This was not surprising. Most juveniles sign immediately, without hesitation or any suspicion that they are relinquishing an important protection.

Wingate expected the worst from the new evaluation. Besides Forgac's earlier finding, he believed experts from the Court Diagnostic and Treatment Center were biased in favor of the state. In his twenty years of practicing law, he had seen some very strange people certified as sane by the center's psychologists, including a man who believed he was a chicken—a highly evolved and intelligent chicken, but a chicken nonetheless.

After meeting with Johnnie for almost two hours, Forgac "found Johnnie Jordan is functioning within the range of borderline intelligence and that he was not psychotic, that he was not displaying a mental or emotional disorder that would make him out of touch with reality."

Forgac was surprised by the "limited variability to [Johnnie's] expression" during the interview. Johnnie spoke "positively" about Mrs. Johnson and her husband, but he showed no sympathy. He did not cry or express remorse, the doctor said. Emotionally he was monotone.

In response to Forgac's questions, Johnnie said he often felt nervous, and had been sad and depressed after social workers removed him from his parents' care. In a mumbled voice, he admitted that he had attempted suicide at least twice. But when the doctor asked about the murder, Johnnie spoke more sharply.

"I don't want to talk about it," he told Forgac. "All I can say is, the voices came into my head telling me to kill her."

After a moment, he added: "She was a nice lady. I was mad about what happened, being taken away from my parents, placed in a foster home, but not at Mrs. Johnson."

Dr. Forgac found no psychiatric excuse for Johnnie's violent behavior. The low IQ test score did not render Johnnie incompetent to stand

trial. Johnnie was completely sane, Forgac reported. He had no hallucinations of any kind or belief that he had special powers. Johnnie's only
unusual fear was of worms, imagined worms, crawling on his skin.

"Although Johnnie Jordan, Jr. reported having had the unusual experience of hearing voices," Forgac wrote, "there was nothing in his clinical presentation, including his thought content or stream of thought,
which would indicate he was acutely psychotic on the day of this evaluation."

As to whether he was sane when he killed Mrs. Johnson, Forgac
determined that Johnnie met the Standard of Criminal Responsibility
in Ohio. "It certainly appears that Johnnie knew the wrongfulness of
his acts at the time they occurred," he reported, citing how Johnnie had
turned away twice before succumbing to his urge to kill, then setting
Mrs. Johnson on fire because he was afraid she would accuse him, and
stealing money from her purse so he could escape. "All these things
indicate he was experiencing normal conflict but eventually followed
through.

"Johnnie Jordan, Jr.'s behavior at the time of the offense was not a
product of mental illness," the doctor concluded. "It appears he was able
to know the wrongfulness of his acts at the time they occurred."

As damning as his report read, Forgac's live testimony would prove
even more damaging to Johnnie. When Prosecutor Bates called him to
the stand, Forgac would say that Johnnie had almost no chance of rehabilitation in prison—juvenile or adult. Peer group influence is
extremely important in juvenile cases because individuals do not form
adult identities until their mid-twenties, he explained. Even if he did
receive extensive therapy, certainly Johnnie would have to be imprisoned for years because of his crime. "If this young man is incarcerated
and at this stage is exposed to criminals and is just limited in his contact
to criminals, that will become more and more a part of his identity," he
told the court.

Johnnie's attorneys asked no questions on cross-examination. Anything Forgac said, they felt, would only hurt Johnnie.

III

Wingate and Meyer had requested a second opinion from Dr. Joel Zrull,
a professor of psychiatry and the chairman of the Medical College of

Ohio, who in previous cases had appeared more sympathetic to troubled juveniles. Wingate almost automatically asks for a second opinion. But in this case, after listening to the tape of Johnnie's confession, Wingate was sure the voices in Johnnie's head meant that his client had not been sane when he bludgeoned Mrs. Johnson to death.

But Zrull's findings were not what Wingate had hoped for. Five months after Forgac's evaluation, Zrull echoed his fellow doctor's basic view, though he tempered it with more sadness and regret.

"There was no evidence of bizarre or unusual thinking except for his allusion to the voices," he reported. The voices, "it would appear, are more a concretization of Johnnie's interpretation of what is right and what is wrong rather than being what appeared to be true hallucinations. He alludes to having experienced voices prior to the incident with Mrs. Johnson but he's had nothing of it since, nor has it been anything that has been pervasive in his lifetime."

Johnnie was able to recall the murder in detail and he knew that he had clearly done something wrong in the eyes of the law. He demonstrated to the doctor that he had "solid thinking capabilities." When asked to interpret the statement "People in glass houses should not throw stones," Johnnie answered, "If they did, they would break windows."

Zrull found "interesting responses to social questions," such as what Johnnie would do if he found an addressed, stamped envelope. Johnnie said he would leave it lying on the street. If he were in a theater where he smelled something burning, Johnnie said he would do nothing until someone else reacted or an alarm went off.

Johnnie was as detached from his environment as he was from his feelings. Asked how he felt about all the foster homes he had been through and what had happened to him in his life, Johnnie was quiet. "It was difficult for Johnnie to respond to this and indeed ultimately [he] said that he really did not know how he felt about what happened to him," Zrull wrote.

Remorse was foreign to Johnnie, or at least the remorse expected of normal people. During this second evaluation, he again showed no sorrow for striking the bus driver, nor for the gang-related drive-by shooting involving his sister. On occasion, "he found himself crying in relation to Mrs. Johnson and that he only hopes Mr. Johnson will be able to forgive him," Zrull reported. But when asked if he wished he could turn back time and not commit the murder, Johnnie sat still, looking at the floor. To the doctor, he appeared depressed, not remorseful.

Almost worse than not understanding his emotions, Johnnie had no one to confide in, Zrull reported. He had never bonded with another person in a normal or a healthy way. Johnnie said plainly that he had never been able to talk to anyone in any meaningful depth; he "feels that if he tells people something, that they simply act as though they understand him when they really do not." He had no ties to anyone who might teach him moral values and behavior; he seemed incapable of trusting anyone.

Finally, Zrull asked Johnnie, what has been the best time of your life? Johnnie was silent for some time. Then he looked directly into the doctor's eyes without sadness or self-pity or sarcasm.

"There has never been no best time in my life," he said.

Of all the findings, that reply struck Wingate most deeply. He and everyone involved in the case knew Johnnie was probably speaking the truth. But the fact that Johnnie recognized just how pathetic his childhood had been was almost unbearably tragic to Wingate. Johnnie had never known happiness or even contentment. From his birth, he had been in a perpetual state of war with life.

With the evidence so far stacked against him, Wingate fought to get a third psychological evaluation. He was certain the voices in Johnnie's head proved him insane. He chose Dr. Gerald Briskin of the University of Michigan, who is both a clinical psychologist and an attorney, to perform the evaluation. Briskin worked as a psychologist in the U.S. Army for five years in the 1950s, served as the director of psychology at Wyandot General Hospital in Michigan, and founded and codirected the Adolescent Psychiatric Service there.

After spending an hour with Johnnie and reviewing his files, Briskin brought bad news to Wingate. Johnnie did indicate remorse. He had been suicidal at times in his young life. But Johnnie was not crazy, Briskin concluded. His background had mangled him, but Johnnie had never been legally insane. The voices in his head telling him to kill and not to kill was his conscience speaking to him.

There was little anyone could do for Johnnie now, Briskin told Wingate. For years, Johnnie had suffered from "severe conduct disorder," a condition described in the American Psychiatric Association's diagnostic manual for children as the juvenile equivalent of a sociopath. The specific behaviors Johnnie had exhibited for most of his life were almost textbook examples of the disorder: "the aggressive behavior, the difficulties with authorities, the stealing, the running away, the inability to maintain an adjustment in school." Johnnie had little self-control, and no firm conscience, but he was not legally crazy.

"His personality is organized in a relatively primitive manner, with a great deal of underlying anger and poor internal controls that permit him to act out impulsively. He does not tolerate stress particularly well, nor does he inhibit his impulses," Briskin would testify later.

Yet Briskin's analysis was the best Johnnie's defense had up to that point. Without character witnesses to testify, without a family support system to help rehabilitate him or even care about him, this finding— that Johnnie was a sociopath—was the only defense he had.

For Wingate and Meyer, success at this point meant getting Johnnie as little time in prison as possible. They hoped for psychiatric care as well. But they knew too well that psychological rehabilitative help hardly existed in prison.

III

Meyer carefully examined Briskin on the stand. Although sympathetic and with some optimism for all children, Briskin had little hope for Johnnie.

In the best-case scenario, Meyer said, Johnnie would spend at least the next twenty years in prison. "Is there any reason to hope that he could come out a functioning member of society?" he asked.

Briskin paused. He could not give the simple response Meyer clearly wanted.

"That would depend on the conditions that he experiences during that period of incarceration," Briskin replied. "It would probably be the most stable period he has ever experienced in his life . . . He has not, to my knowledge, up to this point, ever really had a stable, ongoing relationship with anyone, nor do the records I examined reflect that he was exposed to any significant therapeutic efforts during the course of his contact with Children Services.

"If he were in a stable prison placement, if he could form some relationships there, if he was afforded treatment, if he were exposed to religious information proselytization, considering the fact that he's now just approaching his seventeenth birthday and is not an adult and is still somewhat malleable, it is conceivable that he might make progress and be able to return to civilian life, and make a reasonable adjustment."

III

The prosecution bored in on the cross-examination.

Did Johnnie cry or break down with remorse when Briskin saw him? Bates asked.

No, Briskin answered.

"Do you find that prisons rehabilitate?"

"Not generally," Briskin replied.

In a normal case, Briskin's testimony would have ended there. But in Johnnie's trial, in an attempt to guard against a ruling by emotion, the three-judge panel was allowed to question witnesses directly.

Judge Ruth Ann Franks, who headed the panel, asked what Briskin thought the ideal treatment for Johnnie would be.

"Ideally, he would be placed in an institution for young offenders. Ideally, he would be seen by a counselor on a regular basis. And ideally, he would be involved in group therapy. He needs to establish the ability to form some relationships."

What does "being able to form relationships" mean? Briskin was asked.

"He needs to learn how to trust people. He needs to learn how to control his own impulses with respect to his own needs. He needs to learn how to temper what is expected of him in a kind of a rational, normal type of society and learn how to inhibit some impulses . . . He needs to be able to come to feel that he has some worth and that other people believe he has some worth."

If all this is done, Briskin concluded, Johnnie "*may* begin to develop, internalize some superego, some conscience, internalize a sense of camaraderie with another human being that neither exploits him nor he exploits."

But Briskin testified, there was only a slight chance that Johnnie could conform to society after ten years of incarceration, and only then if he received intense therapy.

And if Johnnie did not receive this kind of therapy? the judges wanted to know.

If Johnnie got little, none, or just some psychiatric help and was placed in a usual crowd of prisoners, Briskin replied, "the prognosis would be grave."

III

Leaving the courthouse that night, Wingate knew with a chill of certainty where his case stood.

"We're facing a firing squad," he mumbled to Meyer. "The only question is, do we get a blindfold?"

19

Over the next few days, Wingate watched his defense erode further. When the prosecution introduced the coroner's photographs of Mrs. Johnson's mutilated body, the head of the panel, Judge Franks, turned away in disgust. The photographs had been described to her in detail, she explained, and she could imagine the rest. The two other judges took the closed envelope of photographs into their chambers. Judge Ronald Bowman, a war veteran, cried when he viewed Mrs. Johnson's torn, swollen, and charred body. Judge James Jensen appeared angry when he returned to the courtroom after he looked at the mutilated human remains of Johnnie's violence and read the coroner's report. All the while, Johnnie sat expressionless.

The night before the final arguments, after all evidence had been presented and the witnesses heard, Wingate had visited Johnnie in jail to explain what co-counsel Meyer intended to say in his closing statement. Johnnie reacted with a stunned look.

"What do you mean?" he asked Wingate, panic lighting his matted eyes for the first time. "You ain't doing it? Why not?"

Johnnie cared less about what was said than who said it. Words never meant much to him. His senses did. He had attached himself to Wingate, not because Wingate was also African-American, but because Johnnie sensed that Wingate cared about him. Wingate was the only one Johnnie trusted to fight for him. Johnnie's response surprised Wingate. Even behind closed doors in talks with his lawyers, Johnnie had been largely mute and had given little evidence of his feelings.

Although he was taken aback, Wingate agreed to give the summation. He phoned Meyer and again went over what would be said in Johnnie's last defense, by him now rather than Meyer.

Together they agreed that he would be direct.

III

"How do you defend an indefensible case?" Wingate began that morning's proceeding, his hands spread, dramatizing his feeling of helplessness.

He knew Johnnie would be found guilty. All he could do was emphasize that Johnnie had not murdered for money or set fire to kill or destroy property. Those acts alone could add forty years to Johnnie's sentence.[1]

Wingate asked the judges to find that Johnnie murdered in a fit of rage. Only afterward, as he sought to escape, did Johnnie realize he would need money to run away. The fire he set was not to further maim or kill, but to erase the murder, to turn the evidence into ash.

The overriding problem with proving their argument, the defense lawyers recognized, was the absence of a reason why Johnnie killed at all. His violence demanded a rationale if they were to convince the judges that the murder was not planned as part of the robbery or arson. Wingate struggled to identify Johnnie's real motive. The only rationale he could come up with was to tie it to the accumulated injuries in Johnnie's past.

"I say now," Wingate told the court, "when you take Johnnie Jordan and you take all the other Johnnie Jordans of the world and you look at those children who from birth have been denied any semblance of a home environment, who have been denied their basic rights of humanity, and you take Johnnie Jordan and he commits this type of offense and you ask why, I'll tell you: Why not? Because a child is nothing more and never will be anything more than the sum total of his or her environment, and the sum total of Johnnie Jordan's life has been nothing— his very existence has been nothing but a crime.

"When you look at Johnnie Jordan, you, the public, the prosecutor, and the news media, and you want to give justification as to why Johnnie Jordan took the life of Mrs. Johnson," he persisted. "The justification you want to give us is that Johnnie Jordan purposely caused the death of

---

1. In a strange twist of the law, a person who even unintentionally kills someone in a robbery attempt will often receive a longer sentence than a criminal who randomly selects and executes a person on the street simply for the thrill of a kill, according to Lucas County Prosecutor Julia Bates.

Mrs. Johnson while committing the offense of aggravated robbery or aggravated arson.

"I think it is so easy for all of us to label things that we do not understand, and we don't understand Johnnie Jordan, because, for whatever the reason, we don't know what makes Johnnie tick. And we haven't had an opportunity to let Johnnie address that."

Wingate wanted to blame the foster care system for neglecting Johnnie, for ignoring his cries, for failing to care for his mental health, and for hardening him in cold temporary homes of its creation. But to blame anyone other than Johnnie was too dangerous in this case. Someone had to be accountable. A system was too amorphous, broad, unsatisfying to blame. The public, the court, Wingate knew, needed a person to condemn.

The crime just did not make sense through adult eyes. But Johnnie was a child, an angry, impulsive child. He was not motivated by greed or destruction, Wingate contended. "Mrs. Johnson was the victim of Johnnie Jordan's unfulfilled need for love, his unfulfilled need for stability," Wingate declared. "He is not a monster and he is not an abomination. He's a child who desperately wanted a childhood."

III

Prosecutor Bates stood before the court with little to prove. Johnnie had murdered Mrs. Johnson. He had confessed. He had taken her money. He had set her on fire.

Anything beyond those facts could only dilute her case. If the court found that Johnnie had not committed the murder for money and that he did not set fire to further maim or damage, but simply to rid the incident from his mind, and hide it from the world, he could possibly leave prison in twenty years. That, Bates felt, amounted to an unacceptably light punishment for a horrendous crime. It was her job to protect the community from Johnnie Jordan.

The disadvantages of Johnnie's life, the uncaring foster homes and his "sad, if not heartbreaking" experiences were unfortunate, Bates said, but "there are maybe hundreds of thousands of these stories in our cities and towns all across this country. And not ever, never can it justify the taking of a life."

Jeanette Johnson had been better than a good person, Bates reminded the court. She was the most giving of people, and Johnnie knew it. He benefited from her kindness. Twice he thought about killing her that evening but pulled back. The third time, he did it. "That's not anger," Bates told the panel of judges. "That's cold, conscious calculation."

He did not hit Mrs. Johnson over the head just once. He hit her fifteen, perhaps twenty times, with an ax. Johnnie broke her skull. He destroyed one of her eyes, her jaw, knocked out her teeth. The judges could look at the pictures again if they wished.

Johnnie stole several dollars and a handful of loose change while his foster mother lay dying. He thought about setting her body on fire, and then labored to do it, which resulted in $900 worth of property damage. He fled the gruesome scene.

"I carry, I guess, a little piece of each case with me, but this case is different," Bates concluded. "This case takes a huge chunk out of every one of us that has been involved, out of those who have listened, those of us in this courtroom, those of us in our community, those of us in our society when someone so young is capable of so much violence against someone who held out her hand to help.

"Put away the sadness, the sympathy, the pain you must feel," she urged. "Judge this case, as you must, on the facts and on the law."

III

Mr. Johnson would not be in the courtroom when the judges returned. He sensed what the verdict would be. He found no comfort in the judgment. I cannot say Mr. Johnson "forgave" Johnnie. Only he could explain in what way he reconciled the murderer with his sadness and pain. There were moments, particularly in his silent pauses, in which I knew he felt more than I could understand and perhaps more than even he understood. Both life and death seemed to weigh heavily on his heart. And in the end, this brought some sort of reconciliation that he felt only Johnnie might understand. He seemed to believe he and Johnnie had been wrecked by the same storm. And although Mr. Johnson could come out into the sunlight, he had not much more life left in him than Johnnie did. Only Johnnie did not yet recognize the prisons he and Mr. Johnson would now live in. Nothing could save his wife now, and nothing could save Johnnie, Mr. Johnson told me. The tragedy simply was playing itself out.

20

After deliberating for only two hours during the afternoon of September 10, 1996, the judges returned to the courtroom. Johnnie stood when Wingate nudged him. He had been before a judge several times before, but he still did not understand court etiquette. He wasn't frightened, although he did feel a familiar sting in his chest spreading to his stomach.

Beside him, Wingate felt time slow down. The courtroom was too still. Behind him, twenty people sat on the prosecution's side of the gallery. All were Mrs. Johnson's friends. No one could be found on Johnnie's side. As in the days and months before, no one came to the trial for Johnnie. It was eerie to see someone that young on trial for his life, Wingate thought. This child was absolutely alone.

Judge Franks delivered the verdict.

"It is the unanimous finding of this three-judge panel," she read, "that the State has proven beyond a reasonable doubt all the essential elements of aggravated murder as set forth in Count 1 of the indictment and that the killing of Jeanette E. Johnson was committed purposely by the defendant Johnnie Jordan while committing both aggravated robbery and aggravated arson on or about January 29th, 1996, and in Lucas County, Ohio."

Wingate heard the pounding of his heart. He had lost big. Guilty of murder, and aggravated robbery and arson. Guilty of murder, yes, he had expected. But not aggravated robbery and arson. No, he thought. Johnnie had not killed Mrs. Johnson for money. Money was an afterthought. The same with the fire. In his entire career, Wingate has lost only two cases in which he believes justice was not done. Johnnie's was one.

Rick Meyer felt differently. The verdict was harsh, he says, and it was expected.

III

Johnnie did not know what to think as he was led back to his cell. He was not surprised that the court found him guilty. He had confessed. But the look on Wingate's face surprised and confused him. He expected to be in prison only until he was twenty-one. Four years would be hard, he thought, but he deserved the punishment.

The night before Johnnie's sentencing a month later, Wingate again tried to explain that the punishment could be much, much worse.

"They can't kill me, Ronnie," Johnnie said.

"No, but they could put you away for a long, long time."

The words did not mean much to Johnnie, and he did not give them much thought.

III

On the morning of the sentencing, Judge Franks began by reviewing Johnnie's decision to waive a jury trial in favor of the three-judge panel. Then she asked, "Mr. Jordan, do you understand what I've just said?"

"No," Johnnie said. "If I may?"

His words, shorn of apparent meaning, indicate how little he understood of the trial. To Johnnie, the judges and lawyers spoke a language wholly different from his own. No one understood what he said or meant. He later explained that he had hoped the judges would allow him to speak up on his own behalf, a practice that was sometimes permitted in juvenile court. But in adult court, there was no such opportunity unless the defendant was called to the stand as a witness. His lawyers had decided not to call Johnnie for fear that his lack of remorse would damage his case.

Meyer and Wingate quietly explained to Johnnie the formality of Judge Frank's question and told him to answer yes.

"Yes, ma'am," Johnnie said.

"Mr. Jordan, you can stand, please," Judge Franks firmly directed Johnnie.

Slowly, Johnnie rose to his feet.

Because Johnnie was a minor when he committed murder, the judge explained, he could not be sentenced to death or to life in prison without parole in the state of Ohio. On the murder charge alone, Johnnie could still be sentenced to life in prison, although he would be eligible for parole after serving twenty or thirty years, Franks continued. In addition, however, there was the matter of time for aggravated robbery and aggravated arson. Those counts could add five to twenty-five years each. Fines could also be imposed, though because Johnnie had no money, this was moot.

III

Rick Meyer addressed the court after the judge finished explaining the parameters of sentencing Johnnie.

"The facts of this case were overwhelming," he acknowledged. "I don't think there was ever any doubt as to what the verdict of the court would be. The only question ever was what your sentence was going to be."

Meyer repeated the plea for sympathy and understanding based on Johnnie's upbringing.

"[We] ask the Court to take this into consideration not because it excuses or explains what he did, but as you look at his past, there is only one inescapable conclusion: He never had a chance. Through no fault of his own, he lost the early part of his life. Through actions of his own, he's now, at the best-case scenario, going to lose the middle part of his life."

The minimum sentence Johnnie could expect was twenty years. Meyer asked the judges to allow the parole board to decide whether Johnnie was fit to return to society after that time, instead of fixing the length of his sentence now. "It seems to me that as a society, we at least owe him some chance somewhere along the line. He hasn't had one up until now," he said.

To bolster his point, Meyer recalled psychologist Briskin to the stand.

Was there reason to hope that Johnnie could fit back into society after twenty years in prison? Meyer asked.

"That would depend," was the most optimistic answer Briskin could give. He repeated his earlier testimony that such a long term in jail would probably be the most stable period in Johnnie's life. If he was given treatment, if he was able to form positive and good relationships with other people in prison, if he were inspired somehow toward some morality, given his youth, "it is conceivable," Briskin told the court, "that he might make progress and be able to return to civilian life and make a reasonable adjustment."

Under cross-examination by Assistant Prosecutor Dean Mandross, who took over the sentencing phase of the case from Bates, Briskin was asked if he had spent merely one hour evaluating Johnnie.

"That's right," Briskin replied.

Did he review all eight boxes of Johnnie's records?

"No," Briskin answered.

Was he aware of the allegations of gun use and gang involvement? Briskin was aware.

When Johnnie spoke of the murder, did he break down and cry?

"No."

"He didn't weep or shake or—"

"No."

"Are you aware when he confessed to the police, he didn't show any remorse?"

"Yes."

"Do you find that prisons rehabilitate?"

"Not generally," the doctor answered.

"[In] forming our own individuality, we first form a group identity. Would you agree with that?"

"No," Briskin said, surprising Mandross. "What we first do is we make an identification with some parent or parent surrogate at the very outset of infancy, in a normal infancy; and that helps us begin to internalize family values, their values. Then we have identification with family. And subsequent to that, we are influenced and identify with various educational societal entities."

As for instilling values, Johnnie had not only missed out on the first two phases, Briskin noted, he had been exposed and raised to mimic brutal values.

"And his peers for the next twenty years are going to be convicts? Correct?"

"That's correct," Briskin replied.

III

Defense attorney Meyer called on Johnnie's group home counselor, J. R. Robinson, to describe the softer side of Johnnie. J.R. described how gently Johnnie behaved with his wife and children and other family members at family gatherings.

"Did he ever express any desires about becoming part of your family?" Mandross asked on cross-examination.

Yes, J.R. said. Johnnie had wanted J.R. to adopt him. "It was a very difficult thing to say no. I tossed it around in my head a thousand times. Johnnie was so needy. Of all the kids at River Road [group home], he was the neediest."

For years afterward, J.R. would kick himself for this answer. He wished he had told the panel how he would have adopted Johnnie, how he trusted Johnnie to be among the people he loved most. But he did not get the chance to say so in court, he said later.

The prosecutor did not give him much of a chance to be complimentary. Johnnie told you that "Mrs. Johnson was extremely nice?" Mandross asked.

"Yes."

"That she had never done anything to him?"

"Exactly."

"Does—on a personal level, does it—does it frighten you that he could do that to someone he—" Mandross began.

Meyer objected. Judge Franks sustained his objection, ruling that J.R.'s personal feelings were not relevant.

III

The last witness called by the defense was Johnnie himself. As part of the sentencing hearing, under the law Johnnie was not subject to cross-examination if he limited himself to giving a statement. Wingate had written one out for him. Judge Franks directed Johnnie to stand.

"I just want to apologize to the family for all the pain and stuff that I caused them for the death of Mrs. Johnson," Johnnie said, mumbling. "And I want to apologize to Mr. Johnson but apparently he's not here, but could you all please tell him that I am sorry for this and I'll be more than happy to serve twenty to thirty years of my life in prison for this crime. But it would make me feel a little bit better if I know that you all one day will forgive me for this, although I can never forgive myself for it. And I would like to just say I'm sorry again and thanks for your time."

Johnnie sat down. The world around him seemed not his own. He was just a minor actor in the scene taking place around him.

III

Now came the state's turn to influence the judges' decision on the sentence. Prosecutor Bates returned to the court to pose two questions: Is Johnnie Jordan dangerous? Will he remain dangerous after twenty to thirty years? The first question was a given, Bates figured. It was the latter question she would focus on.

Bates called Dr. Forgac back to the stand to negate the few hopeful comments in Dr. Briskin's testimony. She set out to prove that Johnnie lacked the fundamentals of humanity and that without these basics there was little hope that he could ever live peacefully in society.

Did Johnnie even cry once when he recounted his crime during the evaluation?

"No," Forgac answered.

Did he express any sympathy for Mrs. Johnson?

"He had expressed that she was a nice lady, that he spoke relatively positively about her and her husband. But other than that, he didn't express any other feelings."

Bates then asked about Johnnie's social maturity.

How would a prison term affect Johnnie?

"If this young man is incarcerated and at this stage is exposed to criminals and is just limited in his contact to criminals, that will become more and more a part of his identity, that rehabilitation will be difficult," Forgac replied.

"Will he become more dangerous?" Bates asked.

Wingate objected successfully.

Bates tried twice more to rephrase her question before she received the answers she wanted.

"Particularly in the next eight or nine years [prison] will have a significant negative effect on the juvenile's life," Forgac said.

Finally, to counter Johnnie's personal plea for mercy, Bates read a statement from Mr. Johnson's friends.

> We cannot express the amount of pain and suffering that you, John-
> nie Jordan, have caused our family. Every day for the rest of our lives we
> will feel the pain and the anger that you have caused us to feel. She gave

you that love, Johnnie, and you violently and unremorsefully took that love away from all of us. No other child will be able to experience that love and support that she gave you . . . Please Your Honors [the statement concluded], we ask you to impose the maximum sentence allowed by the law so that this will not happen to another family.

All the while, Johnnie sat staring ahead.

III

Wingate rose to make the final argument on Johnnie's behalf.

"I know that lives have been taken for something as simple as a pair of name-brand tennis shoes and lives have been taken for something as complex as love. You may have had a jealous husband, you may have had an angry lover, and you may have a fifteen-year-old boy who wants nothing more than to be loved," Wingate said.

"As you sow, so shall you reap," he quoted from the Book of Job. "Johnnie Jordan is our bitter harvest. Whether we want to accept it or not, that's the truth."

Mrs. Johnson did not deserve to die, Wingate acknowledged. "But Johnnie has been dying for fifteen years."

Wingate told the judges that Mr. Johnson had recently "expressed that he wanted to help the defendant.

"If Mr. Johnson, through all his pain, all of his sorrow and his loss, can still extend a hand to Johnnie, I think the court can do no less. So I would ask the court for as much leniency as possible."

III

After a moment, Bates rose. Johnnie's past earned him sympathy. But to her, the matter was less about punishing Johnnie Jordan than it was about protecting the community.

The Johnsons were not a threat, Bates began. "They were not enemies of Mr. Jordan. They were not rival gang members . . . If the defendant is capable of that violence against a good and kind person, someone that he liked—we can't allow that kind of violence to ever be unleashed again against another person.

"I would be a very cold, hard, callous person to have sat through this trial and not feel very, very sad, very, very touched by the incredibly tragic life that was experienced by this boy," she said. "But your Hon-

ors, there are many, many people in our community and in our state
and in our country that suffer that same abuse and they do not kill . . .

"There's still a volcano building and erupting in Johnnie Jordan," she
added. "The defendant's attorney said that society owes the defendant a
chance, but I can't in any way in good conscience support that."

Rehabilitation is worse than a coin flip, Bates concluded. It is "extraordinarily unlikely" that Johnnie would return to society less dangerous after being surrounded by killers, rapists, and thugs. Bates asked the
judges to give Johnnie the maximum sentence.

III

By early afternoon, after two hours of deliberations, the judges
returned to pass sentence.

In a preamble to the announcement, Franks noted Johnnie's childhood "of abandonment and abuse," and said the court took into consideration Johnnie's age. But the judges still did not harbor much
sympathy for Johnnie. "The panel cannot conclude that these conditions serve to control or compel the defendant into his conscious decision to brutally take the life of Jeanette Johnson."

The three judges sentenced Johnnie Jordan, Jr. to the maximum punishment for Mrs. Johnson's murder—life imprisonment with parole eli-
gibility after thirty years. They also sentenced Johnnie to twenty-five
years in prison for aggravated robbery and between ten and twenty-five
years for aggravated arson. Those two counts could be served at the
same time, the judges decided, but only after Johnnie completed his
murder sentence.

According to the terms of the combined sentence, Johnnie could not
go free until he was seventy years old at the earliest. And Wingate knew
that if Johnnie was able to survive in prison that long, he would not
have the discipline record needed to make parole.

21

The sentence left Wingate weak and breathless. He felt the courtroom tilt underneath him. Imagining his young client was still staring
blankly ahead, he kept his eyes on the fine grain running through the
mahogany table dividing them from the court. When he finally looked
up to face Johnnie, he found the boy had turned to him with a dull,
quizzical look, not the grief, disappointment, or even the anger he
would have expected from a client.

"He didn't know what was going on," Wingate recalled, his own eyes
wide with amazement even at the memory. "He looked at me to explain.
I couldn't."

Wingate could find no words for Johnnie as he was led away from
the last place without bars that he would ever see. Shuffling in leg
shackles, tripping on the twice-cuffed pant legs of his oversized bright
orange prison jumpsuit, Johnnie seemed badly miscast as the criminal
in this scene.

When Wingate could sit no longer without being noticed, he stood as
straight and upright as he could, and walked out of the courtroom. He
turned around once, to take in the place and moment that scarred his
faith in the justice system and his personal understanding of reason. He
never wanted to go back. Then struggling past a blur of onlookers, he
rushed to the fourth floor of the Lucas County Courthouse, where,
alone in a men's room stall, he cried as he had not cried since he was a
child.

Wingate found no comfort in thinking how little Johnnie had actually lost. Johnnie had never developed hopes or dreams or ambitions. He
never even thought of a future. The truth is that Johnnie Jordan began
dying as soon as he was born, Wingate thought. But this truth only
deepened his anguish.

III

Wingate was not sure how his legs carried him out of the courthouse that day. He did not remember crossing busy Michigan Avenue or climbing the solid grey stairs to the Lucas County jail. But he found himself staring across a metal table at a shackled child that the media was calling a monster. It was time to explain that they had lost. That, at age fifteen, Johnnie had entered prison and would probably never get out. His life, for all real purposes, was over.

"I'm sorry, Johnnie," he said. "I'm sorry I couldn't do any better."

Johnnie was stunned. Not by the verdict, but by Wingate's words. Few people had ever said they were sorry to him about anything. He didn't know what he should say, or whether there was an advantage to be sought or gained from Wingate's apology.

"I'm sorry," Johnnie finally said, repeating the same words. "I'm sorry for what I done."

He and Wingate both lowered their heads. Neither said another word as the lawyer rose quietly and left. Hoping to shelter Johnnie from his own stinging tears, Wingate looked away as Johnnie's questioning eyes anxiously trailed him. Later he wondered whether Johnnie thought his own apology could change the judges' sentence even after it was rendered, or whether Johnnie recognized and was responding to Wingate's grief.

Johnnie says it was both.

III

In the buzzing halls of the Lucas County Courthouse the afternoon of the sentencing, word spread quickly that Judge Jensen was looking for Ron Wingate. The defense attorney did not want to see anyone, let alone one of the three judges who just hours earlier had sentenced his fifteen-year-old client to life in prison with virtually no chance of parole. But he felt a duty to the court to appear in the judge's chambers.

"I think you deserve an explanation," Jensen began. "I think you deserve to hear why."

The room was dim and quiet, starkly different from the echoing halls of the white domed courthouse.

"If I could have given him more time, I would have," Jensen said.

Though his voice was soft and almost gentle, the words stung Wingate like iodine on an open cut.

If Johnnie was put in an institution where he could get the help he needed—the therapy and education—he could perhaps be rehabilitated, Jensen said. But because Johnnie's crime was so heinous, and had provoked such horror and anger in the community, such a course was out of the question. The law and the public demanded that Johnnie receive harsh punishment. In prison, any prison, he would not get the special help he needed for rehabilitation. If the sentence were shorter, Johnnie would one day reemerge in the community an older, bigger, and stronger criminal. None of his underlying problems would be solved and, in all probability, given the statistical evidence, his antisocial attitudes and behavior would become more severe.[1] In addition, any tenuous support that he might receive from family and relatives would undoubtedly dissipate with time and distance. After twenty years in jail, which was the minimum for aggravated murder, Johnnie would be even less equipped to cope with the world. He would revert to crime, and as an impressionable youth influenced by hardened criminals during critical years of development, Johnnie would pose an even greater threat to society should he ever be released.

When Judge Jensen finished, Wingate painfully shook his outstretched hand, then left without saying a word. He was not thankful for the judge's explanation. His sense of tragedy only deepened.

"The saddest part was that when you reflect on the rationality behind the judges' decision, they were right," he said later, looking into a distance. "It was solid thinking. I might not agree with them, but they were right," he paused, looking ahead, focused and certain in his view. "Still, justice to Johnnie Jordan was never done. I know that at my core."

Judge Jensen, who heads the Toledo Bar Association, refused to discuss the sentence with me and said the two other judges on Johnnie's panel would also remain silent. Judge Franks did not return my calls.

---

1. One study by Donna Bishop, a criminology professor at Northeastern University, and Charles Frazier matched age, race, gender, current charges, and past criminal records of 2,738 juveniles prosecuted as adults with the same number of juveniles who stayed within the juvenile system. Over a two-year period, they found 30 percent of teenagers prosecuted in adult criminal court were rearrested, compared to 19 percent of those in the juvenile system.

Judge Bowman spoke with me, but would not discuss the specifics of the case on the record.

By way of explanation, Jensen at first said his comments might affect any appeal in Johnnie's case. When I pointed out that Johnnie's final appeal had already been denied, Jensen offered another reason.

"We don't think it is wise to let attorneys know how we arrived at our decision in this case because it may influence other cases like this one," he said.

Jensen did confirm that, at his own initiative, he discussed the case with Wingate the evening that Johnnie was sentenced. He did not deny or elaborate on Wingate's recollection. He volunteered that Wingate had done "a fine job" in defending Johnnie, that probably nothing more could have been done on Johnnie's behalf.

III

For years, Wingate has taken Johnnie's sentence as a personal failure.

The comment he had overheard in the courthouse months before still rings in his ears when he thinks of the sentencing: "The law is only as good as your attorney." He had given his all, but the bottom line was his client got the longest sentence, the worst punishment possible. As days stretched into weeks and months, Wingate wanted to be alone. He did not want to speak to anyone. He found it almost impossible to smile.

"I felt rejected, for Johnnie to get that much time," he said later. "It was like the judges saying, 'I hear what you're saying—he's young, he's a kid, he's not ever had a fighting chance, he didn't understand what he was doing or what he had done as an adult would—but you're full of it,' that's what they were saying. I never got them to fully understand, to fully accept those truths."

And yet the law had not been distorted in the case. That fact shook Wingate profoundly. For Johnnie, law and justice functioned as smoothly as they were designed to work in the adult system. Every cog turned as it was supposed to. In the eyes of the law, everything that happened to Johnnie Jordan was absolutely fair. But justice represents something different, Wingate believed. And unless the system changed, true justice would never reach Johnnie Jordan, or the other Johnnie Jordans who were surfacing in the courts of America with alarming frequency.

"I don't think I can ever take another case that will compare to Johnnie Jordan," Wingate said. "No matter what, it's etched in stone."

"How long did it take you to get over it?" I asked.

Wingate looked at me with surprise.

"I'm not over it," he replied gently a full year after the sentencing. "You never get over something like this. This is the case that will stay with me forever."

III

Two years later, his answer remained the same. When he looks at some of his young clients, his mind often flashes back to Johnnie, to Johnnie's eyes at the moment after the sentence was read, when there was no sound, no movement, and Johnnie sat utterly detached.

He sees Johnnie in many of the kids coming before the court now. He likens Johnnie to a ten-year-old "shadow" he had for a day earlier in his career. The boy had stolen to help support his mother, and a juvenile court judge asked Wingate to allow the boy to follow him around, in hopes of inspiring the child to straighten himself out. Afterward, the boy told his mother he wanted to be an attorney, "just like Ronnie Wingate." But recently he learned his "shadow" was on trial for rape. Visiting him briefly behind bars, Wingate thought for a moment he was looking again into Johnnie Jordan's eyes.

"What do you see in Johnnie's eyes?" I asked.

"Society's failures." Wingate's answer was quick. "Always, society's failures, from the beginning to now, the end.

"Everything functioned smoothly, but we can only pretend it worked. That's the secret. All of us on the inside know that it doesn't work in these crazy, young, senseless murder cases, but we have to pretend it does because people can't stand to look at what really stands before us. People are too afraid, like in the witch trials. Justice has to be blind."

22

The day after the sentencing, Wingate returned to the jail and again tried to explain to Johnnie what his sentence meant in real time, in real life. Once again, he found himself looking into blank eyes.

"I didn't really understand," Johnnie said later. "It didn't click on me, what time she [Judge Franks] gave me. She was an old lady was all I remembered."

In the weeks to come, Wingate and Meyer visited Johnnie repeatedly to advise him how to survive in adult prison. For Johnnie, that meant learning the whole new social structure of prison life: which kinds of inmates to stay away from, which ones to show respect to, how not to get taken. Johnnie thought he knew it all from his time at a Department of Youth Services (DYS) juvenile detention center. He was wrong. And though it was no longer their job, his lawyers felt responsible for correcting his cocky naïveté. It was a futile effort.

"I looked at it like it was going to be like DYS," Johnnie recalls, shaking his head in disbelief during an interview at Ross Correctional Institution, his fourth adult prison. "I'd get out in a few years. At DYS, I knocked out a year like it was nothing."

His face wrinkles, suddenly turning wizened and unnaturally old.

"Now it hit me," he mumbles with arms crossed. He kicks the chair next to him, startling the guards whose fingers move to their pistols.[1] "I

---

1. Just after Johnnie kicked the chair, a guard pulled me aside with a warning: "These aren't kids," he told me. "They're animals. You just can't tell what they'll do." Earlier that day, an inmate in the visiting room where I was interviewing Johnnie suddenly pulled a knife and slashed his girlfriend across the neck because he suspected she was having an affair with his friend. "An adult inmate would at least wait 'til he got back on the street" to get revenge, the guard told me. "These kids can't wait for anything; they don't think about cost. They're the most dangerous and unpredictable criminals I've seen, and I've been doing this for twenty years."

get tired of being locked up. My celly, he older, he been down for fifteen years. He came in when he was my age. Now people outside forgot about him. His life went down the drain. If I hadn't just told you about him, you wouldn't even know he exist. No one would. Know what I'm saying? Twenty, thirty years, that's a long time. I can't see it, man. Two years is a long time here. I try to maintain. I've gotten a lot smarter. But man, fifteen years."

He didn't know why his cellmate is serving time, never bothered to ask. He doesn't talk to him. "Most guys that been down for more than five years lose conversation," Johnnie later wrote in a letter from Ross. Johnnie himself doesn't talk to many people. He has made no friends in any of the five state prisons in which he has been serving his sentence. Prison officials move him around often, usually because he gets into fights with other inmates.

During his fourth year, Johnnie filed his own appeal to the Ohio Supreme Court. An earlier appeal, filed by another court-appointed attorney, was denied. But Johnnie said he wanted a chance to defend himself.

"I'd rather it came out of my mouth," he said. "I couldn't put the words in the right spot then [at his trial], but I could now. I'd say what happened and why it happened. And most important, I'd show remorse."

"How would you explain why it happened?" I asked.

"I can't really say why it happened yet," he said. "I don't really know, to be honest with you. I try to keep my mind off of it."

"Does it bother you when you try to remember?"

"No," he replied simply. "It's like it never even happened. I don't have no dreams about it. I don't even think about it, because it wouldn't do me no good. The only thing that reminds me I did it is being in here, in the penitentiary talking to you."

I asked him why he thinks he should be set free.

"Because time ain't doing nothing for me," he said bitterly. "Time don't do nothing but make me worser. You hear a lot of things here and read a lot of things. Now I know how to do worser things and how to get away with them next time. I'm smarter about cops and what to say when they ask me questions. This time they gave me, it ain't doing nothing."

He seemed to believe that he was punishing the judges by learning how to become a more hardened and clever criminal. He clearly did not understand the concept of rehabilitation. He saw no reason to change and even bristled at the suggestion. "What's wrong with the way I am now?" he challenged. "I like myself this way. I don't want to change at all."

Tilting back precariously in his plastic chair with arms folded, he went on:

"They could have given me five days in county [jail], and I would have been rehabilitated. I could have been rehabilitated on the first day. If they just said 'Okay, Mr. Jordan, we'll let you out if you promise you're not going to murder anyone again.' I would have said 'Okay, I won't.'

"I might, though," he admitted slyly. "But I would say I wouldn't kill someone again and they'd let me go free. You understand what I'm saying?"

Law is now a game of words for Johnnie. Rehabilitation means freedom. Freedom is something you get, not something that makes you think or feel differently. Rehabilitation is not something that changes you.

III

When he was not in "the Hole," as he calls solitary confinement, Johnnie frequently phoned me. He often became angry with my questions. He spoke coldly and roughly most of the time. During the first year, I would hang up the phone wondering if he would ever call again. Sometimes, I didn't care. But slowly, our relationship grew stronger, insofar as a journalistic relationship can. There were never any promises or suggestions that he would benefit from the book I intended to write. He knew I would not pay him or his family for their stories. Three years into my research, when Johnnie asked me for money so he could buy soap, toiletries, and maybe a few Little Debbie cakes in the prison commissary, I reminded him that we had discussed this at our first meeting. I could not give him money. I was not paying him for his story. I did not dare tell him that I also believe you can't pay for truth without adulterating it in some way.

Johnnie became quiet after my refusal. "Okay," he said softly. He called again the next day "just to check in." Up to that point, it was the closest I came to feeling that Johnnie appreciated my interest in him. I was the only person in the outside world who always accepted his collect calls.

J. R. Robinson, his former counselor, installed a block on his phone; he had so many children calling him collect that he could not afford their calls. Johnnie's family refused most of his calls. Ron Wingate visited him a few times and, after Johnnie asked, sent him money for clothes and toiletries and even a television set, using Johnnie's grandmother's name because she is the only person allowed by prison regulations to send him anything. She is his only adult relative. Even Johnnie admits his parents didn't count anymore.

Though Johnnie did not seem to like me at first, he phoned after our initial interviews in prison because he had promised to do so, and then began writing letters. It took time to establish boundaries. I was neither a girlfriend nor a mother, and those were the only two types of women Johnnie knew. He classified even his social workers by whether he had a crush on them, or whether they represented a maternal figure. I was neither.

"I don't get you," he said often. "Why you doing this?"

I found myself struggling to answer. "To figure it all out. To help people like the Johnsons. To help other kids from going down your path."

"Why?"

"Don't you want to make it so no one has to go through everything you went through?"

"No," he said.

"Why not?"

"I don't know them," he told me. "Why do you care about people you don't know? That's stupid."

III

Johnnie had a softer side, especially in his letters. He wrote that he didn't have words to recount what was happening in his head. He wrote that he appreciated my letters and our conversations.

One October, he phoned late in the evening. His voice was quieter, not as tough as usual, more like the softer tone of his letters. It took me some moments to identify the reason. He was excited, even optimistic.

"I'm just calling to tell you they're moving me tomorrow," he said.

He had requested the transfer to Mansfield prison many times. It is much closer to Toledo and his family than Ross penitentiary, which is a three- or four-hour car ride away. That morning he had been told to pack. He filled two small plastic bags with a few towels and a blanket. The rest of his belongings he gave away, he said, because his little brothers were still too small to use them and he wasn't permitted to take more than the two bags.

He had not been told why he was being transferred. But several months earlier, Mrs. Johnson's nephew was sent to Ross and, according to guards and other inmates, he had threatened to revenge his aunt's murder. Johnnie was aware of the threats, and although his voice had become tougher and meaner when he talked about them, he professed to be unconcerned.

Now he was being transferred, and he was happy. He had no idea exactly what to expect, but he seemed to anticipate that the world would open up.

"I tell you one thing. I deserve good things to happen to me, I really do. I'm a sweet guy, I really am."

I laughed until he added, "You taught me that."

He wasn't joking. I was surprised. I had never thought of him as sweet, let alone told him so. Perhaps my interest in him had engendered a greater self-respect in himself, a step forward in social development.

"Tell Ronnie I love him, man," Johnnie said when a recording warned of only thirty seconds left on the call.

"You're serious, Johnnie, aren't you?" I asked. "You're not being sarcastic?"

"No, man, I really do. He's the closest thing I ever had to a father."

The call went dead.

|||

The next day, he called again, as I had requested. I wanted to learn how conditions were at the new prison in Mansfield.

"You like it better there?"

"No," he said, his voice dry, hard, and cold again.

"Why not?"

"What do you mean, why not?" he spat out, aggravation brimming in his voice.

"Is the food better?"

"No. Worse."

"What's your new celly like?"

"I don't know, man, I don't talk to him. I don't talk to anyone. I all I got, and nothing going to make it better."

The remains of his family had made new excuses not to visit him. Johnnie was closing down. We both sensed it. In the months that followed, his optimism left him. His enthusiasm was quenched. He would not allow himself to fall prey to disappointment again. Soon, Johnnie would be utterly gone. Only the murderer would remain.

23

Today, Johnnie's world is tilted, skewed, angry, and mean. Action, not thought, constitutes personality. Reflection is dangerous because it often brings anxiety, anger, and then violence. There is no cause and effect, no God, no future, no past, and little reason. In Johnnie's words, "heaven is what you make of it and hell is what you go through." Love comes from the stomach and not the heart, where it mixes with hatred and anger. In Johnnie's world, there are different expressions of caring: the violent ones are often more meaningful than the gentle ones.

Johnnie was secretly pleased whenever J.R. yelled at him. "It meant he cared." He likes the guards to yell at him too, he claims, even when they cuss him out. "It don't bother me," he says, with prison bravado. It reaffirms his sense of strength and being.

In Johnnie's world now, there is right and wrong, only they do not mean much. Nothing is deserved. The air in his world stinks most of the time. Water tastes foul. To think too much is stupid. To build a self and feel too much is for fools.

Very little makes sense to Johnnie. After the court denied his personal appeal in late February 1998, two years after the murder, Johnnie wrote me a tear-stained letter.

> Nothing has ever hurt so bad. I am finally waking up, that I probably will never ever see the streets again. See the streets to see my baby girl grow up. See the streets to see my little sisters and brothers grow up. See the streets to see myself grow up. One thing I can say for myself is I do got responsibility for myself. Responsibility to me means respect for him or herself. A person that own up to their own mistake, no matter what it is that consists of responsibility . . . a person that know when something is wrong and does everything in its might to fix whatever they broke. I know that I ain't gonna always do good, but I'm not going to always do bad. I'm

a survivor and I'm gonna always keep my head above water. Only God can judge me now. Out of all the things that went wrong in my life, this hurt me the most. Not because I can't do what I want, not cause I can't make love to a girl. It's because I can't have another chance or choice. Out of all my homies, a group of five, three dead, one in jail, it seems like I'm the only one failure. A lot of my friends have cried. A lot of my friends have died. I'm the only one that didn't get a piece of the pie.

Jagged pieces of Johnnie's personality edge to the surface in strong and unpredictable ways. He can be gentle, sometimes thoughtful. He can be smart, and he has a dry wit. He has learned to be reflective, but at the risk of sadness and overwhelming anger. He can turn inward for a moment, then come back aggressively. He is a mess of young and underdeveloped personalities.

But Johnnie says he likes himself. He likes who he was on the streets, who he is in the cell on his block, and who he is during our interviews. He admits he's different in each setting. But he likes each part of himself. He does not want to change, not to look different, not grow taller, not get a deeper voice, not grow more facial hair. He sees nothing wrong with staying who he is. "Do you?" he asks as a challenge. Johnnie fights all changes. He is caught in an adolescence he is unlikely to outgrow.

In prison, he rebels against even trifling changes that were for his own benefit. Before his eighteenth birthday, he had mistakenly been placed in a cell block with older criminals. When I requested permission to visit for an interview, the prison reviewed Johnnie's files and moved quickly to correct the error. Johnnie was told he would be moved from his adult cell block at Ross to the less harsh juvenile block so he could attend school. In the juvenile block, he would also have been permitted to earn spending money for the commissary. But Johnnie refused to go and was punished for disobedience.

"I'm gonna go to the Hole," he said, anger tightening his words.

When will you get out? I asked.

"I don't know. Probably never."

He was too angry to think straight. He only knew that he was not moving from his cell, and he'd fight if he had to. Even if he landed back in solitary again.

"They probably will up my security to close [the level for the most difficult criminals with the worst crimes] and send me to Lucasville, but I don't care no more. I don't care about nothing no more. I get tired of it."

Tired of what?

"Everything. I'm at the point where I don't care about nothing, man. I'm tired of everything, period. They're making me not care."

What about school?

"I don't care about school neither," he said.

Is the block you're on now so good you don't want to leave?

"No, man, it sucks. I just not gonna move again." Johnnie was adamant, even though he very seldom got along with his cellmates. He was trying to reach for control of his life and surroundings, which he could never have.

How was the food? I asked.

"The food is nasty, man." Johnnie worked in the kitchen at Ross and saw inmates urinate in the vats of food on their bad days. Lucasville had an even nastier reputation. There, inmates have almost no freedom to walk or read. For only one hour each day, they are permitted to walk around a small boxlike structure outside known as a "dog cage" because it resembles a kennel.

After a month in solitary, Johnnie was moved to the juvenile block at Ross despite his objection. But little else changed as he went to school.

"I'm getting ready to go back into the Hole," he told me soon after. He knew he was spiraling out of control. He can almost predict his own violent outbursts now, but still cannot prevent them.

"People are talking crazy to me, man," he said. He sounded like he was on speed, but he was not. A prison psychiatrist prescribed both sedatives to help him sleep and Zoloft to treat his depression. But he refused to take drugs of any sort, except for weed, which he could still find ways to get in prison. He didn't trust drugs given out by the prison, not even aspirin, and he certainly didn't trust the doctors.

"Nothing I did in my whole life to deserve this," he said.

You took a life, I reminded him.

"Yeah," he said. "Could have took my life. That would be better."

He paused. "I have remorse for her, man," he resumed. "I never thought I had the guts to do nothing like that. I was all talk. When I watched her bleed to death, I didn't feel nothing. No tears came to my eyes. I didn't have no dreams about it later. That bothered me. Not what

I did, but that I didn't feel nothing about it. That bothered me. I thought I'd panic or something."

Johnnie still does not flinch at the memory of Mrs. Johnson's murder. Nor does he have nightmares about it. He never thinks of that night, he says, unless someone brings it up. Then, his only discomfort is the strange look on their faces which he can't identify. He wants to persuade them, as he has convinced himself, that the murder is in the past, beyond his control, an event that happened as the rest of his life happened. He knows that he had some responsibility for it, but not all that much.

"I knew the difference between right or wrong," he says, "but at the time, I couldn't help myself. I still feel that anger. Getting worser by the minute." He stops for a moment, thinking.

"It would have happened someday, to tell you the truth," he says of the murder. "If everything stays the same, I'm probably going to do it again." Then without anger, he adds, "It would probably happen again."

To him, his contradictions are full of truths. He does not see them as a whole, just honest responses to questions. He still believes he should not be imprisoned for such a long sentence. A year maybe, perhaps even five, but not a lifetime. The more time passes, the more he will be lost to the outside world, and that scares him more than anything.

Minutes into a bitter phone conversation one day, I understand why Johnnie is so agitated. He had phoned his older sister collect from prison, and although she finally accepted the call, she said she did not know a Johnnie.

"I had to tell her, 'It's your brother, man.'"

Johnnie's voice is pained, although it attempts disgust. "They're forgetting me already. I don't think they mean to, they just do. This is the lowest time of my life, right here, these last three weeks. I wake up and see things I've never seen before. I need more love and affection and not getting it," he says almost threateningly.

The prison-allotted time for the call expires and Johnnie is abruptly cut off. Two hours later, he fights with a guard and is sent to solitary for a full month.

"I don't have any family, friends, or religion like other guys here do," he writes in a letter from the Hole, three years after his sentencing. "I don't believe in anything that don't exist and don't do nothing for me. I just believe in myself."

24

Alan Konop, the attorney who sued Lucas County Children Services on Mr. Johnson's behalf, fancies himself a small-town lawyer, affable and open. But the twinkle in his sharp blue eyes assures that if you think this man is a small-town anything, you've seriously underestimated him. Life experiences make for richer intelligence, it seems to Konop. And he has had plenty of experience in the system he now challenged on Mr. Johnson's behalf.

Konop married his first wife when he was a junior at the University of Michigan. "That was the fifties, when people did that sort of thing," he chuckles. Their first child came before he graduated. To support his family, he sold insurance, then decided to become a rabbi but lasted only one week at Hebrew Union College in Cincinnati. He returned to Michigan to earn his undergraduate degree in 1959, and then was hired as a social worker in the Lucas County Welfare Department. He liked the work but recognized that there were better ways to make money to support two children. By day, he worked in the welfare system. At night, he earned a law degree at the University of Toledo, where he now teaches periodically. He tells his students that being a defense attorney is not like being Johnnie Cochran. Unlike Cochran, Konop says he loses more cases that he wins. But he adds, "I wouldn't like it otherwise. The system wouldn't be working. There are a lot of guilty people out there. I just try to get a little break so my client will get a lesser offense."

Konop's humble words are deceptive. About a year after the Johnson case, the *Toledo City Paper* featured Konop on its front page, his jutting chin sporting a meticulously groomed white beard, his arms crossed in a formidable pose in front of the Lucas County Courthouse. The headline read: "Preserving the System." Konop was the first of ten lawyers, including Wingate, profiled as Toledo's best defense attorneys.

"It's apparent that the 61-year-old attorney possesses not only a vibrant personality," the text flattered Konop, "but also a passion for people that rivals his love for law."

Not everyone is so complimentary. Critics point out that by swiftly taking Mr. Johnson as a client, Konop—whether intentionally or not—gave his law partner, Don Cameron, an excuse to recuse himself as Johnnie Jordan's court-appointed attorney, an unpopular and unrewarding assignment that no lawyer sought. Then there is the issue of money. Wingate and Rick Meyer spent more than nine months defending Johnnie, and in the process they uncovered a multitude of failures committed by Children Services. "They made only one, maybe two grand off the case," one attorney points out. "Alan Konop, for a lot less time and work, made about a hundred-and-sixty grand off their work. I wouldn't call it all altruism on his part."

Konop says he did not seek out Mr. Johnson to persuade him to file suit against the foster care system that allegedly contributed to his wife's death. Eva Holston, a former client of Konop's, and the Johnsons' neighbor, had phoned Konop and suggested he represent Mr. Johnson. Konop had read of the case in the newspaper and agreed to meet with Mr. Johnson. As a former social worker, he understood the bureaucracy that led to the tragedy.

Konop was particularly impressed by Mr. Johnson's sincerity, he says, Mr. Johnson's lifetime of foster-parenting children, and his charity. Charles Johnson wasn't looking for money. He was looking for reform. Most remarkable, he was almost forgiving of Johnnie.

As the lawyer recalls it, Mr. Johnson said he and his wife would have even foster-parented Johnnie if Children Services had been honest with them: "If they had said, 'Look, he was incarcerated before, he was in detention for hitting a bus driver, he had problems with guns, he had difficulty staying in various homes.' If they had said 'Here's what you're dealing with,' you know something? We probably would have said fine. We can deal with it. But I would have dealt with it differently. I wouldn't have left my wife alone with him. I really feel I could have done something."

Mr. Johnson's main purpose in bringing suit was to expose foster care's deceptions and failures, and force it to change. Without the lawsuit, child privacy laws would have prevented the public from ever knowing many of the raw and disturbing details of how Lucas County officials had handled Johnnie's case, how they failed to inform the Johnsons of the danger Johnnie posed, how they repeatedly ignored the Johnsons' pleas to remove Johnnie from their home, and how they neglected to take care of Johnnie himself or to treat his anger. Konop was drawn to the case because he believed something had gone terribly wrong in the system where he once worked. He also wanted change. And he too was guilty of idealism and naïveté, he now says with a light shrug but with a twinkle in his eyes.

Konop was familiar with each of the agencies involved in Johnnie's case—foster care, juvenile justice, and mental health. "The problem I first saw was that you had three agencies working at the same time on Johnnie Jordan, which is very dangerous. Not all of them mesh," he explains. "They each have slightly different agendas. That's part of the problem. The court is looking only at whether Johnnie Jordan's behavior is proper. Parole is looking at whether he belongs behind bars. And Children Services is looking for a placement for him."

Children Services understood that it did about seventy-five percent of what should have been done. They analyzed the problem pretty well. Number one: Johnnie Jordan couldn't cut it in various homes. Number two: he was so bad, group homes wouldn't even take him. But they didn't admit number three: their failure to tell the Johnsons any of this.

"This is what still bothers me about the agency." Konop's brow furrows slightly. "They still won't admit that maybe they should have gone to the Johnsons. Forget about the law. You don't need to do law to know about informed consent. That's just decency. This is a human thing. They knew damn well they used the Johnsons. They knew this kid was dangerous, ready to blow. They used Mr. Johnson because he was such a nice guy."

In court, Children Services could argue that they fulfilled their primary responsibility of placing Johnnie Jordan in a safe, warm home. Legally it was not their job to protect anyone from him. There is no law that required the agency to make full disclosure of Johnnie's problems to anyone, including foster parents.

The fault was more than poor conduct within Children Services or the other agencies, more than the lack of communication that inevitably exists as each agency spins in separate spheres. It is that none of these agencies is geared to handle complicated or dangerous children in foster care. Children Services is equipped to deal with the temporary placement of children in foster care. But it is incapable of raising kids like Johnnie Jordan, much less addressing their pressing needs. When faced with kids like Johnnie, it inevitably fails. Konop found this problem at the heart of his lawsuit.

By forcing Children Services to confront its failure in Johnnie's case, Konop thought the agency would recognize the need to change.

It didn't.

Konop settled the case without trial, winning just under $1 million for Mr. Johnson's loss, but without getting Children Services to admit wrong.

It was a reasonable win, with a reasonable sum, Konop says today. "If we had gone to trial, there is the issue of government immunity. You can't sue a government agency."

There was also the issue of what standard to use in judging gross negligence. And finally, Konop says, it would have been difficult to find a favorable jury.

Privately, Konop knew he and Mr. Johnson had lost their case for true reform. The agency was as immune to a lawsuit as they were to admitting fault and therefore to all other measures to reform. There was no peace in that truth. The only thing left was to let go.

III

Shortly after the settlement, Mr. Johnson died of cancer.

"To this day, I believe his death was a result of the trauma of his wife's murder," Konop says. "He lost the will to live."

Konop attended Mr. Johnson's funeral, one of the last in the old home of St. Mary's Baptist Church, where Mr. Johnson preached on occasion. Now the foster father was gracefully laid out before the overflowing congregation. He was dead, his wife had been murdered, Johnnie Jordan, Jr. was in prison. Only the system which destroyed them all survives intact.

IV
FALLOUT

25

Mr. Johnson's lawsuit against the Lucas County Children Services "did not have a big effect on us," its new director, Dean Sparks, admits with a strikingly casual, even indifferent, shrug. In fact, it had no real effect at all.

Did the agency make any policy changes as a result? I asked Sparks in his expansive office overlooking downtown Toledo.

"Well, there's been some legal changes in Ohio," he said warily. "But inside, we don't really see a need to change what we do."

Children Services' position is to continue to deny that anything at all went wrong in its welfare agency, and if something did go wrong—after all, Johnnie murdered his foster mother—then primary responsibility lies with some other agency, such as juvenile justice or mental health or, in this interview, both. Misinforming or not informing foster parents of the risk to them, Sparks seems to suggest, is necessary in finding placement for many of the children in foster care. That it resulted in an innocent's death simply is not an agency problem. Children Services' problem is finding safe placements for foster children.

Prosecutor Julia Bates had told me in an earlier interview that she felt awkward in being required to defend Sparks's agency after prosecuting Johnnie Jordan, so she pushed for an out-of-court settlement despite Children Services' wish to fight the case. Both sides seemed to feel that $1 million represented neither a true win nor a significant loss.

Children Services' biggest loss was self-imposed, in the forced resignation of its director, Ellen Jones, after she took up an office collection for Mrs. Johnson's funeral. In the midst of attacks from the media, the agency feared the community would see Jones's gesture as an admission of the agency's fault.

Tamara Cusack, Johnnie's primary caseworker, still works at Children Services in the same capacity. Sparks declined to answer questions about Cusack's role. He was reluctant to talk about the case in general, even in the presence of two agency lawyers whom he insisted sit in and advise him during our interview. Sparks said Cusack did not wish to be interviewed. She did not return any of my phone calls.

In internal memos written by Cusack, she did not take responsibility or even express regret for the tragedy. Mr. Johnson claimed she failed to inform him and his wife of Johnnie's dangerous past and failed to show up at the critical court meeting that would have removed Johnnie from the Johnsons' home and put him in a detention center well before he murdered. She claimed not to have known about the hearing. Because she was out of town, she did not return the Johnsons' urgent calls in the days leading up to the murder. Nobody did.

Cusack also claimed that the agency was unaware that Johnnie had acted out sexually in more than one incident at River Road, did not know that he had a substance abuse problem, nor that he was supposed to receive ongoing counseling after he served time for striking the bus driver. But it is difficult to believe the agency was in the dark about these matters. They were all recorded in Johnnie's files. Rather than accept responsibility, Cusack blamed a lack of communication between agencies: "It continues to be evident that breakdown in communication between DYS [juvenile correction] and LCCS [foster care] had greatly impaired the delivery of appropriate services to this child," she wrote.

Sixteen months after Mrs. Johnson's murder, Sparks said he saw no point in reviewing the case, either with me or in any other fashion. While he agreed that many children are following Johnnie's violent path, and many of those children are the wards of his Children Services agency, he argued that they were not the problem of the foster care system.

"We're here to protect kids from their parents," he said, "not to protect the community from delinquent kids. Johnnie's the kind of kid that is very troubled. There are lots and lots of kids like that. One agency couldn't handle it themselves. Maybe the lesson is we need to do a better job coordinating agencies."

That's as far as Sparks went in his assessment. Any investigation or review of Johnnie's case was intrusive and possibly dangerous, and obviously bothersome.

"Johnnie Jordan is not the first child to kill his foster mother," he said after persistent questioning. "We had one in Columbus. One in Dayton. And that's just in Ohio. There are many more throughout the country. Why are you focusing on this one?"

It didn't matter which case I focused on, I told him, as long as it educated the public about the conditions that had failed to prevent, if not invited, inexplicably violent crimes committed by children. Moreover, Children Services never made reforms or changes after Mrs. Johnson's murder, despite Mr. Johnson's appeals. Even after he fought for those changes with the few resources he had, he still had little or no voice. The agency had not even attempted to examine, let alone learn from, what happened. While recognizing these child murderers would emerge again, Lucas County Children Services especially sought to keep the tragedy away from public consciousness.

There were reasons for that, according to Sparks. But when I asked what they were, he quickly asserted that he was not with Lucas County Children Services at the time, so he could not speak to those issues. He could only talk about what he found when he got there.

"This agency has been traumatized by what happened. When I came in, it was suffering from posttraumatic stress disorder," he joked. "It needed a lot of morale boosting. We need to mend and explain to the community who we are and what we do."

Sparks was director of the children's services department in Montgomery County, Ohio, when a number of babies were killed in their foster homes. He did not want to answer questions about his tenure there, either.

"That was two agencies ago," he said. What he seems to remember most vividly about those deaths was the personal accusations in the media against him, not the tragedy of the lost young lives. "They called me a baby killer," he recalled angrily.

"I've been in this field for twenty-two years. It's not our fault. It's the fault of whoever does the killing. Then the community turns on you, and makes it a lot harder."

Children Services "was an agency that was traumatized by what happened," Sparks repeated, speaking through his greying beard. "You go into a bunker mentality. You get angry with your community, with your press. You get very defensive and shut yourself off. The tragedy is bad enough, but then you get little support from the community.

"You can't point the finger at one agency and say this is your fault," Sparks added, indignant. "The blame lies with Johnnie Jordan."

Few people would argue with that. But Children Services was responsible for Johnnie, a juvenile at the time, and much more could have been done to prevent him from murdering. So Sparks pointed the finger elsewhere, specifically at juvenile justice, which had periodically jailed Johnnie.

"I make an assumption that once he's been in the juvenile justice system, he's not going to come out dangerous," he said. "If they are still dangerous, juvenile justice will keep them. I guess that's not always the case."

After an hour and a half, Sparks came to the gut of the problem as he saw it:

"Foster homes are designed to take care of abused and neglected kids," he said. "The problem is our country doesn't have the in-between for delinquent kids. We have foster homes and kiddy jails, and adult jails. Nothing in between. We have therapeutic homes, but they don't always work and there aren't many of them. Anyway, there are thousands of Johnnie Jordans out there. In this country, there are thousands. So what do you do?" His hands flew up. "Which kids do you work on?"

26

Jack Ford, a Toledo Democrat and minority leader in Ohio's House of Representatives, was not shocked when he learned of the Johnnie Jordan case. With a degree in social work, Ford had been an inspector of foster homes for the state Department of Youth Services in the late 1970s. Back then, the kids he encountered were mostly runaways or incorrigibles. Not like today, he has heard from many of his friends still in social work.

Ford went on to earn a law degree and, fourteen years before he was elected to the Ohio legislature, had started a countywide drug treatment agency. After reading two long articles in the *Toledo Blade* about the Johnnie Jordan case, he started asking questions and listening to the people he knew and trusted in the social services field. What he found out surprised him more than the case itself.

"There are fifty Johnnie Jordans out there every day," he said, still incredulous. "Fifty, and nowhere for them to go until they murder."

Ford introduced House Bill 173, which turned out to be one of the few Democratic-sponsored bills to pass the Republican-majority House that year. Ninety-six of the legislature's ninety-nine representatives approved it. The State Senate passed it unanimously. The measure became known as the Johnnie Jordan law.

Ford pitched the act as "a victims' rights bill from a preventive standpoint." On the House floor he told his colleagues, "It may save another Mrs. Johnson."

But his hopes of reforming the system dwindled with the many diluting revisions he allowed in order to win passage of the measure. The legislators were not primarily concerned with helping the Johnnie Jordans of the world, but being tough on juvenile crime and big on protecting the public. The few who admitted their concern for troubled and destructive kids certainly did not want to come across as sympathetic "to that kid or any like him," as one representative said later.

"It was far too passionate a time," this legislator added, asking that his name not be used because shards of public outrage from the Johnnie Jordan case still reverberate through Ohio politics. "I can only liken it to the Rodney King incident. But in this case, there was a prevailing consensus. It would have been political suicide to stand up before my hometown and say, 'I know this is terrible, horrendous and undeserved what happened to Mrs. Johnson, but let's also look to see how we could have helped Johnnie Jordan to prevent this from happening in the future.' The mood was simply to turn inward. How do we protect ourselves from these monsters in the future?"

The Right to Know law, as the Johnnie Jordan law is also often called, requires children's services agencies throughout the state to inform foster parents about a child's previous conduct. Under certain circumstances, it provides for some children to undergo a psychological evaluation. Lucas County Children Services officials say that prior to the law, its social workers verbally notified foster parents out of good faith if their wards had a troubled past. But Jack Ford was told that passing on such information was the rare exception rather than the rule. Now Lucas County Children Services and similar agencies across Ohio are required to give foster parents a written assessment of the child who is being placed with them, and foster parents must sign a statement acknowledging that they have read the document and are aware of the child's history.

Representative Ford had to wait two years to introduce the second phase of the Johnnie Jordan law. House Bill 332 called for better training of foster parents. Until 1999, Ohio did not require foster parents to undergo any training, although the state Department of Human Services did offer a twelve-hour orientation program for new foster parents plus a twelve-hour refresher class every two years; the latter was often waived, however.

The orientation classes were standard for all foster parents. Those caregivers taking in pregnant children and teenage mothers sat through the same general classes as those preparing for crack babies and troubled children like Johnnie. Most foster parents say they found the classes a formality and a waste of time.

Ford's second bill, written with the aid of his legislative assistant

Cathy Allen, ordered foster care agency directors to provide more specialized training classes to caretakers, based on the needs and conditions of the children placed in their homes. Under this tiered training system, those people who operate treatment foster homes (also known as therapeutic foster homes), which deal with more-troubled children, require more training: forty-eight preservice hours, thirty-six hours during the first year, and thirty hours each year thereafter. The caregivers are paid no more than ordinary foster parents who, under the new law, are now required to undergo thirty-six hours of training before taking in a child, and twenty-four additional hours each year thereafter. Kinship care, the kind of foster care that Johnnie's stepgrandmother once provided, still requires no training. But if the kinship foster care parent asks for such help, or if the foster care authorities advise it, the state must pay for special classes for the guardian.

The Ohio legislature allocated $3 million for the entire training program, which was expected to increase to $6 million with federal matching grants. Each foster parent will be paid a $20 or $25 stipend to attend each three-hour session. Otherwise, the law did not change the amount of money that the state pays foster parents to take care of the children.

A third Ford bill, known as the foster care reform bill, was expected to be merged with a Republican measure introduced by Representative Kerry Metzker. Both call for stricter licensing requirements for foster homes, and require foster care agencies to monitor each child's progress and to assess, by school grades and truancy reports, whether he or she is better off in foster care than in their biological homes.

In response to the dozens of cases of children who died in foster care, some of them killed by their caregivers, the measure also called for an independent Child Fatality Review Board to examine every case involving a child's death. Finally, following news reports of the misuse of foster care funds, the Metzker measure requires foster care agencies to be held accountable for the money they receive from state taxes. Before, these agencies had to answer to no one but their directors.

While these bills move toward reform, they fall far short of the fundamental changes the system needs. Jack Ford recognizes the shortcomings, but feels that the public is not yet ready to listen to people like former director of Children Services Ellen Jones and accept a prescription for radical overhaul.

"Jones is a blacklisted name," said another legislator who is still afraid of aligning himself with the former CSB director's tarnished public image. "The real problem with Ellen Jones is that she was too good for the foster care system. So they used her. But you can't tell people that. They want a fall guy. They want blood. Systems don't bleed. She bleeds."

27

Solution

Johnnie Jordan was lost a long time ago, perhaps before he became a teenager, certainly before he murdered Mrs. Johnson. Warning signs flashed throughout his life. He suffered and witnessed extreme abuse and neglect. He could not adjust to surrogate homes, repeatedly running back to his abusive parents for succor they were incapable of giving. He had difficulties at home, with school, difficulty with his emotions, particularly controlling his anger. Almost everyone who came in contact with Johnnie knew or sensed he was troubled.

Plainly, Johnnie's behavior and record made his probation officer, social workers, and foster parents increasingly anxious. He came to the Johnsons after being kicked out of yet another foster home because of rumors he had a gun. If he was not already dangerous, one teacher warned, he would be soon.

No one disputed that fact. Most were convinced he was destined for terrible things. But there was no place for Johnnie Jordan, nowhere that would address and possibly defuse the explosive potential in him. The therapeutic homes, most of them already overcrowded, rejected him as too dangerous. In the months, days, and hours leading up to the murder, his foster parents, nervous and fearful, repeatedly called for help, realizing that he was about to explode.

"We all waited for the crime that would send him away for good," explained a psychologist at one of the institutions that refused to have anything to do with Johnnie. "We weren't going to bet that we could help him. We didn't have the space for a kid we weren't certain we could help. Frankly, we were fortunate he took only one victim with him. With most kids like this, there can be many, many more."

Certainly mistakes were made in dealing with Johnnie. But the greatest failure was the system itself. The overriding failure was the absence of facilities and programs to identify and head off his violence. His path was not predestined or driven by an innate evilness. Johnnie Jordan was not born a monster, but he developed into a human being who committed a monstrous act. That malignant development could have been arrested. With the right help, he may even have become a healthy asset to society. But today such an outcome is highly improbable, if not impossible. Social workers, probation officers, foster parents, and even some teachers tried to catch Johnnie before he murdered. But they could not do enough within the limitations under which they work. The same is true of the many other violent children living in their foster, biological, or adoptive homes today.

The fundamental problem is that no one system today is designed to handle kids like Johnnie Jordan. None takes full responsibility for them, monitors them, or ensures their safety as well as that of the community throughout their young lives. Like Johnnie, many children coming before juvenile courts have needs that overlap several child care programs and agencies. Such children are labeled "dual-diagnosed" juveniles. They include violent children, mentally ill children, and children with diminished mental capacities who behave in a delinquent or criminal fashion.

Today there are simply "no provisions for dual-diagnosis youths" in the bureaucratic maze of programs designed to help children in need, according to Donna Mitchell, chief magistrate of Toledo's juvenile court. "It is a huge system need."

Among dual-diagnosed children she sees daily are what she calls low-functioning juvenile sex offenders and fire setters, as well as more violent children. Because they are either too young or too mentally deficient, these children have not yet developed the cognitive capability for treatment, Mitchell says. A higher level of understanding and reasoning is necessary for therapy to be effective.

For kids like Johnnie, years of abuse limit their ability to learn in school as well as to mature emotionally. "I don't need to be a psychologist to know that abuse impairs early learning of such things as empathy and sympathy," Mitchell explains. "I see it. These children need treatment so they don't harm themselves or others. But I am in juvenile justice, not treatment. The only place we can put them is in jail with the general criminal population where they only learn more criminal behavior."

Most mental health agencies are designed to treat adults. For children to qualify for help, they must be diagnosed as "severely emotionally disturbed." Few children like Johnnie can satisfy that psychiatric diagnosis. Instead, the obvious signs of their condition—anger and violence—are easy to identify and speed them into the juvenile justice system. Even if diagnosed as severely disturbed, most insurance companies provide limited treatment. Even then, many children in Johnnie's situation are not adequately insured, if they are insured at all.

Regardless of whether delinquent behavior and mental illness are consequences of child abuse, as Mitchell believes, the bureaucracies into which abused children are consigned are not concerned about the roots of the problem. "The question is not even asked about cause," she complains.

Moreover, if a judge finds that a child is delinquent or criminal, the youth cannot be admitted to the state's mental health system for abused children. Even if the crime can be blamed on mental illness, once a crime is committed, the court's only duty is to deal with punishment. "We are responsible and can render only a legal response to illegal behavior, not deal with the roots of that behavior," Mitchell says.

It is imperative to improve the jagged and ineffective cooperation among the panoply of services—juvenile justice, mental health, child protection (foster care), and substance abuse—that deal with dangerous children. Clusters, or representatives, of these various agencies do meet in Ohio to decide exactly what kind of help to provide to a troubled child, as well as who will foot the bill for such services. But these clusters are hobbled by bureaucracy. Representatives must be unanimous when they appear before a judge, both on a course of treatment and the agency to be financially responsible. If one member does not agree, the others have the option to appeal to a magistrate. But because of crowded court dockets and busy caseworker schedules, appeals can take months to sort out. If one representative fails to attend a meeting, the rest of the cluster is forbidden from making any decision. As we saw in Johnnie's case, his Children Services caseworker failed to attend a key meeting (or send a surrogate). Though it never again appeared on a court docket, the meeting was to be rescheduled for weeks later to accommodate the various busy calendars. In the intervening time, Johnnie killed.

Clusters have other faults as well. Because there is a shared decision-making process, no one agency takes full responsibility for the child. He or she is shuttled and pushed among them, and no one takes charge to follow up and monitor the child's overall progress or lack of it. Competition among the services for funds is yet another problem that thwarts cooperation. In most cases, county commissioners parcel out federal, state, and county dollars to the various agencies. In the competition for funds, each agency wants to boast the best success rates. So they pass off their most difficult children whenever they can. None want to be handling the child when he or she explodes.

Being shuffled between services erodes a child's feeling of self-worth and reduces the chance that he or she will form attachments to adults and other children, attachments that are crucial to the child's successful development into adulthood. Troubled children who do succeed often say that the key to their positive outcome was that they became close to someone who really cared about them. Through such relationships, children develop a sense of identity and self-worth, accept the responsibility of a conscience, and find a reason for their existence. Most often, they gain all this simply from the feeling that they are valued by another person.

In most states, troubled children are placed in institutions or therapeutic group homes where they rarely form attachments to underpaid staff members who, working in shifts, are not much more than strangers to the children. Such institutional settings offer little hope or chance for a positive outcome, says Jones, the former director of Children Services. "*If* they are a safe place, that is their only virtue," she adds.

Even such placements are rare, because space and money are limited. The better facilities accept between 5 and 25 percent of applications. And if accepted, children are permitted to stay only a relatively short period of time before they are returned to the environment from which they came. Moreover, because of limited finances, juvenile courts can afford to send only a few of their troubled children to these institutions and group homes even when space is available.

"You have one placement available for about seven or eight kids in need," explains Mitchell, the juvenile court chief magistrate. "How do you decide who's going to get it? Usually you look to who's going to give us the biggest payoff." It will not be the most troubled child or the most dangerous one, she admits, but the child who showed some promise at an earlier placement. The more dangerous children are left to drift until they commit a more serious crime and are confined to a temporary juvenile detention center, where their slide toward even more horrendous crimes is accelerated.

Over the past two decades, a colder, meaner, and more violent juvenile criminal has emerged, and the juvenile justice system struggles in its response to this growing danger. Juvenile courts were designed in the 1800s to aid and reform wayward youth, not violent ones. Today the juvenile justice system is more like the adult penal system, taking criminals off the streets and warehousing them for reasons of public safety. Unlike adult criminals, however, almost all troubled and violent children will return to the streets by their twenty-first birthdays, in the middle of the statistical age group that is most prone to commit violent crimes.

Mitchell is pessimistic about the future of the typical troubled juveniles who pass through her court. "If we don't deal with the child who has criminal tendencies now," she warns, "we'll pay later. And we're not dealing with them now."

III

Ellen Jones has a solution. She wants to set up a separate foster care agency within the juvenile justice system designed especially for troubled children. Take them out of their criminal environments, away from their abusive parents, the detention centers, the standard foster care system, and even their nonabusive biological parents if their parents can't handle them, she proposes, and place them instead in a stricter, closely monitored home with adults who are educated and trained to deal with problem children. She offers a rough sketch of her vision, which she insists is not only practical, but would also save money and lives in the long term. She has dreamed about such a program for fifteen years.

"This would be a service for all those children who don't fit in," Jones says. "Children who have been thrown out of multiple foster care placements, children who have been abused and have begun to abuse others, children who can't stay at home because they are too dangerous, children whose parents cannot handle them, children who are on parole or probation but who have not yet cognitively committed violent crimes and have no good, safe, caring, and secure home in which to live." Jones does not worry about how to select the right children for this kind of special care. As a former referee in juvenile court, a group home director, and a director of Lucas County Children Services, she has learned from experience that these difficult children stand out clearly to most social service workers and teachers.

"We're not talking about just behavior problems here," she explained. "We mean the hopeless kids, the kids who do not fit anywhere, the ones some teachers claim are just plain evil."

Aberrant behavior in most of these children starts early, according to Magistrate Mitchell. By age seven, they may be fire setters or bullies who take sexual advantage of younger children, or even beat helpless or aged adults. "We try not to put them in detention at that age," Mitchell said, for fear they will learn even worse behavior. But the alternative is to allow them to remain free, and so they usually continue to bully, disrupt, and victimize others. By the time they are eleven or twelve years old, many are uncontrollable. By fourteen or fifteen, they are very dangerous.

The special foster care service that Jones proposes, as part of a juvenile justice department, would maintain greater oversight of children. Unlike regular foster care, in which both parents often work outside the home or divide their attention among many foster children, special foster care parents would be well paid to spend more hands-on time with the children in their care, somewhat like the staff at River Road Group Home. But unlike a group home, these parents would be responsible only for one, two, or perhaps three children. They would act more as parents, rather than professional staff who are taught to keep a distance from their wards. The children's free time would be filled, and they would be constantly supervised, much as in therapeutic group homes, but without the rotating staffs which typify most institutional bureaucracies. Group and individual therapy as well as empathy training and anger management would be standard for all children in this special foster care system. These sessions could not be taken cavalierly, as they are in too many juvenile detention centers today. Achievement reports would be reviewed regularly by foster parents, parole officers, and judges. If a child resisted and refused to make progress, he or she would risk a term in juvenile detention.

Rather than taking these very troubled children completely out of society and dumping them into jails with juvenile criminals, this special foster care system would expose them to society in constructive ways. They would learn by example how a healthy family operates, so that ideally, they could create healthy families when they are adults, rather than mimic their own abusive parents.

Jones believes that such a system could attract highly qualified professional foster parents who would make relatively long-term commitments and attachments to the children in their care. "If we take this seriously, and the caregivers know what they're getting into and are trained to handle it, it will work," she says. "There's a wealth of idealistic professionals who could and would do this if they got the proper support. They can meet the challenge. I've seen it done."

With more money and more intensive support, the special foster care service for troubled children could be more selective in choosing the caregivers, encouraging people with professional backgrounds such as nurses, mental-health-care workers, police officers, psychologists, and probation officers to enter the program. Jones would tap into the reservoir of idealistic and energetic adults who are turned off by red tape and senseless procedures that are based less on individual children's needs than on bureaucratic structure. These highly trained foster parents would be well versed in the warning signs of extreme violence and in the potential dangers these troubled children pose to other children, to themselves, and to the caregivers.

As it is, too many good caregivers flee the regular foster care system because they do not receive adequate support from the agency. They often feel that they spend more time struggling with foster care's bureaucracy than helping the children. When caseworkers do not respond to their concerns or suggestions, or do not thoroughly inform them about unique aspects of foster children in their care, foster parents become angry and quit. Money is also a complicating factor.

"We have never given foster parents good compensation for caretaking," Jones admits. Payment is based on estimates of the cost of a child's upkeep, typically about $13 a day. "The result is that we're getting foster parents who are not able to make ends meet on their own, who are fostering for money because they can't get better-paying jobs elsewhere. We're desperate."

Jones proposes to pay special foster parents on a professional scale $35,000 to $50,000 a year, up to ten times more than most regular foster parents earn, but still far less than the cost of a child's year-long stay at a juvenile prison or in most therapeutic group homes.

In most counties across the country, as was the case in Ohio, training for foster parents is seriously inadequate, if not almost nonexistent. Few foster parents get to know other foster caregivers well, or ever speak to the directors. In Jones's special foster care system, a small group of foster parents would train intensely together along with "respite" caregivers. For every seven families, Jones suggests two respite families who would substitute on weekends or for vacations when the main caregivers need a break. Together, she hopes, the families would form larger bonds, building a small community.

The juvenile justice foster care service would also include a strong mental health component. Children would be required to visit a counselor or psychologist once a week on their own, and once a week with a foster parent or parents. Good counseling, when the child is ready, is crucial. Conducting sessions more frequently, rather than less frequently, minimizes the stigma that some children attach to them, opening the door for the time when the child is ready to seek help or gain trust. Such an approach could have helped Johnnie Jordan.

"I had a counselor," Johnnie told me. "She probably would have helped if I had gone to her, if someone made me go see her. But I didn't want people thinking I was crazy, so I didn't go, and when I did, I didn't listen."

Even with the special foster care service, juvenile prisons would be needed for children who commit egregious crimes and need to be removed from society at least for some time. Sentences in juvenile prisons should be extended beyond an inmate's eighteenth or twenty-first birthday, for those children who suffer from delayed or diminished mental capacities to get a greater opportunity to benefit from rehabilitative services. But most of these facilities today are ineffective, as demonstrated by the high number of recidivists. They operate much as adult prisons, warehousing troubled children rather than attempting to rehabilitate them. Violent abuses in boot camps and other detention centers do not scare children into changing their behavior. Studies show that abuse merely fosters abuse. Only teaching and counseling children in a humane environment will encourage them to live a good life.

III

A special foster care program, one that separates and retrains troubled children before they become more violent criminals, is our chance to stop another Johnnie Jordan. For in today's systems, most children following in Johnnie's destructive path will explode. They too are destined to become casualties of a bureaucracy that is less intent on rehabilitation or even justice than on simply removing them from the community in the name of protecting the public. In adult prisons, realistic hope of rehabilitation is abandoned when the gates slam shut. If only one or a few young lives and those of their victims were lost this way, it would be a tragedy. But today there are too many entirely innocent victims— too often young children shot down in schools and playgrounds. Without reform, more are certain to die. The young murderers can be stopped before they kill. But because there is little alternative in place, we wait for their crimes and then raise them in adult prisons where they become even more dangerous criminals. Helping dangerous children become nonviolent and even useful citizens would cost us little, certainly less than the destruction they wreak and the bills for their incarceration. More important and priceless are the lives, young and old, vulnerable and innocent, that would be saved.

28

Johnnie phoned from prison shortly after his nineteenth birthday. Seconds into his call, I sensed he was different. His voice was low, deep, and edgy, but without the sharp agitation and meanness that often came through on his ugly days. His words came swiftly, as if he were afraid.

"Bad," he said when I asked how things were going. "Me and my celly got into it today. I was ready to go off on him," he told me soberly, almost fearfully. "I hit my limit."

Perhaps he feared his new cellmate, I thought; perhaps he was being raped or abused. But no, nothing in particular made him angry. The man had said nothing. He had done nothing. Yet somehow, he had gotten on Johnnie's nerves, triggering rage. Even after the guards pulled Johnnie off, the anger remained deep and strong. Several hours later, alone, Johnnie smashed his fist against the prison's cinder-block walls.

"I hit my limit," he repeated, almost to himself. "I just hit my limit. I can't be here no more. I can't. I hit my limit. I don't know what I might do." He paused. "I'm afraid of myself too." His voice trailed off.

"What do you mean?" I asked.

"The only time I felt this way was last time," he said. "It was the last time I called J.R. I told him I didn't know what I was going to do. This is that same call again."

His words about the days leading up to Mrs. Johnson's murder—of his call to his counselor for help—were so flat they shook me.

"Johnnie, you think you might do it again? That you could after all this?"

"What? Kill somebody?" he answered easily. "Yeah, anyone could. I think it's inside all of us."

"What's inside us?"

"Angry."

"You're angry at what?"

"I don't know," his voice trailed off again, not frustrated or pleading, but disinterested in exploring the reasons. "I just can't do this anymore. I been down a long time. I don't even care. I'm afraid of what I might do."

"Johnnie, you can't kill someone again," I told him firmly. But I could not think of a reason to give him, a reason that might change his mind. Remorse and regret would not stop Johnnie from his powerful rage. Not fear, not the promise of a future. Johnnie had nothing. If he killed again, I said instead, he would likely be put to death. He was silent for several moments.

"But it's the same feeling," he said finally. "I think I might do something and I can't stop it. Back then I didn't care though. I was too young. I didn't know. I wasn't thinking about anything, not even thinking about getting caught. I didn't care. I'm trying to think now."

Still, Johnnie's anger was dangerously unswerving, immune to reason, it seemed, and all-consuming. He recognized that. But he could not get beyond it.

He had asked prison officials for help weeks ago, filing paperwork to request counseling. He had thought of talking to someone before. But now, for the first time, he realized that he needed help to control himself. He sensed he would kill if he did not get help quickly, and he did not want to be killed by the state as punishment. I also believe that Johnnie, deep inside, does not want to take another life.

But in his application for counseling, Johnnie did not mention his anger. He said he has learned that the less specific his requests, the better off he is. He wrote only that he wanted "someone to talk to." Prison officials had not responded. I suggested he see the prison doctor that afternoon about his crushed hand and ask the doctor to arrange a session with a psychologist.

Too late, he told me. After two o'clock, the medical staff leaves for the day.

Ask the head guard on his block for emergency help, I urged him.

"Psheww," he said. "I won't even waste my breath."

We talked some more, as I tried to find some angle to diffuse his anger.

"I got a lot of stuff going on inside me now," he said finally. "Family stuff."

He was quiet for several moments. When he continued, his voice was clearer than I had ever heard it, not clouded by anger or self-pity, but smooth—even pure—and unusually introspective, as if he had a revelation and the truth almost stunned him.

"The reason I'm here is because of my family," he began. "I don't mean I killed someone for them. I just mean I cared about them too much. I wanted to be with them or at least near them so bad. You know how, as a little kid, you go out and stay in some doorway all night till you're real cold and hungry, just to see them? You don't even think about why they don't come to you. Now they, like, disown me, and not because I killed no one, but because they never really cared.

"The thing is, I cared too much. Everything I did was for something [his family] that was never really there. I lived in something they told me, that never was real. The real stuff, the stuff J.R. told me, I never believed. I couldn't because it was the opposite of what my family told me. I trusted something that wasn't there because I had to choose. Now I'm just angry," he said, although sadness, not anger, grew in his voice. "I don't care what I might do ever again."

The phone signaled a final warning that his call, strictly limited by the prison to ten minutes this time, would be terminated in ten seconds.

"I don't care anymore and nobody cares about me," he told me coolly. "It's too late. The truth is, no one really cared about me. It was all a mistake and it brought me here."

III

A week later, Johnnie phoned again. He was about to lose his front teeth. He did not know why.

"All I know is that the motherfuckers are loose," he said. "And if I lose the motherfuckers, I ain't gonna call you no more."

I laughed.

"When I don't call, you know why," a smile came through in his voice.

His anger had clearly subsided. I asked how he had calmed it.

"I don't know," he said in a low voice. "All I know is that it will come back. It always does. And next time, it will be worser than the last time. I can feel it, like last time, like Mrs. Johnson."

He turned the conversation to Ron Wingate, his former attorney, whom he had been calling, asking for bedsheets and other items he felt he needed. Johnnie had become more petulant with each call even after Wingate, several weeks earlier, explained that he was in the midst of closing a death penalty case. When it ended, he was scheduled to enter a hospital for surgery that had been postponed for a month because of the trial. Johnnie said he understood, though clearly he did not.

In his child's mind, people are either alive and healthy, or dead. And like a child, Johnnie expected he could ask for favors in a demanding tone. He did not take into consideration that Wingate had not been his attorney for years or that the money he sent Johnnie came out of his own pocket. When he asked Wingate for new sneakers, Johnnie made clear he wanted the name brand, not the knockoffs.

Now he needed to be reassured that Wingate was not making excuses. Yes, I told him, I understood that Wingate had undergone serious surgery.

Johnnie fell quiet. Wingate had not been exaggerating just to put him off, as people so often did throughout his life, and even more now.

"I don't want to lose him, man," he said softly, almost to himself. "You gonna pray for him?" he asked me. It was a request from the young Johnnie, the one I thought was lost, who still felt adults could change his world miraculously. He knew I don't attend any church or shul, but he was asking me to pray for his friend. It was one of the few requests he made of me.

"Are you?" I asked him.

There was a silence between us.

"For him, I might," he said low and soft again. "For him. Not for me though. I'll never pray for me. But for Ronnie, I would. If there is a God, I'd talk to him directly. I'd do anything for Ronnie."

There was no question that a compassionate heart still beat in Johnnie Jordan, Jr., though it was buried, muffled, and dying. A part of Johnnie cared for some people perhaps more than himself, despite feeling alienated and rejected by our world, the world we once wanted him and other children like him to be a part of. But there was also still a part of Johnnie that may kill out of a sudden wild internal rage, an anger that has never been seriously treated nor dealt with professionally, an anger that could strike someone closest at hand, or even the person he cares about most.

III

Although Johnnie recognized that he cared too much about his family, he could not remain unmoved when he learned his mother was back on the streets smoking crack.

"I miss my mom," he said, his voice thick with concern. "I feel bad for her. When my grandmother said my mom was trying [to stay sober], I felt so bad for her I had to cry right there on the phone."

Even though he recalls the painful times his mother was not there for him, and even while incarcerated and hoping perhaps above all else that she would visit him or write him, he worries for her safety. He has not heard from her since his arrest at age fifteen.

"I know she loves me," he tells me poignantly, "because all mothers love their kids. She can try to throw me out of her life, but I know she still loves me."

III

Not long afterward, Johnnie found that there was an inmate at Mansfield Correctional Institution one year younger than he.

"This dude used to live across the street from here," Johnnie explained. "From his home, he could see Mansfield. It's sad, man, no one ever looked out for him."

Now, Johnnie does. "I try to correct his mistakes. I mean, I don't tell him what to do, I just give him my opinion. I want him to know that he could turn out like me if he's not careful. I know he's like me too. I was so mad when I was growing up, all the time I was mad, so when someone tries to show me love, I think they're out to get me. He needs to take the help before it's too late."

Why are you helping him? I asked.

He paused for a long time.

"I don't know, man," he said. "I guess you could say I done a lot of thinking since I was fifteen. I don't want him to be like me."

29

Conclusion

What happened inside Johnnie Jordan, Jr.—why Johnnie committed the brutal murder of his foster mother on that cold January night—will always be a mystery which neither science, philosophy, nor psychiatry alone can explain, though each holds its truths.

J. R. Robinson, who knew Johnnie better than anyone as his counselor, friend, and father figure, offered a simple answer: "Johnnie is a system's kid," he said with a wide shrug. "He basically grew up in the system. No question his parents are responsible. Second, the system didn't do everything it should do. In some ways, it couldn't. It wasn't designed to. Third, you got the environment where Johnnie lived. Johnnie was into gangsta rap, and gansta rap is not telling kids to be nice people. He lived in places where violence is normal and where you can get guns easily. A lot of people felt—almost everyone who knew his situation, in fact—that it was just a matter of time before he exploded. With all these things, we create our own little monsters. Johnnie was one of them."

J.R. recognized that his explanation was far from complete. Certainly children in Johnnie's straits are far more susceptible to becoming criminals, but not all susceptible children become bullies or commit murder. Some turn out fine. What drove Johnnie Jordan over the edge? What was he trying to show or gain from taking an innocent life? Or did he have a purpose?

To many of those familiar with the Johnson case, Johnnie fit the profile of a qualitatively new type of juvenile criminal—harder, meaner, colder, one who is said to show no regret, no remorse, and no sympathy. One, they claim, who has no capacity for empathy and no conscience.

These children are viewed as dangerous predators for whom and about which nothing can be done. They are headed toward murder, and those around them know it.

Many of the anecdotal fears I had heard when I began investigating Johnnie's case seemed to have materialized during the past four years. But only the most striking cases are brought to national attention, such as the eleven-year-old Michigan boy, Nathaniel Abraham, who shot to death an eighteen-year-old stranger outside a convenience store. Before the murder, Nathaniel's mother had pleaded with juvenile court several times for help with her son, who had run afoul of the police numerous times. While recognizing the danger Nathaniel posed, neither the court nor social services could intervene until the boy murdered.[1]

Several months later, a six-year-old boy in Flint, Michigan, shot to death a six-year-old classmate. Like Johnnie, this child lived in miserable environments throughout his life. His last home was described as a crack house. His father languished in jail; his mother abused drugs regularly. Yet resisting the tide of public opinion, state prosecutors determined the child had not fully understood the concept of murder and thus should not be tried as an adult. Prosecutors turned instead to a teenager who illegally kept the murder weapon loaded in the home with the child.[2]

Perhaps we do live in an increasingly aggressive, competitive, and violent culture, as many critics complain. Certainly that was Johnnie's world. On his mean streets, love and kindness are a luxury he almost never enjoyed and emotion is a weakness. But Johnnie's life is not un-

1. Abraham was determined to be borderline retarded, with the emotional age of six. He was the youngest American ever charged and convicted of murder as an adult. The judge refused to sentence him as an adult, however, saying that to do so would destroy any hope for rehabilitation. Abraham will remain in juvenile detention until he turns twenty-one, when he will be released. Prosecutors argued strongly against his sentence, urging instead that he be evaluated at that age and transferred to an adult prison if he is not clearly rehabilitated by then. Judge Eugene A. Moore, who created a firestorm with his decision, said he hoped to alert the public that "our youth are in trouble" and that the state should devote far more resources to rehabilitating troubled teenagers before they become adult criminals. ("Young Killer Sentenced to Juvenile Facility," *Washington Post*, Jan. 14, 2000; "Boy Who Killed Gets 7 Years," *New York Times*, Jan. 14, 2000.)
2. The number of children under eighteen serving time in adult prisons more than doubled between 1985 and 1997. Seven in ten of those juveniles who received adult punishment in 1997, the latest year for which state prison records are available, were convicted for violent offenses like murder, robbery, and assault. (Justice Department report, Feb. 28, 2000.)

like that lived by many children throughout the world struggling for dignity as though it is survival. A surfeit of guns, media and cultural violence, and lack of parenting are also factors that partially explain this phenomenon. But these young murderers—white or black; poor, middle-class, or rich; rural or urban—have fundamental similarities reaching beyond race, socioeconomic status, or geography. They share traits that lead to their murderous rages, or, in other cases, their planned executions.

All these children had been severely abused. While some were physically abused, all felt emotionally battered, shamed, and humiliated. Johnnie certainly did. He remembers too well the jibes he received at church and school from his schoolmates and the distasteful looks on his teachers' faces when they spoke to him. When the Johnsons refused to adopt him, when they called Children Services to have him removed from their home, Johnnie went over the edge. He murdered Mrs. Johnson, in my view, not so much as an expression of power to kill, as it was an attempt to take control, or perhaps to overpower another humiliating rejection.

Many young murderers claim to have experienced extreme pain and terror in early life and were unable to express their outrage. Like Johnnie, some did not even know the feelings inside of them, or could not identify them. Johnnie could not absorb the abuse he suffered. He failed to incorporate it into his reality. His mind firmly insisted on a false image of his family life, and he would allow nothing, including truth, to remake that fantasy world. His abuse began before he had words to express his feelings and continued into his teens. Even now, Johnnie lacks the language that might help him, yet at times he can communicate very effectively.

"I can't put the words to express how I feel," he wrote to me from prison. "A lot of people know the surface side of me. The side they see while I'm working or just going through the day. But there's another side of myself that people never see. I don't even know what it is. It's a part that's full of a thousand thoughts. A part that understands without words. The inside of me has so many moods that the outside never shows."

Abuse and subsequent detachment from feeling, however, are only partial explanations. They do not answer the question why some victims of such violence and abuse kill but most do not. Why is it that we all have different thresholds of violence, rage, and murder? Where are those invisible lines?

Dr. Lonnie Athens, a criminologist whom Richard Rhodes profiled in his book *Why They Kill*, believes that four phases precede violence: "brutalization," "belligerence," "violent performances," and "virulency." Intervention at any of these phases can prevent violence, he argues. If so, then it is possible that Johnnie could have been stopped a number of times before he murdered. Some who knew him said that he was a sensitive child, even a caring person. From Mansfield Correctional Institution on August 18, 2000, he wrote me: "I can be hurt by things that don't seem like much to you. People being inconsiderate, being taken for granted, being told half truths, being deceived or manipulated." It may be that Johnnie's sensitivity made him more vulnerable to hurt and humiliation he could not acknowledge or process, which then turned to rage and violence.

Like Rhodes, who found answers in Athens's work, I believe that individuals like Johnnie are conditioned to be violent by absorbing violence. Most have witnessed or suffered violence, cruelty, or sexual abuse and become inured to such injuries, accepting and even embracing such pain as part of their lives. This conditioning is a greater cause of violence than genetic inheritance, health, or poverty, though I believe those are all powerful and dangerous factors.

Based on the research and work of Dr. Athens, Rhodes attacks the "prejudice that has comforted us," the prejudice which holds that violent criminals are different from the rest of us. There is a presumption in society that criminals are brain-damaged, mentally ill, genetically inferior, or simply born monsters. Athens and Rhodes, both of whom survived the abuse they experienced as children, insist that criminals are like the rest of us and are rarely crazy. Refuting theories that murderers kill in bursts of unconsciously motivated fury and in spite of themselves, Athens contends that most violent criminals whom he has interviewed planned to be violent and felt completely responsible for their crimes. Adult criminals are, in fact, just like us, he argues, but they choose to act in a manner different from us. They simply make an unforgivable choice we would not have made. With children who are raw with hurt and humiliation, however, there are opportunities to intervene before they make the wrong choices.

Dr. Hershel Thomas, a clinical psychiatrist, has traced the seemingly irrational and implausible violence of young men after rejection and shame. Shame triggers a physiological response, Thomas argues. Emotions begin in our body, not our brain; the brain simply registers and stores the emotion. When shame, rejection, humiliation, or pain occurs, it often manifests itself first in the stomach or the chest. It did so with Johnnie. The morning of the murder, he complained of not feeling well. He often complained of stomachaches and chest pains when unwanted change occurred in his life, as it so often did in his nineteen foster homes.[3]

Not all children turn violent in reaction to rejection and shame. Thomas found that three factors are very influential in this regard.

First and most important is the significance to the child of the person who rejects him or her. In Johnnie's case, he had grown deeply attached to the Johnsons. They were more important to him than anyone recognized at the time. The more he cared for and respected them, the deeper his anger became when he was rejected. Moreover, Johnnie had already suffered a long string of rejections. Thomas believes that one harsh rejection can bring an outburst of violence, but violence is more likely when a series of rejections occur over time. This view comes as no surprise to people who work with juvenile murderers. When such a child erupts in violence, he or she often explains that someone "dissed" them. Disrespect is of paramount importance to children who exist in a world where they feel little or no acceptance.

The second factor relates to how surprised the child is by the rejection. If he anticipates it, he can handle it better. Though Johnnie had plenty of warning that the Johnsons were about to reject him, he refused to heed the signs until the morning of the murder. He persisted in his own cloistered world, as children of abuse often do to combat and control what is going on around them.

The final factor deals with the extent of the shame the child feels. Were there witnesses to the humiliation? Yes, in Johnnie's case. Teresa Edwards, whom Johnnie respected and had wanted as a mother earlier— only to be rejected by her, too—knew the Johnsons were trying to get rid of Johnnie.

3. Girls generally turn anger inward, abusing themselves more than others, while boys are more likely to look for an outward release to the anger. But statistical trends suggest that girls are becoming just as outwardly dangerous in their fury as boys.

After experiencing these kinds of scenarios, Thomas says, it is critical for the child to talk to an adult whom he trusts and respects, like a parent or teacher, to discuss the hurt openly and try to come to terms with it objectively. Johnnie had no one available to whom he could admit his vulnerability, no one to comfort him and express continuing love for him despite the rejection, at the crucial time. He reached out for J. R. Robinson, the only person he trusted, but Robinson unfortunately was out of town and unreachable.

III

The greatest tragedy in cases like Johnnie's is that many teachers and caregivers read danger signs in children but fail to act until it is too late. There are almost always warnings. Johnnie had been diagnosed with "conduct disorder," a condition that is termed "sociopathic" when applied to adults. Other children hoard guns. Some build their rage on social rejection. If these signs are ignored, the outcome is predictable.

When I became interested in this subject, I found teachers and social workers who would point directly to this child or that one and say he was well on his way to becoming a serial murderer or some other kind of criminal. In some instances, they would make these disturbing predictions within the child's hearing. They would give up on children as young as five and seven years old, allowing them to drift through their classrooms or placements, hoping the child would not harm anyone while under their watch.

"I just hope I'm not around when he explodes," one teacher said to me of a child I tutored. She believed that there was nothing she nor anyone else could do to straighten him out. "Whether it's genetics or environment, it's over for this child. Move on to another."

I did not believe that was true. After writing this book, I know it is not. The problem is adults allowing children who are already well on their way to sociopathic behavior—children who clearly exhibit ominous warnings—to continue freely down such a path. Just as disturbing are the parents who turn a blind eye or are in denial of their children's bullying or maladaptive behavior, attraction to violence, or interest and accumulation of weapons, especially guns. In my research, I could see the patterns of behavior that led professionals to proclaim that a child was a ticking time bomb. But I came to believe that it was a self-fulfill-ing prophecy only if nothing was done for the child.

A first step toward a solution is anger management and behavior modification. These programs already exist. Johnnie was supposed to enter such classes on three different occasions. He never did. None were followed through, both because of caseworker negligence and because there was little faith that such programs work, often even among the program directors.

"You give a kid an hour, maybe two, a week in therapy with someone he doesn't know or trust and you think that's going to change him?" one teacher who is also an assistant principal told me. "With the way managed care is today, they don't even see the same doctor twice. Each time, they start from the beginning with someone they know doesn't really care about them and doesn't believe in them. You think that's going to change him? Now, that's stupid. This kid needs intensive work. Something that will entirely submerge who he is now and brainwash him if need be. Who's going to let you do that?"

Such programs may be inadequate, but they deserve better than an out-of-hand dismissal by a teacher whose opinion is certain to influence a child's willingness to receive help. These programs need to be taken seriously and revamped to effect change. To do nothing at all is to wait until a child such as Johnnie kills, and then to punish him by placing him behind bars where rehabilitation is highly improbable. What is likely instead is that this fifteen-year-old, after spending most of his life in prison, will become a meaner, more dangerous, more vicious crimi-nal.

There should be a threshold of danger for children. If they cross that line, they forfeit their right to freedom and should be placed in a special home designed to deal with their anger and their behavior, an intensive, rehabilitative environment of the kind that unfortunately does not exist today. They require a strict program, with strong oversight and therapy, until they are ready to reenter society. This is the only way to both protect society and allow these children a fighting chance to straighten out their lives. Ellen Jones's program would create a new ser-vice, separate from the general foster care service of today, run by the juvenile justice system, with foster parents who have a good understanding of the needs of troubled and dangerous children like Johnnie. Such a program, I believe, would have saved Mrs. and Mr. Johnson, as well as Johnnie Jordan.

The truth of this story is that Johnnie Jordan did not have to kill. He chose to. His mind had been distorted and stunted by abuse. His sensitivity had been smothered by a bureaucratic maze that ignored and destroyed his integrity. There is never justification for murder. But there are reasons why children kill and why, if we do not heed their cries of pain and intervene decisively to help them, we will see countless more children who murder.

30

Epilogue

For all of his adult life and half of his teenage years, Johnnie Jordan Jr. has lived in cages. He has almost adjusted, or as much as he can with the constant frustration and agitation that buzz in his mind.

"I don't know what's going on," he tells me periodically in his still young, confused voice. When I ask him to explain, he says simply: "I'm tired. I'm tired of everything—that really speaks for itself."

He hasn't given up on life completely, though he's tried. Suicide seemed the solution to him many times, not because he would go to a better place, but because he desperately wanted out—out of prison, out of his body, and out of his mind. He found through his failed attempts that he couldn't take his life. Instead, he has adopted a manner of being he began developing as a child in reaction to conditions beyond his control. "I don't really care," he says. "I don't care if I live or if I die, so I don't really have fear. If I can't prevent it, I guess it's over."

He lives, day by day, in a routine. At 6 A.M., the guards wake him and other inmates on his block with banging bars and loudspeakers. At 6:35, they go to breakfast. But Johnnie usually stays behind in his cell. He's not hungry, he says. At 8, he goes to school, sometimes. In jails for juveniles, attendance is mandatory. In adult prisons, it's not. He takes regular classes to prepare for the GED, a high school equivalency exam, which he has failed four times. He signs up for other classes as well. He recently received a certificate from his "problem solving class." There wasn't much for him to learn in that class, he claims. "Some dudes it helps, I guess. But not me so much. I don't put myself in those situations. I never do anything that bad."

School ends at 10:45 and a half hour later, he's back in his "pod" for lockup and count time. Chow is at 11:30, he says, and he sometimes goes. After lunch, the inmates on his block play dominoes, cards, or watch TV. Johnnie sometimes joins in; otherwise, he keeps to himself and occasionally reads. His favorite books have violence in them. Others bore him.

At 1:15 or 2:30, depending on random scheduling to prevent break-outs, three times a week Johnnie has "rec" time when he works out with jump ropes, does push-ups, and runs on a concrete track. Then he show-ers and returns to be locked up for another count time. Dinner is at 4:30, after which "I kick it with a couple of my dudes," talking about life, cracking jokes, playing cards. "We don't talk about me though," he says. "I don't talk to people like that."

He hasn't learned much, he tells me, but his letters and our conver-sations indicate that he has matured to some extent despite the stagnant confines of his grey, artificial life. He remains, for the most part, the child he was when he was first incarcerated, though his voice has deep-ened, his muscles have defined themselves, and he has grown several inches taller.

"Just when I seem to understand life, something that I don't under-stand happens," he writes from Mansfield Correctional Institution. "Just when life begins to taste sweet, sour flavored reality fills my mouth." The younger Johnnie believed he understood life, and that his understanding was invincible. The younger Johnnie never linked the foul taste in his mouth to his feelings or moods. But now Johnnie has had time to notice these things. He's not always on the move or on the run.

His life is held still within bars. "I'm quiet," he says. "So I do a lot of thinking." Some things he thinks about a good deal. Others, especially those that elicit emotions, he avoids. This is his way of controlling him-self. He has always struggled with acting before thinking, or more accu-rately, reacting without reason. He doesn't blame the environment in which he was raised. "When I was younger, I was like every kid. I do what other kids do. But then early on, I do what I want to regardless of what other people say about me or what they tell me to do." He doesn't know why it was that way. It was just him, he guesses with a shrug. Some things he doesn't try to explain; some things just happen. Like Mrs. Johnson's murder.

"What happened to Mrs. Johnson, it just happened," he tells me in the very same words he used when I first met him. He shrugs too, as he did then. But there is an older, heavier depth to his gesture. It is not a shrug of dismissal anymore, as though he'd like to shoo that fly of memory away, and as if he could. There is more meaning, more sadness, whether for himself, Mrs. Johnson, or Mr. Johnson, he's not sure.

"No, I didn't want to kill her," he goes on in a more serious tone than he had at age fifteen. But again his words are jarringly unchanged. "I didn't mean no harm to no one. I guess that what happens. Not my intention though."

His intentions rarely conformed to his actions when he was younger, but now they do more often. When he does well in classes, when he's able to help a younger inmate with advice, Johnnie's spirits seem higher. He doesn't make this connection, however. Only when I ask him what he did that day do the two of us agree that he feels good about himself, for the moment.

But depression often strikes quickly, sometimes because of the monotony of his days, sometimes following an angry outburst. Johnnie never sees the darkness as a brief spell of clouds in his head; he sees it as truth and eternity. I've found nothing I can say will ease the depression, which often spirals uncontrollably back into anger and rage. At a more peaceful, thoughtful time, I asked him what he looks forward to, so that I could remind him of these things during his next spell of darkness.

"Look forward to?" he repeated my question quietly, thoughtfully. "Right now, I can't really say. I don't think about the future. I live day by day. Sometimes I try to think about leaving the spot—getting free."

"Do you have hope?"

"Don't know if you call it hope," he answered after a moment. "But I think I got a chance, somewhere down the line."

"What about goals?"

"I ain't got no goals or anything like that. I just hope everything work out for the better." Johnnie stopped for a while. His voice slowed almost to a mumble. "I hope this is not the place I'm meant to be the rest of my life."

I said nothing. Johnnie was silent for another moment, but then continued, which surprised me. He had lingered on the possibility instead of quickly moving on.

"I always felt I had a plan in life, a destiny to get to. I never got there. I don't know what my purpose was. I just know it shouldn't be this." He looked down for a moment, then added, "But, this might be it."

There was no self-pity in his voice, only wandering thoughts exploring new territory.

"Is that fate then, Johnnie?" I asked. "Fate that brought you here and fate that killed Mrs. Johnson?"

"Fate?" he asked back. "Mrs. Johnson? No, not Mrs. Johnson. I ain't too familiar with fate. Whatever guided me to that, it was a mistake. But I don't know what 'fate' means. They say everybody got a purpose, that God has a plan. But me personally, I don't believe in that."

"Why not?"

"Because it don't make sense. [Prison] just makes me worser," he said, repeating his words from our earliest interviews. "That anger or whatever just builds in me. The pressure builds in me getting a lot worser than before. What's the point of that?"

III

There are truths he has learned in prison, Johnnie finally admits without allowing that these truths have changed him—such as trying to take control of his life as much as possible and modify his behavior if he can. He wishes he had learned this lesson much earlier, especially that he had participated more in his legal defense. He's not sure the outcome would be different, but he would like another chance.

"Ain't no telling what the future looks like. Right now, ain't no possibility," he says solidly. Without freedom, there is no future in Johnnie's world, only more day-by-day. "I got to make something happen. I got to go back to court. I got a fifty-fifty chance. It's just a matter of time. I can beat it by myself. Don't need no lawyer."

Johnnie's plans make little sense. He has expended all of his appeals. He knows little of the law. But it is still too difficult for me to remind him of this. It seems clear as he continues, however, that hope for freedom is not the key point, at least not the only one.

"Even if I lose," Johnnie continues, "I don't care. I just want people to look at me and hear where I'm coming from. Not look like I'm dangerous and scared to be around me or have me around their kids. I'm just like any average person. I got an anger problem, but a lot of people do. I just want people to know where I'm coming from. I want to be normal."

"Do you think you're normal, Johnnie?"

"Yeah," he declares clearly, plainly, and without offense.

The phone goes dead, the allotted time for prison collect calls expires bluntly, without warning. But Johnnie calls back the next day.

"I just want you to know that I haven't lied to you or to myself," he tells me. "But sometimes I wonder if being honest causes more pain than not being honest."

I never truly understood Johnnie's continued compulsion to be open and truthful, especially after his honesty nailed his conviction. Truth is still important to him, as important as love would be to some, or breathing to others. Lies, half truths, information kept from him when he asks for it, these infuriate Johnnie beyond simple anger. I always found his insistence on truth admirable, but often I wondered if he realized that had he not told the truth to his probation officer and then to the detectives, had he not confessed voluntarily, there would have been no evidence to convict him. More than likely, he would have gone free.

"Yeah," he says in a slow whisper, he recognizes that. "It was the truth though," he states, but then adds with twinging anger. "Maybe if I had known then what would happen, I wouldn't have told though."

III

In his final letter, Johnnie writes of another lesson that he has learned, one of the few changes he has allowed in himself.

"I don't be judgmental of others because I now understand that we all must overcome something that is potentially self-defeating." Something in Johnnie is growing. Increasingly, flashes of intelligence and insight come through in his letters. Sometimes I have wondered if he in fact wrote the letters I read, or whether another inmate helped him. But when I ask him to elaborate his thoughts on the phone, it is clear they are his own. Still, he struggles with the steps of maturity and often on the personal implications. What there is in himself that could be self-defeating, for example, he still won't say. He's still not sure he knows. While he tries to take more control of his situation and himself, he has accepted that anger and fury are part of who he is, not a weakness he must overcome.

What he does know, he tells me, is something he doesn't understand. Something vital, though he doesn't know why.

"I will always search within myself more tentatively to find the words now. I never thought words had anything to do with what was going on inside me. But now I see they connect something to my feelings.

"You'll be surprised to find in me a new place in you," he concludes in big, sprawling, angular letters falling to the left.

"think of me please!

Your friend in the struggle of life,
Johnnie Jordan
#337–207
Mansfield Correctional Institution
P.O. Box 778
Mansfield, Ohio 44901[1]

"When you write that book," he asks me in a call later, "will you give them my address so they can write to me?"

I tell him I'm not sure, and I try to warn him of the angry letters he might receive.

"That's okay," he promises. "I can handle that." Given his years of neglect and abuse, any reaction is better than none to Johnnie.

"Why, Johnnie?" I ask. "Why would you want that?"

"I want them to know I'm alive. I'm dead to them now. I want to be alive. I never really was out there, least not as an adult."

But as time wears on him, Johnnie begins to lose his struggle for life. If his next appeal gets denied, as he senses it will, he says he will end all ties to people on the outside. He wants me to contact his former attorney and his siblings and explain why he wants to talk to them.

"My people don't even know if I'm dead or alive right now." He had not heard from his family in eight months, and if he cuts his ties with them, he will not feel so discarded and forsaken. Or so he believes. "It also takes stress off me. I won't have to worry about them."

Life is ultimately precarious to Johnnie, both on the inside and outside worlds. He knows that his life, or anyone else's for that matter,

1. Johnnie has since been moved to: Toledo Correctional Institution, 2001 East Central Ave., Toledo, Ohio 43608.

could be extinguished as randomly as Mrs. Johnson's. He has never known life to be different.

"If my baby daughter or family or Ronnie die on me while I'm in here, it will kill me. So I rather not know."

"You want to forget them?"

"Nooo! What I'm saying is, if I don't know, it ain't gonna hurt me." Frustration stinging his voice, he struggles to explain. "It's like a mother when her house burns down. It's better if she don't go to the hospital and see which of her kids lived. It's better if she don't know. It's better if she just move on."

"Even for the children?" I ask.

Johnnie pauses.

"It don't really matter," he answers, a tough pride flickering in his voice. "Kids got to take care of themselves. I did. I raised myself."

"So you're saying good-bye, Johnnie?"

"Naw, man, not good-bye. I just want them to lose all memory of me, that's what I want, like I was never born. It's not good-bye 'cause I never really was alive."

The great, unpardonable sin is to murder the love of life in a human soul.

—*John Gabriel Borkman,* Henrik Ibsen

METHODOLOGY AND
ACKNOWLEDGMENTS

This book would not have been possible without the help of Ron Wingate, J. R. Robinson, Dr. Barbara Baker, Ed Pendleton, Ellen Jones, Rick Meyer, and others who put their careers and reputations on the line with their honesty. This was not an easy or painless task for them, or for anyone involved. But I do believe they made a critical and brave contribution toward understanding what happened to Johnnie Jordan, and what is happening to other children who are following in his violent path.

Those who contributed to this book faced a great deal of opposition. Child privacy laws posed the greatest legal roadblock to telling this story. These laws were written with the intent to protect children, their identities and their pasts, from public attention. But more often than not, these secrecy laws are used to protect criminal abuses and failings within child welfare and juvenile justice systems. Because all juvenile records are kept strictly secret, the public rarely sees any evidence of the abuses that children face, or what really goes on behind the closed doors of their worlds. It is often not enough to print the children's first-person stories by themselves, even when bolstered by adult accounts, without facing liability concerns. In Johnnie's case, fear that his life story would expose the failures of certain agencies and individuals led Lucas County officials to try to cover up the truth of what happened to Johnnie Jordan at the expense of reforms that could have prevented another child who murders from taking another life. Within the child welfare system, well-meaning adults risk a great deal if they agree to tell the truth about a child who has been wronged. If foster parents or social workers breach these so-called privacy laws, they face not only the loss of their jobs, but also lawsuits. While I was researching this book Lucas County

Children Services sent letters to all nineteen of Johnnie's foster families, ordering them not to speak with me and warning them of dire consequences if they did. I am grateful to those foster parents who did talk to me, some on the record, most on background, and a few on deep background. They did so so that we all may gain some greater understanding of Johnnie and children like him. Children Services also alerted caseworkers and urged them not to cooperate. I am grateful to those social workers who did talk to me, both on background and off the record, despite the risks, providing me clues and the confidence to pursue different avenues I might not have explored without their direction. Equally brave were Eva Holston and others who recounted for me the days and months leading up to Mrs. Johnson's murder. It took a great deal of strength to relive those times.

Without Lucas County Children Services' approval, I was fortunate to gain access to all of the agency's files on Johnnie, his parents, and his siblings. These voluminous files include Johnnie's psychiatric evaluations, neighbors' and teachers' transcripts, as well as caseworker and foster parent reports from throughout Johnnie's childhood. These records were invaluable in reconstructing Johnnie's past. I am thankful for the psychologists and psychiatrists who remembered Johnnie and granted me interviews despite the threat to confidentiality. I also acquired Johnnie's parole, probation, and juvenile justice files, as well as his school and medical records, and relied on juvenile and adult court records, physical evidence, and recorded testimony. When the court records contradicted autopsy reports or several of my interviews, I pointed out the discrepancies in footnotes. All these files, I believe, gave me a far greater wealth of clues and documentation of what happened to Johnnie than I could have extracted from children who grow up in the privacy of their biological or adoptive homes. In private homes without records, I would have had to rely primarily on interviews and risk the interference of hindsight. In contrast, these reports provided me with thousands of snapshots that enabled me to better chronicle Johnnie's life.

A great tragedy of Johnnie's life, however, is that no one person, certainly not his parents, knew him well. Each relative, acquaintance, foster parent, or teacher, knew him during different parts of his life. Their recollections fell together like pieces of a puzzle. I was fortunate to interview members of Homebuilders programs and after-school programs, and counselors who remembered Johnnie, as well as members of Johnnie's family, his few "associates" or friends, neighbors, and several teachers. While not all these interviews appear in this book, I greatly appreciate each of those who contributed to my understanding. Aside from interviews or situations where I was present, I quote only conversations in which both parties agreed to what was said and how it was said.

With the help of the Lucas County Sheriff's Department, I was able to hear the original recordings of Johnnie's confessions and review the detectives' written notes during and after the case. I very much appreciate the help of Detectives Denny Richardson, Ernest Lamb, and Bruce Birr for their firm recollection of facts of the case, as well as their willingness to recall the events as they saw and felt them.

No one, not even those who won the criminal case against Johnnie, was proud of what happened, Prosecutor Julia Bates told me. I greatly appreciate her honest assessment of Johnnie and the politics surrounding his case. Assistant prosecutors John Weglian and Dean Mandross were also tremendously helpful in reviewing how and why they made decisions in Johnnie's trial. Juvenile court judge James Ray and Lucas County's chief magistrate of juvenile court, Donna Mitchell, took political risks by speaking honestly about this case that perhaps some other justice officials might not have. Their insights were invaluable.

Ironically, those closest and most hurt by the murder case were most cooperative. Charles Johnson's care and inspiration carried this book before and beyond his death. His thoughts, help, and interviews are priceless to me. He taught me a great deal, not just about this case but also about myself. I can only hope to do his wisdom some justice. Though he had perhaps the most to lose, Johnnie Jordan, Jr. was also honest and forthcoming. He allowed me to interview him for hundreds of hours, both in prison and over the phone. Some correctional facilities made it difficult for me to see Johnnie for interviews. Like many people, some prison officials and guards seemed dubious of my intentions in the case.

In researching and writing this book, I encountered a great deal of suspicion and blame. Why, I was asked frequently in the course of thousands of hours of interviews, did I choose *this* case to write about? Why, they seemed to be saying, was I picking on this particular community?

Even a clerk at the Lucas County Records Office was at times reluctant to allow me to inspect public records because she was suspicious of my interest and found it "freakish." Several times, I had to prove to her that the files I asked from her were public records which she could not legally withhold. But those more deeply involved in the Johnnie Jordan case understood the importance of this book.

There were many reasons I chose to examine Johnnie Jordan's case. Though I told few people, I found Mr. Johnson's quest for understanding and reform moving. I became more determined to pursue answers to the questions he had begun to ask when I witnessed the reckless and disrespectful attempts by various child welfare agencies to forget this case and move on, bent on closing their eyes and refusing to learn any lessons from what happened. I also believed I had a greater wealth of clues to the mystery of child murderers with Johnnie's many files. But most often, I told people who questioned my interest in Johnnie Jordan that frankly, it did not matter which child I chose to profile as long as I could bring forth some way to understand and cope with the horrors of their seemingly inexplicable actions, in the hope of preventing such crimes in the future. There were lesser factors as well that stoked my interest in Johnnie's case. Toledo, Ohio, is symbolic. It represents the saturation of children committing violent crimes throughout the country. These brutal crimes are carried out not just in inner cities. This is a problem reaching deep into America, even Middle America. And the crisis of young anger we face extends beyond geography, race, and socioeconomic backgrounds. I did not select Johnnie because he is black, as some suggested. I was encouraged by his guileless honesty. That honesty was critical. Johnnie did not hold out hope that he could somehow get out of prison or receive better treatment if he told me certain stories or gave twisted accounts. Nor did he hesitate to tell the uglier truths of what happened. Finally, my interest in this case was cemented by the convictions of people who were involved in Johnnie's case, particularly Ron Wingate, J. R. Robinson, and Ellen Jones, who resisted a strong tide of public opinion to do what they felt was right. Whether I agreed with them or not, I found their courage remarkable.

But even as I explained my rationale for investigating the genesis and ramifications of Johnnie Jordan's evolution into a child who killed, few people in Lucas County looked forward to such an investigation. Far from eager to learn from the case, many were instead more worried about how the book would portray the community. Most people wanted to erase Mrs. Johnson's death from the community's conscience and memory. I sincerely believe that Charles and Jeanette Johnson deserved more.

The suspicion, blame, and distrust of a pained community, as well as overly strict child privacy laws, made this case very difficult to investigate and explore at times. But I deeply admire and appreciate the help of those who cared enough to look beyond the community's wounds and, in some instances, their personal feelings of failure, to find some truth in what happened to Johnnie Jordan, why he murdered, and what this portends for cities across the country that are grappling with the same problems.

I especially appreciate the honesty and integrity of those who cooperated in this book, who took both professional and personal risks, who relived the most painful times, all because they want to see a better life for our children and for those who care for them. Their bravery, sincerity, and hope will always remain inspiring to me.

PERSONAL ACKNOWLEDGMENTS

On many personal and professional levels, this book was a great challenge for me. Without the encouragement and support of family and friends, I could not have completed it. My husband, Craig Whitlock, a reporter for *The Washington Post*, discussed every turn and aspect of Johnnie's story and was particularly helpful in his knowledge of public records and how to fight reluctant authorities for them. My father, Robert Toth, painstakingly edited and re-edited each chapter. My mother, Paula Toth, kept me well fed, and took care of my family when I was unable to. My brother, John, and sister, Jessica, consistently offered encouragement. Finally, Dr. Richard Footer and Marla Horowitz put me on bed rest which, among other things, concentrated my efforts. Their care of my son and me during my pregnancy allowed me the comfort and peace to complete my work.

Keith Korman, my agent at Raines & Raines, gave me confidence to pursue this project from the beginning, before the many incidents of young violence around the country came to the forefront of national news. Dominick Anfuso, my editor at Simon & Schuster, and then The Free Press, again gave me the great opportunity to contribute to this field. His support has meant a great deal to me.

I am most grateful to John Kyle Whitlock, my son, who patiently listened to *Johnnie Jordan*—a stark introduction to the world of books— read and re-read before and after his birth. His future, as well as the Johnsons' past, gave this book special meaning. But most important is the wonder Kyle has brought into my life, now and forevermore.

SELECT BIBLIOGRAPHY

BOOKS

Barden, Renardo. *Juvenile Violence*. New York: Marshall Cavendish, 1994.

Butterfield, Fox. *All God's Children: The Bosket Family and the American Tradition of Violence*. New York: Knopf, 1995.

Capote, Truman. *In Cold Blood: A True Account of a Multiple Murder and Its Consequences*. New York: Signet Press, 1965.

Cocozza, Joseph J., ed. *Responding to the Mental Health Needs of Youth in the Juvenile Justice System*. Seattle: National Coalition for the Mentally Ill in the Criminal Justice System, 1992.

Coles, Robert. *Children of Crisis: A Study of Courage and Fear*. Boston: Little, Brown and Company, 1967.

Coles, Robert. *The Moral Intelligence of Children*. New York: Random House, 1997.

Coles, Robert. *The Spiritual Life of Children*. Boston: Houghton Mifflin, 1990.

Cournos, Francine. *City of One*. New York: W. W. Norton & Co., 1999.

Dutile, Fernand N., ed., and Cleon H. Foust, ed. *The Prediction of Criminal Violence*. Springfield, Ill.: Charles C. Thomas, 1987.

Erikson, Erik H. *Childhood and Society*. New York: W. W. Norton & Company, 1963.

Ewing, Charles Patrick. *Kids Who Kill*. New York: Free Press, 1990.

Gibbons, Don C. *Society, Crime, and Criminal Careers: An Introduction to Criminology*. 2d ed. Englewood Cliffs, N.J.: Prentice-Hall, 1973.

Hubner, John, and Jill Wolfson. *Somebody Else's Children: The Courts, the Kids, and the Struggle to Save America's Troubled Families*. New York: Crown Publishers, 1996.

Humes, Edward. *No Matter How Loud I Shout: A Year in the Life of Juvenile Court*. New York: Simon & Schuster, 1996.

Hunter, Mic. *Abused Boys: The Neglected Victims of Sexual Abuse*. New York: Fawcett Columbine, 1990.

James, Oliver, ed. *Juvenile Violence in a Winner-Loser Culture: Socio-Economic and Familial Origins of the Rise in Violence Against the Person*. London: Free Association Books Ltd., 1995.

Karr-Morse, Robin, and Meredith S. Wiley. *Ghosts from the Nursery: Tracing the Roots of Violence*. The Atlantic Monthly Press, 1998.

Kozol, Jonathan. *Amazing Grace.* New York: Crown Publishers, 1995.

Landau, Elaine. *Teenage Violence.* Englewood Cliffs, N.J.: Julian Messner, 1990.

Lang, Susan S. *Teen Violence.* New York: Franklin Watts, 1994.

Langone, John. *Violence: Our Fastest Growing Public Health Problem.* Boston: Little, Brown and Company, 1984.

Lefkowitz, Bernard. *Our Guys: The Glen Ridge Rape and the Secret Life of the Perfect Suburb.* Berkeley: University of California Press, 1997.

Lewis, Dorothy. *Guilty by Reason of Insanity: A Psychiatrist Explores the Minds of Killers.* New York: Fawcett Columbine, 1998.

Monahan, J. *Predicting Violent Behavior.* Beverly Hills: Sage Publications, 1981.

Morrison, Blake. *As If: A Crime, a Trial, a Question of Childhood.* New York: Picador, 1997.

Moser, Rosemarie Scolaro, ed., and Corinne E. Frantz. *Shocking Violence: Youth Perpetrators and Victims.* Springfield, Ill.: Charles C. Thomas, 2000.

National Center for Injury Prevention and Control. *The Prevention of Youth Violence: A Framework for Community Action.* Atlanta: Centers for Disease Control and Prevention, 1993.

Prothrow-Stith, Deborah, with Michaelle Weissman. *Deadly Consequences: How Violence Is Destroying Our Teenage Population and a Plan to Begin Solving the Problem.* New York: Harper Collins, 1991.

Rhodes, Richard. *Why They Kill: The Discoveries of a Maverick Criminologist.* New York: Alfred A. Knopf Inc., 1999.

Richardson, Brian A. *About Juvenile Violence and Its Prevention.* Huntington, N.Y.: The Bureau for At-Risk Youth, 1992.

Satterthwaite, Marcia. *Juvenile Crime.* Philadelphia: Chelsea House, 1997.

Shengold, Leonard. *Soul Murder Revisited: Thoughts About Therapy, Hate, Love, and Memory.* New York: Yale University Press, 1999.

Terr, Lenore. *Too Scared to Cry: Psychic Trauma in Childhood.* New York: Harper & Row, 1990.

Van Hasselt, Vincent B., ed., and Michel Hersen, ed. *Aggression and Violence: An Introductory Text.* Needham Heights, Mass.: Allyn & Bacon, Inc., 2000.

Walker, Robert. *Psychology of the Youthful Offender* (3rd edition). Springfield, Ill.: Charles C. Thomas, 1995.

Wilson, James Q., and Richard J. Herrnstein. *Crime and Human Nature.* New York: Simon & Schuster, 1985.

Wilson, James Q. *Moral Judgment: Does the Abuse Excuse Threaten Our Legal System?* New York: Basic Books, 1997.

Wilson, James Q. *The Moral Sense.* New York: Free Press, 1993.

ARTICLES AND JOURNALS

Andrew, June. "Memory and Violent Crime Among Delinquents." *Criminal Justice and Behavior.* September 1982. 9 (3):364–371.

Appelbaum, P. S., R. Z. Jick, T. Grisso, D. Givelber, E. Silver, and H. J. Steadman.

"Use of Posttraumatic Stress Disorder to Support an Insanity Defense." *American Journal of Psychiatry.* Feb. 1993. 150 (2): 229–34.

Ash, P., and A. P. Derdeyn. "Forensic Child and Adolescent Psychiatry: A Review of the Past 10 Years." *Journal of the American Academy of Child and Adolescent Psychiatry.* Nov. 1997. 36 (11): 1493–1502.

Betz, Cecily. "Childhood Violence: A Nursing Concern." *Issues in Comprehensive Pediatric Nursing.* July–September 1995. 18 (3): 149–61.

Borum, Randy. "Assessing Violence Risk Among Youth." *Journal of Clinical Psychology.* October 2000. 56 (10): 1263–88.

Brennan, Patricia A. "Biosocial Risk Factors and Juvenile Violence." *Administrative Office of the United States Courts.* December 1999. 63 (2): 58–60.

Burton, D., D. Foy, C. Bwanausi, J. Johnson, and L. Moore. "The Relationship Between Traumatic Exposure, Family Dysfunction, and Post-Traumatic Stress Symptoms in Male Juvenile Offenders." *Journal of Trauma Stress.* January 1994. 7 (1): 83–93.

Corder, B. F., B. C. Ball, T. M. Haizlip, R. Rollins, and R. Beaumont. "Adolescent Parricide: A Comparison with Other Adolescent Murder." *American Journal of Psychiatry.* August 1976. 133 (8): 957–61.

Cormier, B. M., and B. Markus. "A Longitudinal Study of Adolescent Murderers." *Bulletin of the American Academy of Psychiatry and the Law.* 8 (3): 240–60.

Cornell, D., C. Miller, and E. Benedek. "MMPI Profiles of Adolescents Charged with Homicide." *Behavioral Sciences and the Law.* 6: 401–407.

Cornell, D., and G. Dewey. "Prior Adjustment of Violent Juvenile Offenders." *Law and Human Behavior.* Dec. 1990. 14 (6): 569–77.

Di Iluio, Jr., John J. "The Coming of the Super-Predators." *Weekly Standard.* Nov. 27, 1995.

Dugger, Celia W. "A Boy in Search of Respect Discovers How to Kill," *New York Times.* May 15, 1994. p. 1.

Duncan, J. W., and G. M. Duncan. "Murder in the Family: A Study of Some Homicidal Adolescents." *American Journal of Psychiatry.* May 1971. 127 (11): 1498–1502.

Famularo, R., T. Fenton, and R. Kinscherff. "Child Maltreatment and the Development of Posttraumatic Stress Disorder." *American Journal of Diseases of Children.* July 1993. 147 (7): 755–60.

Famularo, R., and T. Fenton. "Early Developmental History and Pediatric Post-traumatic Stress Disorder." *Archives of Pediatric Adolescent Medicine.* Oct. 1994. 148 (10):1032–1038.

Famularo, R., R. Kinscherff, and T. Fenton. "Posttraumatic Stress Disorder Among Children Clinically Diagnosed As Borderline Personality Disorder." *Journal Mental Disorders.* July 1991. 179 (7): 428–31.

Famularo, R., R. Kinscherff, and T. Fenton. "Symptom Differences in Acute and Chronic Presentation of Childhood Post-Traumatic Stress Disorder." *Child Abuse and Neglect.* 1990. 14 (3): 439–44.

Farrington, David, and Rolf Loeber. "Epidemiology of Juvenile Violence." *Child and Adolescent Psychiatric Clinics of North America.* October 2000. 9 (4): 733–48.

Grisso, Thomas. "Law & Psychiatry: The Changing Face of Juvenile Justice." *Psychiatric Services.* April 2000. 51 (4): 425–62.

Grisso, Thomas. "Society's Retributive Response to Juvenile Violence: A Developmental Perspective." *Law and Human Behavior.* June 1996. 20 (3): 229–47.

Haller, Lee. "Forensic Aspects of Juvenile Violence." *Child and Adolescent Psychiatric Clinics of North America.* October 2000. 9 (4): 1056–4993.

Heide, K. M. "Juvenile Homicide in America: How Can We Stop the Killing?" *Behavioral Sciences and the Law.* Spring 1997. 15 (2): 203–20.

Hennes, H. "A Review of Violence Statistics Among Children and Adolescents in the United States." *Pediatric Clinics of North America.* April 1998. 45 (2): 269–80.

Lawrence, Jan S. "Neutralizing Inmate Violence: Juvenile Offenders in Institutions." *Children and Youth Services Review.* Spring 1979. 128–31.

Lewis, Dorothy. "Toward a Theory of the Genesis of Violence: A Follow-Up Study of Delinquents." *Journal of the American Academy of Child and Adolescent Psychiatry.* May 1989. 28 (3): 431–36.

Pope, Carl E. "Neutralizing Inmate Violence: Juvenile Offenders in Institutions." *Crime and Delinquency.* January 1981. 27 (1): 127–34.

Rapp, Lisa, and John Wodarski. "Juvenile Violence: The High Risk Factors, Current Interventions, and Implications for Social Work Practice." *Journal of Applied Social Sciences.* Fall–Winter 1997. 22 (1): 3–14.

Russakoff, Dale. "Horror That Burned into Littleton Minds." *The Washington Post.* 5/15/99. A3.

Scott, Charles. "Juvenile Violence." *Psychiatric Clinics of North America.* March 1999. 22 (1): 71–83.

Steiner, H., I. G. Garcia, and Z. Matthews. "Posttraumatic Stress Disorder in Incarcerated Juvenile Delinquents. *Journal of American Academic Child and Adolescent Psychiatry.* March 1997. 36 (3): 357–65.

Walsh, Anthony. "Genetic and Environmental Explanation of Juvenile Violence in Advantaged and Disadvantaged Environments." *Aggressive Behavior.* 1992. 18 (3): 187–99.

Zalsman, G., A. Frisch, M. Bromberg, J. Gelernter, E. Michaelovsky, A. Campino, Z. Erlich, S. Tyano, A. Apter, and A. Weizman. "Family-Based Association Study of Serotonin Transporter Promoter in Suicidal Adolescents: No Association with Suicidality but Possible Role in Violence Traits." *American Journal of Medical Genetics.* April 8, 2001. 105 (3): 239–45.

Zalsman, G., N. Horesh, R. Arzi, D. Edelist, D. H. Even, S. Tyano, F. Poustka, and A. Apter. "Psychosocial diagnosis in Psychiatrically Hospitalized Adolescents." *Compr. Psychiatry.* May–June 2001. 42 (3): 223–27.